CRISIS AND CLASS WAR IN EGYPT

About the author

Sean F. McMahon is assistant professor of political science. He is editor, with Dan Tschirgi and Walid Kazziha, of *Egypt's Tahrir Revolution* (2013) and author of *The Discourse of Palestinian–Israeli Relations: Persistent Analytics and Practices* (2010).

CRISIS AND CLASS WAR IN EGYPT

SOCIAL REPRODUCTION, FACTIONAL REALIGNMENTS AND THE GLOBAL POLITICAL ECONOMY

SEAN F. MCMAHON

ZED

Zed Books
London

Crisis and Class War in Egypt: Social Reproduction, Factional Realignments and the Global Political Economy
 was first published in 2017 by Zed Books Ltd, The Foundry,
17 Oval Way, London SE11 5RR, UK.

www.zedbooks.net

Typeset in Sabon by Swales & Willis Ltd, Exeter, Devon
Index by Ed Emery
Cover design by Kika Sroka-Miller
Cover photo © Guy Martin/Panos

A catalogue record for this book is available from the British Library.

ISBN 978-1-78360-503-3 hb
ISBN 978-1-78360-502-6 pb
ISBN 978-1-78360-504-0 pdf
ISBN 978-1-78360-505-7 epub
ISBN 978-1-78360-506-4 mobi

Printed and bound by CPI Group (UK) Ltd, Croydon, CR0 4YY

À ma petite pomme de terre

[A]ll science would be superfluous if the form of appearance of things directly coincided with their essence.

Marx – *Capital Volume III: The Process of Capitalist Production as a Whole*

'I built it with my hands. Straightened old nails to put the sheathing on. Rafters are wired to the stringers with baling wire. It's mine. I built it. You bump it down – I'll be in the window with a rifle. You even come too close and I'll pot you like a rabbit.'

'It's not me. There's nothing I can do. I'll lose my job if I don't do it. And look – suppose you kill me? They'll just hang you, but long before you're hung there'll be another guy on the tractor, and he'll bump the house down. You're not killing the right guy.'

'That's so,' the tenant said. 'Who gave you orders? I'll go after him. He's the one to kill.'

'You're wrong. He got his orders from the bank. The bank told him, "Clear those people out or it's your job."'

'Well, there's a president of the bank. There's a board of directors. I'll fill up the magazine of the rifle and go into the bank.'

'The driver said, "Fellow was telling me the bank gets orders from the East. The orders were, 'Make the land show profit or we'll close you up.'"'

'But where does it stop? Who can we shoot? I don't aim to starve to death before I kill the man that's starving me.'

Steinbeck – *The Grapes of Wrath*

CONTENTS

FIGURES AND TABLES

Figures

Tables

ACKNOWLEDGMENTS

Despite appearances, writing is always a social process. This book is only possible because of the enriching relations I have been privileged to live. Sadly, I cannot fully acknowledge all of them because doing so might expose some people to the violence of the Egyptian state form.

My thanks, first, to Kim Walker, and everyone at Zed Books, who supported my manuscript, improved the book's presentation and worked to accelerate its publication; the American University in Cairo for facilitating my research; and the Department of Political Science at the University of Lethbridge for generously providing me an academic home away from home where I was able to initially develop this analysis.

Almost 20 years ago, Fred Judson patiently introduced me to a Marxian analysis I, then, ideologically rejected. Fred did not impose. Instead, he taught, he genuinely taught, and in so doing he allowed me to come to my own understanding of class analysis on my own terms and in my own time. It is a testament to his teaching that students continue to learn from him long after last being in his class. More recently, but still years ago, Sandra Rein proffered claims and made arguments about the dialectic, money form of value and 'capitalism' that continued to echo in my head as I wrote this. Even when we are separated in space and exist in different times Rein remains a valuable interlocutor.

D.T. and Harry Cleaver have been singularly helpful colleagues in the present moment. D. patiently listened to me talk about derivatives, and his perceptive questions always encouraged me to take my analysis deeper. Harry Cleaver proved more responsive to a cold-email than I could have ever hoped. He gave generously of his labor-time, and provided me invaluable insights through his texts and emails.

Will and Red made the daily trips into Tahrir Square with me in late January and early February 2011. We were shot at and tear-gassed together. Their companionship was indispensible to my singular experience of the eruption of crisis in Egyptian society, and it was in our conversations during our walks (and runs) around downtown Cairo and back from Tahrir Square that I first articulated some of the germs of this analysis. A. provided me – so many of us – a safe, well-stocked sanctuary during those explosive days, and again in November 2011. If not for Kristine, this book would be dedicated to her :)

Egyptian workers assisted and protected me in Tahrir Square in January and February 2011, and others provided me relief in November as our battles raged on Mohamed Mahmoud. I do not know their names, and they surely do not know mine, but their actions and those moments were inspirational, representing for me the real possibilities for workers' solidarity. Egyptian workers in student form have helped with this book since the outset. Undergraduate students in my classes were some of the first to critically engage and demand further development of my dialectical analyses of the eruption of crisis in Egyptian society and changing class relations and their expressions in different governing alignments and Egyptian state forms. A number of graduate students also helped with research for this book. I trust those I would otherwise thank by name know who they are and how much I appreciate their labor-time.

Throughout, my Egyptian friends have provided me some of my kindest relations. They called to warn me of state incitement against 'foreign agents' and encouraged me to leave Tahrir Square for my own safety. They accompanied me to Tahrir Square, and were even pressed into duty as my translator. They have spent countless hours sharing their thoughts with me. They have been generous with me to the point of endangering themselves. If fair weather friends abandon you in difficult moments, then my Egyptians friends are some of the best miserable weather friends a guy could ever hope to have.

Douglas and my parents never let the strength of our connections wane. Communication with them was always encouraging and reminded me that I was not alone, despite my having not left my flat for days on end. Douglas's living of life is an empowering inspiration to me.

Finally, my most profound appreciation and gratitude goes to Kristine. She is intensely loving and unwavering in her support. Kristine improves the quality of every endeavor, even the already sublime joy of writing. There is no one with whom I would rather fight life's struggles.

* * *

Parts of Chapter 4 were originally published in McMahon, Sean (2013) 'Egypt's social forces, the state and Middle East order,' in Dan Tschirgi, Walid Kazziha and Sean F. McMahon (eds), *Egypt's Tahrir Revolution*, Boulder, CO: Lynne Rienner Publications, pp. 151–72, and are used with kind permission of Lynne Rienner Publications.

CHAPTER 1

Introduction

Appearance and essence

Egyptian society is at war. Appearances of this ongoing war have been misrepresented as revolutions. Starting on 25 January 2011 eighteen days of protest convulsed the country. Street battles raged in Cairo, Alexandria and Suez. The headquarters of the ruling political party was burned. Internet service was severed. Public spaces were occupied and made the objects of sieges. A vice-president was appointed. Nine hundred protestors were killed. The long-serving president resigned. On 11 February the military, in the form of the Supreme Council of the Armed Forces (SCAF), took power. Later, a constitutional referendum was voted on and adopted. A parliament was elected, dismissed and reinstated. Two rounds of hotly contested elections produced a new president. A Constituent Assembly charged with drafting a new constitution was constituted, disbanded and reconstituted. The two most senior members of SCAF were forcibly retired by the newly elected president. The executive seized all judicial and legislative powers. A new constitution was popularly approved. Protests against the president again swelled in the summer of 2013. The minister of defense deposed the president who had recently appointed him. More protestors were massacred. The minister of defense was promoted within the military and resigned his position to contest and win the presidential election in 2014. Another constitution was adopted. And parliamentary elections were held.

Appearances are often deceiving. Egyptian society has yet to produce a revolution. January 2011 was a particular eruption of the universal crisis of capitalist relations and processes. The reproduction of working-class life was endangered by surplus capital appearing in food price inflation and, in dialectical fashion, this posed an existential crisis for capital in the Egyptian social formation. Political expressions and moments since 2011 have been of intra-capitalist class and inter-class struggles between the factions of productive, commercial and finance capital, and between capital and the working class. In 2011, the military as productive capital disposed of its junior partner, predatory capital, vulgarly labeled the Mubarak regime, and aligned with the Muslim Brotherhood as commercial capital to defer the crisis and extend the relations of the commodity form in Egyptian society. After having consumed commercial capital's use-value, in 2013 productive capital disposed of its junior partner and replaced it with finance capital, represented by the state forms of the Gulf Cooperation Council (GCC). During these moments, capital has unrelentingly attacked, and further weakened, the power of the working class and the value of its labor-power commodity under the cover of reform; constitutional and legal reform, technological reform, currency reform. The contradictions that produced the appearances of crisis in 2011 and 2013 have sharpened during these moments, and Egyptian society is building to a higher-stage crisis. The coming eruption of crisis will be more socially extensive and intensive, more violent, and will take the lives of many more workers.

Recent Egyptian politics are not as they have been represented. The 25 January 'revolution' was a particular expression of the general crisis of neoliberal capitalism that has been differently deluging societies since its eruption in 2007. Egyptian society's particular crisis was a crisis of reproduction of daily life. Mass protests by a working class weakened in relation to capital and in possession of a labor-power commodity devalued by food price inflation crystallized out of an environmental crisis, Benthamite mental conceptions, neoliberal processes of accumulation, including privatization, legal arrangements such as the Commodities Futures Modernization Act (CFMA) of 2000 and the Troubled Assets Relief Program (TARP) of 2008, and the technology of derivatives. Egyptian society did not change *because* of 25 January. Egypt's recent political history represents the forms of expression of ongoing changes.

Egyptian society is comprised of the working class and three factions of capital: productive capital, commercial capital and finance capital. When the working class faced an acute crisis of social reproduction in 2011, its weakness in relation to capital meant it was incapable of realizing revolutionary change. In the crisis moment, productive capital rescued the commodity form in Egyptian society by replacing one faction of unproductive capital with another in the bloc governing the Egyptian social formation. In 2013, productive capital again disposed of its junior partner in the governing alignment; this time replacing commercial capital with finance capital, represented by the GCC state forms. Politics in Egypt since 2011 have been defined by intra-capitalist class struggle. The reforms capital has realized through these moments have been possible because of the weakness of the working class in Egypt, and have further weakened the political power of workers and devalued their labor-power commodity.

The contradictions of capitalist relations and processes continue to sharpen. The eruption of crisis to which Egyptian society, like the global capitalist totality of which it is a part, is building will present the working class with another revolutionary opportunity. Unless the working class is able to alter the balance of forces in its favor by, *inter alia*, thinking in class terms, rather than the fetishisms of nation and religion, the coming crisis will produce even more reactionary relations and political forms of expression that seek disastrously to paralyze the movement of society.

Analytical framework: materialist dialectics

Materialist dialectics is a philosophy, theory and method. The philosophy is critical – dialectics, the theory is of labor value, and the method is of seven inner-related elements.

Marx's ontology is a totality of relations and processes, *not* things. It is a social rather than an individual ontology. Dialectically, it is an ontology of 'inner relations' and 'mutually dependent processes.'[1] Relations constitute the reified things nondialectical thinking sees – capital, for example, is not a thing but a social relation between labor and capital. And 'processes actually interpenetrate'[2] such that a change in one process, say organization, means a change in other processes, circulation, exploitation, reproduction, accumulation.

Change is constantly occurring in this matrix of internal relations and co-dependent processes.[3] A causal philosophy of change presumes an external relation. A condition of stasis is changed by the intervention of an exogenous stimulant. This is precisely why nondialectical thinkers are so often surprised by manifestations of change and compelled to explain them. Dialectics, on the other hand, understands the contradictions *internal* to the totality, the totality of capitalism in Marx's case, as the propellant of this constant change. Contradictions are 'the incompatible development of different [and dependent] elements within the same relation.'[4] The commodity, for instances, reifies and internalizes capitalist contradictions. By way of simple example, the commodity has a use-value and an exchange-value, but only one of these incompatible values can be realized at any one moment. The commodity can be sold for its exchange-value, but then it cannot be consumed for its use-value. Or it can be consumed for its use-value, but then it cannot be transformed into its exchange-value. Contradictions, such as capital's interest in paying labor as small a wage as possible in the factory but needing moneyed consumers in the market or developing and implementing technology that produces surplus-value in the short term only to displace the producers of value in the long term, are never resolved. The standard representation of the dialectic as the thesis-antithesis-synthesis misses the mark in this regard. More accurate is the conceptualization Marx suggests at the end of *Capital*, volume I: dialectical thinking sees an affirmation, its negation, and 'the negation of the negation.'[5] Contradictions are always further internalized, turned in on themselves again and again in a system of perpetual movement or on a grander scale.[6]

The social relation between labor, the class whose only commodity is labor-power, and capital, the class that owns the means of production, is the first contradiction of capitalism. This relation is contradictory because while it is capital that constitutes labor in capitalism and labor that makes possible the capitalist class the relation is antagonistic – capital's goal of accumulating surplus-value can only be realized at the expense of labor. The relation is such that each class needs the other to be and cannot continue to relate to the other if it is to realize itself. The social war fought over capital's attempts to impose the commodity form and appropriate unpaid labor-time from the working class and human beings resisting their own proletarianization and battling to free time from capitalist production produces technology, such as the spinning jenny, and ideas, such as the strike and the union. Societies change because classes fight. Class struggle is the engine of social motion.

The capitalist mode of production is a totality of internal relations and co-dependent processes that are always in contradictory tension. Negations and antagonisms produce constant change and movement. In contrast with commonsensical thinking that is surprised by the dynamism of capitalist societies, materialist dialectics knows '[c]apital is not a thing, but rather a process that exists only in *motion*.'[7] Capital is value in motion. It is constantly being advanced. It is forever producing commodities. It is being realized every time the commodity transforms into money. It continuously circulates back to be advanced again. A crisis occurs when the flow of value is constricted too much or stops completely.

Marx highlights the capacity of the dialectic to perceive and study motion in the postface to the second edition of *Capital*, volume I. It is also here that he explains the materialism of his dialectics in contrast with the idealism of Hegel. Says Marx: '[m]y dialectical method, is, in its foundation, not only different from the Hegelian, but exactly opposite to it. For Hegel . . . the real world is only the external appearance of the idea. With me the reverse is true: the ideal is nothing but the material world reflected in the mind of man, and translated into forms of thought.'[8] Marx continues: '[t]he mystification which the dialectic suffers in Hegel's hands by no means prevents him from being the first to present its general forms of motion in a comprehensive and conscious manner. With him it is standing on its head. It must be inverted.'[9] Marx inverts the Hegelian dialectic, he stands it on its material feet, by recognizing that '[t]he mode of production of material life conditions the general process of social, political and intellectual life. It is not the consciousness of men that determines their existence, but their social existence that determines their consciousness.'[10] The dialectic needed to be demystified, needed to be righted because 'it regards every historically developed form as being in a fluid state, in motion, and therefore grasps its transient aspects as well.'[11] Hegel's dialectics got the idealism wrong, but its value remained the philosophy's power to understand a society constantly in flux.

Dialectics is 'in its essence critical and revolutionary.'[12] Cleaver makes the point that part of this criticality lies in the revelation that the 'analysis of every category and phenomenon must be two-sided' because 'there are always two perspectives, capital's versus the working class's.'[13] Moreover, each class perspective on a phenomenon is two-sided. This means that a commodity has a use-value and an exchange-value for the working class *and* a use-value and an exchange-value for capital.[14] These values are contradictory. From the working-class perspective, food has the use-value of providing workers with nutrition. The exchange-value of the food commodity determines workers' access to it; with wages unchanged, the higher the exchange-value, the more limited the workers' access. From the perspective of capital, the food commodity is useful because it forces workers to labor for capital to obtain the wage needed to be able to consume it. The exchange-value of food for capital is a source of profit.[15] The contradictions are rife. The working class needs food to live and capital 'depends on making hunger permanent among the working class'[16] – no one would work for others if we could adequately feed ourselves. The tendency is that the working class wants a food commodity with a lower exchange-value so it can have qualitatively better nutrition. Concomitantly, capital wants a food commodity with a higher exchange-value so it can accumulate quantitatively more money. To understand how these antagonistic class values are wielded and realized, in whose interest and at whose expense, is to conduct political analysis.

Marx's labor theory of value is dialectical. It is critical. It is material. It captures fluidity. And it is relational.

A commodity is any article that 'satisfies human needs of whatever kind.'[17] As already suggested, such useful articles have a dual character. A commodity has a use-value. Use-values are material – utility is a physical property – and qualitative. A commodity is also a bearer of exchange-value. Exchange-value is the social 'mode of expression' of an equation between two commodities and a quantitative relation;[18] some quantity of this commodity is exchangeable for this quantity of another commodity. Exchange-values can be realized because all commodities embody a common element: value. Value is the '[s]ocially necessary labour-time . . . required to produce any use-value under the conditions of production normal for a given society and with the average degree of skill and intensity of labour prevalent in that society.'[19] When supply and demand are in equilibrium and commodities are represented as having the same exchange-value what is really being expressed is that the commodities took the same amount of socially necessary labor-time to produce.

Value is a fluid concept because the amount of labor-time socially necessary to produce a commodity changes. A change to the conditions of production – for example, the reorganization of labor-power to make it more efficient or the introduction of new technology – will reduce the labor-time socially necessary to produce a commodity, and thereby reduce the commodity's value. Any innovations that increase the productivity of labor, that speed production, reduce the value of the commodity produced by reducing the amount of labor-time objectified in it. Because labor-power is a commodity like any other in the capitalist totality, its value, too, is dependent on the socially necessary labor-time required to produce it (this is why Dunayevskaya speaks of the value theory of labor).[20] The 'labour-time necessary for the production of labour-power is the same as that necessary for the production of means of subsistence; in other words the value of labour-power is the value of the means of subsistence necessary for the maintenance of its owner.'[21] Extending the conceptual dynamism further, the means of subsistence determining the value of the labor-power commodity are 'themselves products of history, and depend therefore to a great extent on the level of civilization attained by a country.'[22] Stated otherwise, 'the determination of the value of labour-power contains a historical and moral element.'[23] As Harvey explains, 'the value of labor-power is highly variable, depending not only on physical needs but also on conditions of class struggle, the degree of civilization in the country and the history of social movements.'[24] Ultimately, none of the factors in the labor theory of value are fixed. They are products of history, and they change.

The total value of a commodity (C) is comprised of three elements: constant capital (*c*), variable capital (*v*), and surplus-value (*s*). Stated algebraically, $C = c + v + s$. Constant capital is the value of the means of production consumed in production. A drill bit or an overhead crane is constant capital. It is what Marx calls dead labor. Variable capital, on the other hand, is the value of the labor-power commodity consumed in production. The workers on the factory floor are variable capital and their value is determined by the socially necessary labor-time required to produce their means of subsistence. This is Marx's living labor. Constant capital transfers value to the new product in the production process. It loses some value that is objectified in the new commodity. Living labor transfers *and adds* value to the commodity in the production process. It does not receive an equivalent for the total value it objectifies in the commodity. The increment is appropriated by the capitalist. '[S]urplus-value [*s*] is the difference between the value of the product [C] and the value of the elements consumed in the formation of the product, in other words the means of production [*c*] and the labour-power [*v*].'[25] Again algebraically, $s = C - (c + v)$. Surplus-value is what bourgeois economists fetishize as profit.

The value objectified in a commodity is a social relation.[26] However, '[a] thing can be a use-value without being a value.'[27] Natural energy such as oil has a use-value for capital and it has no human labor-time objectified in it. Also, not all articles are commodities. A woman who uses her labor-time to paint a canvas to adorn her wall produces a use-value but not a commodity. In order to be a commodity, the article, be it oil or a painting, must possess 'use-values for others, social use-values.'[28]

Materialist dialectics method is dialectical and studies the organization of society for the production, circulation and accumulation of value. Marx identifies six elements of social organization, what Harvey refers to as moments, in footnote four in chapter 15 of *Capital*, volume I: '[t]echnology reveals the active relation of man to nature, the direct process of the production of his life, and thereby it also lays bare the process of the production of the social relations of his life, and of the mental conceptions that flow from these relations.'[29] These elements, and the dialectical relations constituting and changing them, are represented in Figure 1.1.

Figure 1.1 Seven elements of materialist dialectics

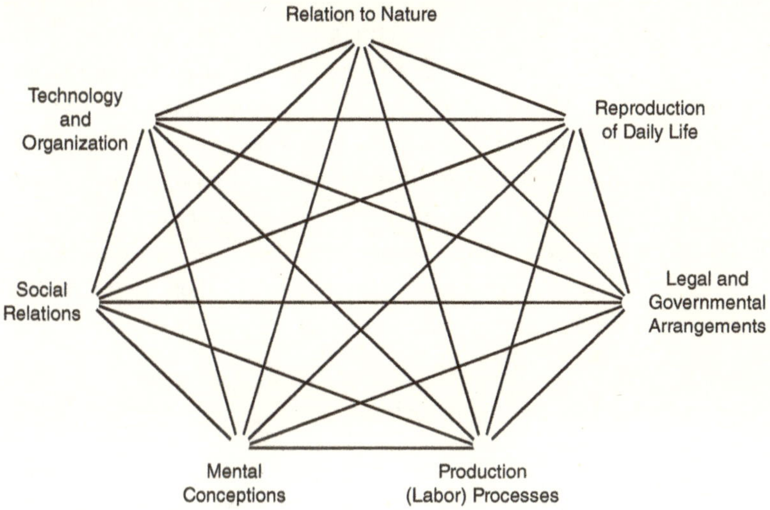

Relation to Nature

Technology and Organization

Reproduction of Daily Life

Social Relations

Legal and Governmental Arrangements

Mental Conceptions

Production (Labor) Processes

Source: David Harvey, 'The enigma of capital and the crisis this time'

Governmental arrangements are not explicitly named in the footnote, but the central and indispensable role played by the state form in the development, extension and intensification of capitalism is an idea that pervades Marx's analysis.[30] Among other things, the state form provides the force required to realize primitive accumulation and is necessary for the legal contract that is credit.

Capitalism is the totality of these inner relations and co-dependent processes. Again, there are no causal relations here. '[N]o process comes first, and each one can be said to determine and be determined by the others.'[31] Of course, this does not mean that one process – for example, reproducing daily life – cannot have a greater effect, at one temporal moment, on others than they do on it. In Marx's vocabulary, the word 'cause' is used to reflect this asymmetry in interaction.[32] No one moment is always determinant in the ensemble.

Such dialectical thinking about the material conditions of history has immediate and significant analytical implications. Commodity society is complex; it is not reducible to one factor. The political is not autonomous. The state form relates to how and how much value is produced and how and what quantity of surplus-value is appropriated. Our species being's relation to nature will not be changed without a change to our ideas. Catastrophic climate change will persist and intensify so long as human beings continue to conceive of nature in bourgeois terms as a source of surplus-value. And the reproduction of daily life, and its negation, death, is dependent on and changes with our social relations. People eat and people starve because of the balance of power between classes. Ultimately, the particular interaction of these seven general moments is the history of different social formations.

Vulgar and fetishistic literature

The present volume's critical contribution lies in its thinking about recent Egyptian history in terms of materialist dialectics' philosophy, theory and method. Much of the literature on recent Egyptian history belongs to one of two corpuses: vulgar politics or fetishistic studies. The first and least valuable corpus is bereft of all three facets of materialist dialectics. The fetishistic studies are considerably more valuable. They are non-dialectical and idealist rather than materialist, but they also have a loose connection with materialist dialectics' method to the extent that they relate political power and wealth.

Vulgar politics

The vulgar politics produces the dominant, commonsensical assessment of recent Egyptian history. It is particularly responsible for propagating the interpretation that Egypt experienced a revolution in 2011, much of it under the rhetorical guise of 'the Arab Spring.'[33] The corpus's understandings are wrong because they are philosophically, theoretically and methodologically inadequate. In philosophical terms, the literature is orthodox, meaning it conceives of change in causal terms. It assumes an Egyptian society that was static and stagnant until other regional changes 'cascaded' over it as a result of 'demonstration and diffusion effects.'[34] The cause of this wave of change is reduced to the singularity of the self-immolation of Mohamed Bouazizi in Tunisia. To answer Gause's question in critical terms, it is precisely non-dialectical thinking that caused such texts to 'miss the Arab Spring,' and that continues to cripple the corpus's research. No amount of attention to the differences between militaries and rulers and 'poorly implemented liberal economic policies' is going to understand social dynamism so long as the philosophical assumption is one of social stasis.[35]

The vulgar politics also starts from the assumption that the political is autonomous from the other moments of Egyptian society, say production processes. This, in turn, produces a singular obsession with the 'regime.' In the outmoded tradition of transitology, some scholars in this corpus wondered whether the Egyptian regime would undergo democratization.[36] Others saw the regime exhibiting a robust or recombinant authoritarianism.[37] In both cases, pride of analytical place is given to the military, *as an institution*.[38] Like so much of the discipline of political science, the texts of this corpus are apolitical; apolitical in the sense that the struggle for power is often absent from the 'analyses.' Springborg talks about the 'administration of justice the SCAF inherited with the fall of Mubarak,' and Albrecht and Bishara contend that the Egyptian military is 'governing by default.'[39] It is incredible that scholars talk as if the levers of political power and apparatuses of the state form just happened to fall into the military's hands; as if the military does not have interests in governing Egyptian society.

Overwhelmingly, this corpus is bereft of coherent theoretical analysis. Goldstone is entirely arbitrary in referring to 'sultanistic dictatorships,' 'elites,' 'ethnic and religious groups,' 'classes,' 'students,' 'professionals,' 'cronies,' 'the young population,' 'conservatives,' 'populists,' Islamists,' and 'modernizing reformers.'[40] The same can be said of Kandil's mishmash of 'parasitic businessmen,' 'the construction class,' 'the upper class,' 'the middle class,' 'superrich' and 'monopoly capitalists.'[41] Even the corpus's political economy texts, which could reasonably be expected to be theoretically informed, if not based in the labor theory of value, are theoretically incoherent. Henry's references to 'civil society,' 'support associations,' 'interest groups,' 'bully police states' and 'bunker republics,' along with his equating the dominance of finance capital with democracy and review of internet usage, are a nonsensical case in point.[42] The near total lack of theoretical rigor exposes this corpus for what it really is – neoliberal ideology.[43]

The ideology is expressed across the corpus through its juxtaposition of democrat*ization* and authoritarian*ism*. Authoritarian and democratic are different forms of government. These are the equivalents. The asymmetry the corpus posits between democratization and authoritarianism makes a positive process of the first noun and a negative, singular result of the second. To affix the suffix 'ism' to a word is to form a noun of an action, criticism, for example, or to name the completed action of a process, say plagiarism. By speaking of authoritarianism as a finished process this corpus reinforces its own assumptions regarding social stasis. To affix 'ism' is also 'to form a term denoting a peculiarity'; a colloquialism, for example.[44] In the present instance, talking about authoritarianism makes the Egyptian form of government distinct while concomitantly normalizing and generalizing democracy. By linguistic sleight of hand, the peculiarity of the powerful is transformed into the general. Finally, to append the suffix 'ism' is to derisively make of a noun a doctrine having a distinctive character. By speaking of authoritarianism and democratization the vulgar politics makes the former a singular doctrine while the latter, in comparison, is made a common process. This is a linguistic embedding of Arab exceptionalism. It is instructive that those processes valued by the vulgar politics are named with the suffix 'tion' (i.e. democratization, trade liberalization and globalization) and those it opposes are rendered 'isms' (i.e. authoritarianism, terrorism). This corpus is, in essence, just as much a doctrine as that which it ossifies and singularizes. The vulgar politics is democraticism, neoliberal democraticism.

This ideology serves two notable and interrelated purposes. It dilutes and distorts the idea of revolution beyond all recognition, and in so doing allows for the deployment of the Egyptian experience to negate the very thing it wasn't. As much as it speaks of revolution, the vulgar politics does not generally bother to conceptualize it. For Hale, the term revolution is 'used loosely to refer to leadership ouster accompanied by mass protests,' and according to Barany a revolution is an act that requires the support of a state's military to succeed.[45] Revolution is much more than this, and not this.

Revolution is a process. It is not a moment or a singularity. It is 'a dialectic of transformations across all [seven] moments' of a social formation.[46] Revolution is our species' transformation of our relation with nature, technology, social relations, mental conceptions, production processes, governmental arrangements and the reproduction of daily life. Capitalism as a mode of production is revolutionary. It overthrew feudal society and continues to transform social relations and processes. Whereas earlier modes of production were essentially conservative, the abiding need to accumulate relative surplus-value means capital can never afford to treat the existing form of a production process as the definitive one.[47] The drive to accumulate makes everything transitory. As Marx says in the *Communist Manifesto*, and this should not be read to suggest any of the determinism that is inaccurately ascribed to Marx as a result of the emphasis in this particular text, the technical basis of commodity society is revolutionary because the 'bourgeoisie cannot exist without constantly revolutionizing the instruments of production, and thereby the relations of production, and with them the whole relations of society.'[48] Capital must forever be looking for ways to accelerate production and reduce its use of labor-power. This, in turn, means that ideas and social relations, among the other elements, are also forever changing. The introduction of machine technology, for example, radically transformed social relations by increasing the quantity of the surplus population, reproduction of daily life by extending the length of the working day and our species' relation to nature by requiring natural power sources to fuel the machines and illuminate factories after sunset. Capitalist production for the sake of accumulation means 'constant revolutionizing,' 'uninterrupted disturbance' and 'everlasting uncertainty and agitation.'[49]

In this social tempest, only the proletariat is a revolutionary class. This is the class free of the means of production that must sell its labor-time in wage slavery, whether its members are actually successful in being exploited for a wage or not. It is in a value relation with capital, and is its negation. Class is *not* a wage relation. A proletarian who receives a higher-than-average wage is not of a different class. (S)he is working in an industry that accumulates more than the average rate. The proletariat is revolutionary because it can end its exploitation and alienation only by abolishing the capitalist mode of production and its relations, and it has nothing to lose in doing so. The capitalist class owns the means of production and accumulates by expropriating unpaid labor-time. It is comprised of three factions: productive capital, commodity capital and money capital. Productive capital synergistically transforms production processes, nature, technology, ideas, social relations, governmental arrangements and daily life in order to produce and accumulate surplus-value on an ever-expanding scale. It is in the production process that value and surplus-value are created. Productive capital can continue to accumulate only so long as it is relatively empowered in the capital–labor relation. Commercial capital accumulates by receiving a distributive share of the surplus-value expropriated from the working class. Productive capital provides this share because commercial capital helps it realize surplus-value. Commercial capital is conservative and reactionary because the more powerful productive capital becomes as a result of its constant transformation of production, the smaller is the share it must provide commercial capital; commercial capital accumulates less and risks being relegated to the working class. Commercial capital wants to slow or reverse productive and social transformations so as to retard or undo the disadvantageous rebalancing of its force relation with the other factions of capital. Finance capital accumulates at the expense of productive and commercial capital.[50] It takes its share of surplus-value from both. Money capital facilitates the transformation of production and society because it is powerful in relation to both factions, in the present moment particularly productive capital, as a result of finance capital's relative mobility. Within the primary contradiction of capitalism – the labor–capital social relation – the proletariat is revolutionary and all factions of capital are reactionary because while capital needs to perpetuate the relation so as to continue to infinitely accumulate surplus-value, the proletariat must destroy the relation in order to end the expropriation of its finite living time.

Two crucial conceptual points follow from this. First, the only revolution that will produce a new society serving the interests of workers, the only one worthy of the name, is a revolution realized by a working class empowered in relation to capital. Capital, as a social relation, revolutionizes the other elements of a society, but unless social relations are revolutionized such that labor is empowered in the class struggle whatever appearance of change there may be, and no matter how spectacular, it will not signal a revolution that is propelling society forward. The contradictions of the capitalist unity produce progress and change as well as the possibility of the empowered working class that must destroy the limits of the unity to realize a revolution. Second, such revolutions do not transfer the machinery of the state from from one hand to another, or leave it as an arbiter, but rather smash it.[51] The irreconcilable antagonisms between capital and labor necessitate the state form. The state form creates the order necessary for accumulation by oppressing the working class, often with the coercive instruments of the military and police. The replacement of the bourgeois state form is a violent enterprise because, as E. H. Carr observed, 'no ruling class ever abdicates of its own accord.'[52] When its order is threatened by an empowered working class, the ruling class calls on its police forces and military to use violence to protect the state form through which it accumulates. Thinking such as that of Barany is quite backwards – the military *never* realizes a revolution. To realize an actual revolution the working class must violently overcome the military and police as the primary bulwarks of social forces bent on arresting revolutionary social change.

Much as the experience of the Soviet Union is used ideologically to delegitimize Marxian analysis rather than state capitalism, the vulgar corpus is declaring the failure of the Egyptian revolution rather than neoliberal capitalism.[53] Revolution must be properly conceptualized lest the 'failure' of its misrepresentation continue to be proffered as a cautionary tale to reinforce neoliberal capital's TINA (There Is No Alternative) Syndrome.

The vulgar politics is neoliberal ideology. It is bereft of critical philosophy, a sense of social interrelatedness and analyses produced by the labor theory of value. Fetishistic studies are similarly non-dialectical, but do countenance a modicum of materialist dialectics' method. They are also not informed by the concept of value.

Fetishistic studies

Marx introduces the concept of fetishism in chapter one of *Capital*, volume I. For the present purpose, a fetishism is the illusory surface appearance of an underlying social reality. It is the representational mask that hides the reality of social relations beneath it.[54] The money form mediating exchange of commodities, for example, disguises the social relations that obtain between the producers.[55] Marx is clear in the appendix of *Capital*, volume I: 'Capital is not a *thing*, any more than money is a *thing*. In capital, as in money, certain *specific social relations of production between* people appear as *relations of things to people*, or else certain social relations appear as the *natural properties of things in society*.'[56] Prices and wages in the sphere of circulation that mediate interactions between individual consumers in the market disguise the real exploitative social relations that exist in the sphere of value production in the factory. Other fetishistic illusions include the national economy and the rate of profit.[57] As Marx explains in *Capital*, volume III, 'the analysis of the real, inner connections of the capitalist production process is a very intricate thing and a work of great detail; it is one of the tasks of science to reduce the visible and merely apparent movement to the actual inner movement.'[58] The concept of value as socially necessary labor-time pierces the fetishistic veil of apparent movement. Analysis conducted in terms of the labor theory of value descends below the level of surface appearances to understand the actual essence of capitalist relations. While fetishisms are socially real, the objectively real is known only in value terms.

This corpus is fetishistic because while attention is focused on the Egyptian working class, the frame of analytical reference is the national economy. Notable authors such as Abdelrahman, El-Mahdi, Beinin and Soliman examine the Egyptian social formation in isolation.[59] This analysis is non-dialectical. Egyptian society, any society for that matter, can only really be understood as a part of the global capitalist totality. This is precisely why Lenin was adamant that '[t]o separate "foreign politics" from politics in general, or, still worse, to contrast foreign politics to home politics, is fundamentally wrong.'[60] What is commonly known as domestic politics is a particular form of appearance of the universal relations and processes of global capital. The two spheres interrelate through the state form. Further to its non-dialectical thinking, the corpus's philosophy of change is causal. Change is not assumed to be constant. Instead, the emphasis is on explaining change, with the conceptualization being of the noun, not the verb. El-Mahdi's tellingly entitled 'Labour protests in Egypt: causes and meanings' even goes so far as to invoke the notion of 'demonstration effects' that characterizes the vulgar politics corpus.[61]

Penetrating the fetishism of the national economy by thinking dialectically has profound implications. It reveals an Egyptian working class in relation to labor and capital on the global scale, and the particularities of Egyptian society in relation to the global neoliberal totality in crisis. Curiously, this kind of critical thinking was being done before 2011. In his 2009 'Workers' struggles under "socialism" and neoliberalism' Beinin linked the wages of Egyptian textile workers to the global political economy by observing that '[i]n order to flourish, the [Egyptian textile] industry must export successfully and compete with China, the rising star in the global textile and clothing industry. This translates directly into downward pressure on wages.'[62] He made this point in the context of crisis. Similarly, in their introduction to the same edited volume, El-Mahdi and Marfleet connected the struggles of millions of working Egyptians to the vicissitudes of global capitalism: '[t]he global crisis which began in 2008 has affected the [Egyptian] economy profoundly, with huge falls in foreign investment, tourism, remittances and other key sources of income, relentlessly increasing pressures upon the poor.'[63] Disappointingly, these critical inclinations did not survive the maelstrom of 2011. The non-dialectical philosophy evident in the volume's subtitle, 'The moment of change,' clearly demanded a shift to explaining the 2011 appearances of change rather than continuing to relate Egypt's social dynamics to global capitalist relations and processes in crisis. Not only does this post-2011 penchant to separate Egyptian society out of the global capitalist crisis come disconcertingly close to the kind of exceptionalism on which Orientalism thrives, it is also curious given the corpus's attention to neoliberalism. After all, capital's neoliberal moment was initiated by the global monetary crisis of 1971,[64] and a distinctly neoliberal crisis of financialization racked the world a mere three years before January 2011. It beggars incredulity to think that a crisis that continues to flood the USA and inundate Greece, Ireland, Spain and Portugal is not deluging Egypt in some form.

Capitalism is perpetually in disequilibrium because accumulation is a contradictory process. Crises occur when capitalism is too far out of balance. They are attempts to bring bourgeois society back into equilibrium. Crises are dialectical moments; they 'are moments of transformation in which capital typically reinvents itself . . . [and] are also moments of danger when the reproduction of capital is threatened by the underlying contradictions.'[65] They are opportunities for accumulation and negations of the reproduction of capitalist social relations.[66] According to Cleaver, a crisis is a 'crisis of power between the classes.'[67] Working-class strength played a prominent role in the last three great crises of capitalism – the last twenty-five years of the nineteenth century, the Great Depression and the 1970s. Each crisis was capital's means of restoring its conditions of accumulation by restoring its control over the working class.[68] The 2008 general crisis, however, was generated by the global weakness of the working class.[69]

'Crises are essential to the reproduction of capitalism.'[70] Crises are in-built to the global totality of capitalist production and circulation. They are not accidental, and they are not driven by human avarice, though this can certainly exacerbate them. Crises are a necessary, instrumental part of how bourgeois societies are organized to produce commodities. Crises are necessary because how capitalism produces commodities tends to be too successful. Global production succeeds in producing and accumulating capital. In fact, it results in the production and accumulation of too much capital; too much capital in the sense that profitable uses cannot be found for the accumulated capital. When this happens, crises ensue as means of devaluing or destroying capital so that the surplus quantity can (again) be put to profitable use. As Marx explains in dialectical fashion in 'Wage labour and capital,' '[b]ut capital does not live only on labour. A lord, at once aristocratic and barbarous, it drags with it into the grave the corpses of its slaves, whole hecatombs of workers who perish in the crises.'[71] Crises are sacrifices of productive forces. Of course, these sacrifices, the costs of this devaluing or destruction of capital, are never equally or uniformly distributed across societies or classes in society. The consequences of the 2007/08 crisis in the USA are a case in point: laboring homeowners have lost trillions of dollars of equity, while financial institutions are again accruing hyper-profits. The same can be seen on the global scale: the 2003 American invasion and subsequent occupation of Iraq destroyed billions of dollars of capital in Iraqi lives and infrastructure and created opportunities for capital to again accumulate in the form of reconstruction contracts.

'[C]apital never solves its crisis tendencies, it merely moves them around.'[72] The crisis tendencies of capitalist social relations cannot be solved because, as Marx explains in *Capital*, volume III, '[t]he ultimate reason for all real crises always remains the poverty and restricted consumption of the masses, in the face of the drive of capitalist production to develop the productive forces as if only absolute consumption capacity of society set a limit to them.'[73] Capital accumulates for the sake of accumulation, and this accumulation tends to produce an insufficient consumption among the working class that negates accumulation. Crises are moved in space and time.[74] The rolling of the 2007/08 crisis from the USA to Europe and Africa evidences the spatial relocation. Debt, the bringing of yet-to-be-produced future value into the present moment, either for states or the working class as consumers, is one way of temporally shifting capitalism's crisis tendencies. The process of privatization by which public goods are commodified and transformed into new sites of accumulation is another way to defer the crisis tendency.[75]

Understanding crisis in dialectical and value terms necessitates a reconceptualization of politics, particularly as crisis is more and more frequently used as a governing mechanism. Politics is the class struggle for power to apportion the gains and losses of the production, realization and destruction of value. In reality, political battles in capitalist societies are not waged to solve economic crises, but rather to distribute their opportunities and costs between different classes in society and/or other societies. Despite the pronouncements of the bourgeois press, the 2007/08 crisis was not resolved; instead its costs were imposed first on working-class home-owners and debtors, and then it was moved from the USA to Europe via such mechanisms as the Federal Reserve's program of quantitative easing. Everywhere this crisis has been realized the distribution of effects has been the same, if not differentially intensive – the working class's wages, in the present form and the deferred form of pensions, have been reduced in absolute and relative terms and state services providing goods primarily to the working class have been degraded and/or transferred to private, for-accumulation ownership, while finance capital has accumulated ever more surplus-value and power.

In the particular terms of Egyptian society, penetrating the fetishism of the national economy and relating Egyptian society to global neoliberal capital in crisis reveal that in 2011 the working class was weak in relation to capital, not strong. This weakness is discussed extensively in the literature. Farah talks about the long-term erosion of the power of Egypt's subordinate classes since the 1990s.[76] Bush and Ayeb make a similar point regarding the marginalization of Egypt's agrarian labor.[77] Most instructively, Beinin explains that '[in January 2011, the independent labor movement] had no nationally recognized leadership, few organizational or financial resources, limited international support, no political program, and only a minimal economic program.'[78] Furthermore, '[o]n the eve of the overthrow of President Hosni Mubarak . . . there were only three trade unions independent of direct control by the regime.'[79] As if to prove Marx's point in *The Eighteenth Brumaire of Louis Bonaparte* that '[w]homever one seeks to persuade, one acknowledges as master of the situation,'[80] Beinin points out that '[s]triking or protesting workers commonly sought to co-opt rather than openly contest the regime's power by calling on Mubarak or a cabinet minister to visit them and hear their grievances.'[81] Even after the 'revolution' this corpus erroneously contends was realized in large measure by the working class, Beinin observes that 'independent trade unions are nonetheless the strongest nationally organized force confronting the autocratic tendencies of the SCAF . . . [b]ut that is not yet saying much.'[82] Egyptian workers are not *sui generis*. Capital's neoliberal counter-attack has weakened them in their relation with capital just as it has undermined the power of Canadian, Japanese and Chinese workers.

Egyptian society's protests in 2011 were protests of a weakened working class, not an empowered one. Because their underlying philosophy is not dialectical, the fetishistic studies mistakenly conflate the eruption of ongoing class war with revolution. Not all forms of appearance of change are marks of revolution. Revolutions are only produced and realized by an empowered working class.

The fetishistic studies are vaguely materialist dialectical in method in the sense that they make connections between power and wealth. Abdelrahman, for example, exposes the false separation of the 'political' and 'economic' in Egyptian society, and identifies the attempt by those in power to assert an ideological hegemony that recasts the revolution as one for a stripped-down liberal democracy that realizes 'freedom' and not 'economic' struggles for justice.[83] Similarly, El-Mahdi argues that 'the labour movement [in Egypt] is an outcome and a signifier of the neoliberal rupture of the post-1952 labour–state pact, both in its hegemonic (ideational) form and its domination (material) elements.'[84] However, the texts in this corpus overwhelmingly understand class struggle as an object of study, not the motive force of history. This produces a powerful misconception of neoliberalism within this corpus. Prevalent among these texts is the idea that neoliberalism is a 'model' or collection of deleterious 'reforms.'[85] Neoliberalism is 'a *political* project to re-establish the conditions for capital accumulation and to restore the power of economic elites.'[86] The material violence of dispossession and the ideal construction of economic rationality and the market serve this end by further extending the commodity form's colonization of all aspects of life. Neoliberalism is not a thing, or a collection of things. Neoliberalism has to be understood in dialectical terms, as a relation and moment between capital and labor in which the former is waging and winning a savage war against the latter. Affixing the suffix 'ism' reifies this relation. The ideas and processes associated with the neoliberal relation – transnationalization of production, privatization, deregulation, trade liberalization, social atomization, monetarization – are capital's arsenal in its war against the working class. The working class is globally weak in relation to capital because it has been losing, for more than forty years now, the push-and-pull struggle to produce and accumulate surplus-value as capital and has succeeded in making itself more mobile, heightening destructive competition between segments of the working class fractured by states and privileging the value of money over employment.[87]

The bourgeois terms 'crony capitalis(t/m)' and 'corruption' must be understood in light of this dialectical conceptualization of the neoliberal relation. Marx shows in the final section of *Capital*, volume I, that the state form was integral to the development and extension of capitalist social relations. The state form was instrumental in transforming a peasantry exploited by feudal lords into a proletariat selling its labor-power to capital. The history of capitalist society is 'anything but idyllic.'[88] In fact, it is written 'in letters of blood and fire'[89] and much of the violence was the state form's. The image of a recently (over)active, but historically passive, state is bourgeois myth serving bourgeois interests. It is ahistorical to speak of 'crony capitalis(t/m)' in connection with the privatization of state-owned industries or the awarding of government contracts as if they are aberrations to or perversions of otherwise normal capitalist relations.[90] It is also to offer a quick and valueless moral judgment in place of a political assessment of a capitalist tactic in the neoliberal class war. Amin makes a similar point about 'corruption.' Much like the state, 'corruption . . . is an organic and necessary component in the formation of the bourgeoisie.'[91] The extensions of the commodity form and the neoliberal class relation are global processes, by no means exclusive to the imperialized world. The 'cronyism' and 'corruption' associated with the Mubarak regime are no different, qualitatively, than those associated with the Bush presidency and its connection to the Enron scandal and the awarding of contracts to the vice-president's Halliburton. Cronyism and corruption are general because they are some of the means capital uses to accumulate through dispossession rather than production in the neoliberal historical moment.[92] After all, the privatization of state industries so often seen as corrupt is, in essence, the neoliberal equivalent of the Enclosures Act's commodification of social goods and subsequent transfer to private ownership for the purposes of accumulation. It is imperative that these tactics be understood in the context of the neoliberal counter-attack on labor.

A dialectical conceptualization of the neoliberal relation also ensures that political outcomes be seen as the products of class struggle, and not simply the choices of capital. There is a tendency to speak of the imposition of neoliberal relations and processes on and in Egypt.[93] This makes sense within an imperial epistemology, but it is also apolitical. It overlooks the fact that what the literature calls 'authoritarian regimes' had political and material interests in willingly subscribing to and enforcing a project intended to (re)concentrate power and wealth. By the same token, seeing only imposition by the state, or by capital through its state, ignores constant working-class contestation. Capital never gets everything it wants because it is in a power *relation* with labor. The relation may be severely unbalanced as it is in the contemporary neoliberal moment, but it remains a relation. Whatever the imposition – say, an act of trade liberalization – it is realized through capital's relation with labor and is less than capital wanted. Ultimately, the neoliberal relation must always be humanized. Neoliberalism is not some *deus ex machina*. It is a forty-five-year-old collection of tactics and weapons deployed by capital to serve its project which has been differently parried by labor and produced a class relation balanced overwhelmingly in capital's favor.

In addition to its non-dialectical thinking confusing forms of appearance of change with revolution and caricaturing the neoliberal relation, the fetishistic corpus remains focused on apparent social movement because it does not deploy the labor theory of value. In contradictory fashion, it is precisely because the vaguely materialist dialectical studies produce analyses of wealth, and *not* value, that they miss the essence of recent Egyptian history. The most glaring example of this is Joya's pseudo-critical study. She sees a 'revolution' because her concerns are with the 'huge wealth gap'[94] and workers' demands for 'better wages, lower food prices, affordable housing, the right to adequate health care and a better educational system.'[95] She is not particularly sanguine about Egypt's future because she doubts there will be a 'radical redistribution of wealth in Egyptian society.'[96] This analysis is conducted exclusively in terms of the money fetishism. Similarly, El-Mahdi sees an emerging workers' movement, imbued with a rising class consciousness, articulating political demands after the rupture of the hegemonic ruling pact that governed Egypt from 1952. Despite statements about objective conditions, El-Mahdi, too, does not penetrate below fetishistic appearances. Her emphasis on hegemony is idealist. It misses the material reality that workers protested not because they were empowered, but because they were disempowered; the protests were not about the workers making gains, but rather about their being unable to sustain further losses. Furthermore, her analysis is conducted exclusively in terms of price; in other words, the money fetishism. She distinguishes between white-collar and blue-collar workers using wages. Wages are the money name for the exchange-value of labor-power in the market. Now, money matters, but not essentially. Wages matter *in relation to* productivity in the factory. They are the dependent variable in relation to capital's rate of accumulation.[97] During the Keynesian historical moment, capital allowed labor to earn more wages because it accumulated surplus-value by increasing productivity.[98] Money is a mask and analyses conducted in its terms conceal, rather than elucidate, the real social dynamics and power relations in a society.

For its abiding interest in the working class, this corpus is curiously silent on the military as the biggest consumer of labor-power, and appropriator of unpaid labor-time, in Egyptian society. Not unlike the vulgar politics, it understands the military in institutional terms as having corporate interests in the national economy. This undertheorization of the military is the direct result of the corpus's failure to deploy materialist dialectics' labor theory of value. Focusing on the money fetishism means focusing on the market in the sphere of circulation. The Egyptian military's social importance is in the sphere of production. Its essential significance lies in how it produces and accumulates surplus-value. By not deploying the labor theory of value the fetishistic studies fail to conceive of the military as productive capital in the Egyptian social formation.

These insufficiently materialist analyses do not conduct the 'intricate and detailed' work of the labor theory of value needed to apprehend the essence of social relations. As a result, they do not see the devaluation of the Egyptian working class's labor-power commodity, in relation to capital locally and in relation to labor-power and capital globally. They also fail to see the ephemeral confluence of interests between Egyptian labor and different factions of Egyptian capital that were manifested in the so-called 25 January 'revolution.'

One final engagement with a fetishistic study that does not appear as one at first blush: Achcar's *The People Want: A Radical Exploration of the Arab Uprising*. In a direct refutation of my thesis, Achcar contends that the upheaval in Arab societies 'is neither a symptom of the general crisis of globalised capitalism, nor even a symptom of the crisis of "neoliberalism".'[99] According to his reasoning, 'the hypothesis that the Arab crisis is basically just an avatar for the global crisis does not hold up under examination.'[100] Achcar gets the matter so wrong precisely because of his reasoning. Achcar uses the word 'dialectic,' but like the authors of other texts in the fetishistic corpus, he does not conduct his analysis in terms of the radical philosophy. He marginalizes the importance of class struggle and tends towards an economism. He disregards the disempowerment of Egyptian labor in the face of capital's unrelenting neoliberal attacks and relies heavily on World Bank documents; which, it must be noted, are the only references that follow his dismissal as an 'analytical shortcut' connections made between the crisis washing across Arab societies and capital's global crisis. Achcar's language is also heavily causal. This would be acceptable given Ollman's explanation that Marx uses the word to draw attention to an asymmetry in inner relation of the seven elements of his materialist dialectics method, except Achcar does not conduct his analysis in terms of the seven elements. Instead, he, in good causal fashion, reduces the study to two elements. Finally, Achcar does not conceptualize phenomena dialectically, from the two perspectives of capital and labor. This is evident in his characterization of the American occupation of Iraq as a 'disaster' and 'debacle.'[101] While it is most assuredly a disaster for the working class, Iraqi and American, it is just as assuredly a boon for capital. Evidently, it needs restating that wars are waged because they have use-values for capital. In methodological terms, Achcar's study is not materialist dialectical. He examines the relation between productive forces and the existing relations of production, not between the dialectically related seven elements. Our species' relation to nature, for example, is nowhere in his analysis. It is instructive in this regard that while Achcar cites Marx, he cites *A Contribution to the Critique of Political Economy* and not *Capital*, volume I, or the *Grundrisse*. Achcar does not draw methodologically on Marx's predominantly methodological texts. Moreover, the Althusserian notion of superstructure that informs so much of his analysis has so little significance to Marx's method that he speaks of it only once in *Capital*, volume I, and then only in a footnote.[102] Finally, Achcar's philosophically and methodologically limited analysis is conducted in fetishistic terms. His repeated references to 'crony capitalism' are just more of the same ahistoricity. Much more problematic is his political economy of money. Achcar talks extensively about oil rents and their circulation between the Arab world and the USA, for example. He says nothing, however, about oil as a natural power replacement for human labor-power that allows capital to produce use-values without increasing exchange-values while concomitantly threatening working-class power. His discussion remains comfortable in the market and never dirties itself in the factory. Ultimately, Achcar's *The People Want* is the kind of wrong-headed analysis that is produced when Marx's name, but not his philosophy, method or theory, is invoked.

The studies in the fetishistic corpus are based on an individual ontology, reproduce the illusion of a national economy and do not use the labor theory of value. They conflate the eruption of class conflict with revolution, do not connect Egyptian society's particular crisis in 2011 to the ongoing crisis of global capital, misconceive the neoliberal relation and working-class power in relation to capital and never penetrate below the level of surface appearances. What is necessary to properly understand the essence of recent Egyptian history is an analysis that combines critical philosophy, radical political economy and a method of interacting social elements.

Before moving on to adumbrate that necessary analysis, concluding mention must be made of two texts that are neither vulgar politics nor fetishistic: Hanieh's *Lineages of Revolt: Issues of Contemporary Capitalism in the Middle East* and Amin's *The*

People's Spring: The Future of the Arab Revolution. Both texts are unlike any in the two corpuses because they realize dialectical analysis, in the sense that they understand Egypt as a particular part of the global capitalist totality. They do not reproduce the fetishism of the Egyptian national economy. At the same time, they do not examine the inner relation of all seven elements of historical materialist method. The present volume shares these texts' critical philosophy and overcomes their methodological incompleteness. The reason, however, that I see a crisis of a weakened working class where they see revolt or revolution is because we conduct different value analyses. Ultimately, it is only the detailed use of Marx's labor theory of value that allows for penetrating analysis of the actual movement of recent Egyptian history.

Structure of the book

Egyptian society has yet to realize an actual revolution. The spectacular 2011 appearance of change was a particular expression of the ongoing crisis of global neoliberal capitalist relations and processes. It was the product of the dialectical transformation of the totality of capitalist society which, most importantly for the Egyptian instance, endangered the society's reproduction. Egypt's particular crisis has not been solved. Neither has the general crisis, for that matter. Moreover, the manner in which it has been temporally deferred is setting the stage for a bigger crisis in the future. This crisis will again threaten Egyptian workers while also providing them with the opportunity to realize genuine revolutionary change.

I realize my analysis over the course of five chapters. In the second chapter, I historicize the dialectical development of crisis in Egyptian society. I explain in value terms how the crisis crystalized out of the interaction of our species' destruction of our metabolic relation with nature, neoliberal mental conceptions, the processes of accumulation by dispossession, financial technology, legal and governmental arrangements, reproduction of daily life, and changing social relations. More specifically, I show how bourgeois consumption of natural sources of power and conversion of food into biofuel, thinking in terms of freedom and Benthamite self-interest, extraction of land and privatization of workers' value, derivatives, the Commodities Futures Modernization Act (CFMA), Troubled Assets Relief Program (TARP) and quantitative easing, food price inflation, and an increased rate of exploitation so imbalanced the working class–capital dialectic as to threaten commodity relations in Egyptian society. The so-called 'revolution' was the mode of appearance of capital's dumping of value destruction on the Egyptian working class, and this endangering of the reproduction of working-class life posed an existential crisis for capital in Egyptian society.

In Chapter 3, I descend below the surface appearances of Egyptian society and lay bear the ruling ideas and relations in their essence. I expose the fetishisms of the social formation, including freedom and social justice, and conceptualize it as capital. The 'corrupt businessmen' associated with the Mubarak regime were predatory capital that accumulated through processes of neoliberal reform. The Ikhwan (Muslim Brotherhood) is commercial capital. It is reactionary because it represents the interests of merchant capital. The military is productive capital. It accumulates through the processes of production of department I and department II commodities, transportation and communication, and land extraction. My conceptualization produces five significant insights into the inner relations of Egyptian society, including the military and the Ikhwan's need for each other, and how the military must govern in coalition with another capitalist faction and that it chooses its junior partner.

In Chapter 4, I tell the story of the changing inter- and intra-class relations of Egyptian society since the eruption of crisis in early 2011 in two moments. Moment I begins with productive capital, as the senior faction in the governing bloc, disposing of its junior faction, predatory capital, and aligning, in a union of necessity, with the commercial capital faction. The relations of Moment I realized processes such as trade liberalization, debt assumption, reducing the price of the Egyptian currency and subsidization, and were expressed in forms including the Political Parties Law and productive capital's 2012 awarding of the presidential election to the personification of commercial capital. Moment II also began with a disposal – productive capital disposed of commercial capital after it had exhausted the Ikhwan's use-value, and chose as its new junior partner in governing finance capital represented by the GCC state forms. The processes of Moment II include the privatization of land and reform of legal arrangements, and the relations have appeared in, *inter alia*, the mental conception of national crisis, the technology of the 'New Suez Canal' and the 2014 constitution. Through both moments capital has savaged the working class, devaluing its labor-power commodity and disempowering it.

In Chapter 5, I extend today's analysis into tomorrow to anticipate the future of Egyptian society. It is dire for the working class. The contradictions of global capitalist relations and processes that produced crisis in Egyptian society in 2011 have been raised to a higher stage since 2007/08 through the extension of processes such as quantitative easing by major central banks. Moreover, the irreconcilable contradictions particular to Egyptian society, specifically the accumulation by dispossession necessary and ultimately impossible for the productive capital–finance capital bloc, are sharpening to another crisis. The eruption of the coming crisis will provide another revolutionary opportunity, but so long as the power disequilibrium between capital and the working class so favors capital, the coming explosion will be more reactionary and more violent than in 2011 and 2013.

CHAPTER 2

Dialectical development of Egypt's crisis moment

Introduction

The ongoing class war in Egyptian society erupted in early 2011. The working class, and with it capital, in the Egyptian social formation faced an existential crisis. In this chapter I analyze how Egypt's particular form of expression of neoliberal crisis developed through the inner relations and mutually dependent processes of global capital. I pay particular attention to how speculative inflation of food prices on the global level threatened reproduction of the Egyptian working class's life.

First, a note on Egypt's import. For as much as has been written and said about recent Egyptian history, almost all of it assumes that Egypt is significant. Rarely asked or answered is the question: why does Egypt matter? Nationalist sentiment and/or myopia are partially responsible for this. For Egyptians, and some scholars of or in Egypt, Egypt matters because it is Egypt. For capital's media, Egypt's significance is similarly tautological. Egypt matters because it matters to the imperial powers. In 2011, Egypt became singularly significant as it transformed into a spectacle. While spectacular events produce, circulate and accumulate value, they are *not* important as the media represents them. In fact, the relation between events and importance is contradictory; the more spectacular the event, the less socially important (i.e. World Cups, Olympic Games, the bringing down of the World Trade Center towers). Short-term events and spectacles are what Braudel called the 'dust' of *histoire événementielle*.[1] They have no lasting effects and are eventually swept into the wastebin of history.

Like capital's media for which they so often serve as 'experts,' scholars who fashion themselves advisors to imperial princes also see Egypt's significance in tautological terms.[2] Egypt is significant because it is a significant actor in a region that is significant to the USA. Other scholars register Egypt as important in its own terms. Korany, for example, rationalizes his and El-Madhi's *Arab Spring in Egypt: Revolution and Beyond* on the grounds that Egypt is 'the most central and populous country of the Arab world.'[3] This rationalization is insufficient – it does not explain how global and regional space is configured such that Egypt is central to it, or why geographic centrality and a Malthusian interest in population matter, but at least it does not take as given Egypt's import.

Such texts fetishize Egypt. Texts that assume that Egypt matters invest it with an innate value and/or power that are not innate at all but are rather the product of human labor.[4] Texts that see Egypt's importance in tautological terms and imagine Egypt's significance as following from some inherent quality fetishize Egypt through their state-centric individual ontology. According to Cohen, a fetishism is '*if elements . . . which must be united are initially severed, they come to be joined indirectly on an alienated plane, in illusory forms. Division in what needs to be unified leads to duplication.*'[5] Conceiving of Egypt in the singular, rather than as a duplicate product, in relations with other duplicates, of the dialectical process of dividing the global working class and gathering some of its members together under the illusion of the nation is fetishistic.

To be clear, Egypt is important. Its import is not ontologically prior to capitalist relations and processes, however. Egypt matters because the objectification of human labor in the technology of the Suez Canal has a use-value for capital. It is this technology that makes the appearance of relations and processes in Egypt more important than those in, say, Bolivia or Norway. What is important in the capitalist mode of production is what is important to capital.

Marx knew immediately that the Suez Canal revolutionized global capitalism.[6] The canal produces value, which is then available for expropriation by capital, by facilitating a change in the spatial location of commodities.[7] A full 8 percent of the world's seaborne trade, more than double the quantity of commodities that transit through the Panama Canal, passes through the Suez Canal.[8] The higher rates of value creation following on from the transnationalization of production and its just-in-time techniques are dependent on the predictability of transport produced by the Suez Canal technology. Furthermore, the Suez Canal raises the general rate of profit for capital by shortening the average turnover time of commercial capital.[9] According to the World Shipping Council, compared to traveling around the Cape of Good Hope, the Suez Canal reduces the distance between the Persian Gulf and London from 11,300 nautical miles to 6,400 nautical miles. In other words, the distance is reduced by 43 percent. In temporal terms, the movement is accelerated from twenty-four days to fourteen days.[10] Surprisingly, and counter-intuitively, at least at first blush, the canal even accelerates the movement of commodities between places such as Singapore and New York.[11] The International Energy Agency's numbers are a little different – the Suez Canal speeds the change of spatial location from the Persian Gulf to Europe by fifteen days and to the USA by eight to ten days – but its importance is the same: the canal reduces capital's reproduction period by reducing the quantity of time capital is objectified in the commodity form and, thereby, accelerates accumulation.[12]

Egypt is a form of appearance of social relations that are important to capital; considerably more important than some other expressions of relations in the imperialized world. Egypt matters because, as Sabatani says in Zola's masterpiece *Money*: 'Suez, why, it's capital.'[13] It is capital producing value. It is capital accumulating surplus-value. Egypt is important because of its dialectical relation with global commodity society – the technology of the Suez Canal is useful in the contemporary moment of capital and the contemporary moment of capital is produced, in considerable part, by the technology of the Suez Canal.[14]

Producing the crisis of reproduction

According to Ollman, 'dialectical research begins with the whole.'[15] It is only fitting, then, to start my detailed analysis with man's relation to nature.

Relation to nature

Johnstone and Mazo, in their 'Global warming and the Arab Spring,' note that '[a] proximate factor behind the unrest [in 2011] was a spike in global food prices, which in turn was due in part to the extreme weather throughout the globe.'[16] They go on to catalogue how drought and fires in Russia, Ukraine and Kazakhstan, record spring rainfall in Canada, drought and dust storms in China, 'winter kill' in the USA, drought in Argentina and torrential rains in Australia in 2010 destroyed global crop yields, including those of wheat and maize.[17] The World Bank makes much the same point, seeing climate change adversely affecting harvests.[18] Of course, the destruction of our biosphere is a global phenomenon. The air workers in Egypt breathe is heavily polluted, as is the water they consume and the soil in which their food is grown. In 1992, the World Health Organization (WHO) and the United Nations Environment Programme (UNEP) observed that 'pollutant concentrations [in Cairo] regularly exceed WHO guidelines.'[19] And contrary to the classist indictment leveled against agricultural laborers regularly offered when the pollution becomes particularly oppressive, the organizations also noted that 'the main pollution problem in Cairo results from motor vehicle traffic and from the high density of industrial activities in the Greater Cairo area.'[20] In 1990, Egypt emitted 75 million metric tons of carbon dioxide; by 2003 it was emitting 140 million metric tons.[21] The deterioration of public transportation and explosion in motor vehicle use since the early 1990s have meant that, according to measures of pollutants such as particulate matter less than 10 microns in diameter (PM10), sulfur dioxide, carbon monoxide and lead, Egypt's air was some of the most polluted in the world by 2011. Egypt's PM10 measure of 138 meant its air was more polluted than that of India, China and Mexico.[22]

At the turn of the millennium Egypt was in a water crisis with a reduction of average water availability.[23] Moreover, the reduced water to which Egyptian society had access was increasingly polluted. According to the Egyptian Center for Economic and Social Rights, 'Egypt's main source of freshwater, the Nile, is subject to unsustainably and shockingly high levels of industrial, agricultural and domestic wastewater pollution.'[24] Egypt was the region's largest polluter in terms of daily emissions of organic water pollutants,[25] but that is not all that was being dumped into the Nile. Pollutants into the Nile from production also include asbestos, mercury, arsenic and radioactive materials, including uranium and cesium.[26] This has disastrous consequences for the health of Egyptian workers, to say nothing of the destruction of animal populations and habitats and biodiversity, and further pollutes and degrades a soil already intensely exploited, including with fertilizers and pesticides, for agricultural production. The soil of the Nile Delta is so poisoned by polluted water, in fact, that its products sicken and kill livestock.[27] And in dialectical fashion, the plummeting fertility of the degraded and despoiled soil intensifies further the use of fertilizer.[28]

The Johnstone and Mazo article and the World Bank report do not relate the crisis of our biosphere to capitalist production, historically or in value terms. Those texts that calculate the economic costs of environmental degradation are no exception. They deploy the perverse bourgeois logic that the economy is the referent and nature is somehow external to it so as to colonize all of nature with the money form.[29] The crisis of the environment and climate change are anthropogenic. They are the products of our species' 300-year history of consuming fossil fuels, particularly coal and oil; what the United Nations' Intergovernmental Panel on Climate Change (IPCC) characterizes as our civilization's dependence on fossil fuels.[30] In dialectical fashion, it is our species' consumption of natural sources of power that is primarily responsible for destroying our species' relation to nature.

Our 'civilization,' as it were, is capitalist. Why is it dependent on fossil fuels? Why are coal and oil so important in the capitalist mode of production? According to Marx,

> [i]f an instrument of production has no value to lose, i.e. if it is not the product of human labour, it transfers no value to the product. It helps to create use-value without contributing to the formation of exchange-value. This is true of all those means of production supplied by nature without human assistance, such as land, wind, water, metals in the form of ore, and timber in virgin forests.[31]

Unlike labor-power or machinery, coal and oil are means of production supplied free of charge to capital by nature. While coal and oil have a price, they do not have value; no human labor-time is objectified in them. As such, the commodities enable capital to produce use-values without increasing their exchange-value. In money terms, the use of natural sources of power enables capital to produce commodities without increasing the price of the commodity. Moreover, natural sources of power have two use-values specific to the capitalist class. First, the dialectical relation between the process of mechanization and the control and use of natural energy increases productivity, which, in turn, devalues the commodity by reducing the amount of variable capital objectified in it, thereby enabling capital to accumulate more surplus-value. Second, natural energy is a weapon against the working class. Like science and machinery, natural power is inimical to the worker.[32] Natural sources of power enable capital to reorganize production processes in space to better exploit geographic differences in the value of labor-power (when capitalist manufacturing was tied to running water the sites of production were relatively limited; the transportability of coal and oil means surplus-value can be produced anywhere) and cast more workers into the surplus population. Capital consumes natural power in place of human labor-power because it helps decompose working-class power.[33] Our species' metabolic relation with nature is being destroyed by fossil fuel consumption because of how natural power subsidizes capital's production of surplus-value and the manner in which these free instruments of production help erode working-class power.

Global consumption of natural sources of power produces and/ or intensifies the processes of desertification and salination and coastal erosion in Egypt. Desertification is a peril in the Middle East and 28.6 percent of arable land in the Nile Valley is threatened with further degradation.[34] Concomitantly, in 2007 the IPCC 'declared Egypt's Nile Delta to be among the top three areas on the planet most vulnerable to a rise in sea levels.'[35] In 2009, then environment minister George Maged said, 'many of the towns . . . in the north of the Delta will suffer from the rise in the level of the Mediterranean with effect from 2020, and about 15 per cent of

Delta land is currently under threat from the rising sea level and the seepage of salt water into ground water.'[36] Maged downplayed the threat; in 2009 salination was already destroying agricultural land in the north Delta. Similarly, in 2009, in some places, 100 meters of coast were already being lost to the sea each year.[37] The *Arab Human Development Report 2009* gives a good sense of how dire the situation is: '[a]n increase in the Earth's temperature by three or four degrees would raise the sea level by approximately one metre, creating 6 million refugees in Egypt, with 4,500 square kilometers of agricultural land in the Delta flooded. Even if the sea level rises by one one-half metre, it could create two million refugees.'[38] The 1-meter rise would also threaten the city of Alexandria. If consumption of natural sources of power continues to melt all of the Greenland and western Antarctic icecaps, the Delta will be submerged to the northern outskirts of Cairo.[39]

Natural power and food prices and crises are often linked. This only stands to reason; after all, a food crisis is a crisis of the energy needs of human beings. According to Harvey, 'a response to fuel scarcities in recent times has been to go back to the land for fuel (ethanol, in particular), and this has had the predictable consequence of rapidly increasing food and other raw-material prices.'[40] The World Bank makes the same point: 'higher crude oil prices encourage greater use of food products such as corn, vegetable oil and sugar in the production of biofuels.'[41] This shifting of food products from energy for human beings to energy for machines, in turn, inflates the price of the remaining food stocks available for human consumption. (If ever there was an indictment of the perversity of bourgeois values it is that people are made to starve so machines can be powered. Dead labor living vampire-like off the soon-to-be-dead, indeed!) The relation between fuel and food again has a use-value for capital: increasing the exchange-value of both commodities devalues labor-power. This has specific regional implications. Oil-extracting state forms such as those of Saudi Arabia and Kuwait are integral to capital's war on the working class, including Egypt's working class. The oil commodity disempowers the working class, and when its price is inflated the working class's labor-power is devalued. Furthermore, the inflation of the price of oil prompts the conversion of food to fuel, which curtails the supply of the remaining food and inflates its price. Egyptian workers are locked in a circuit in which increases in the price of oil, driven because it is a free subsidy to capital in production, devalue the labor-power commodity while transforming human energy to machine energy and increasing food prices, which also devalues the labor-power commodity. Then the working class whose labor-power commodity is devalued has to access the food at inflated prices when it is imported into the society. The oil of the region is no friend of the Egyptian worker.

Our species is destroying the biosphere by consuming natural sources of power such as coal and oil because they are free means of production for capital and one of its weapon in the struggle against workers. The accelerating destruction of our metabolic relation with nature is the product of the contradiction of capital pursuing infinite accumulation against the finitude of nature.

Mental conceptions

Seeing in the world free and exploitable means of producing use-values that are bearers of exchange-value, and valuing the accumulation of exchange-value above preserving a sustainable metabolic relation with nature, are bourgeois mental conceptions. Ways of thinking about life and the world are not natural, nor are their relative social powers. They do not have an existence independent of the material conditions of production and circulation. The class or factions dominant in material relations regulate the production and distribution of ideas. Our present historical moment is ruled by finance capital and its neoliberal ideals.

'The founding figures of neoliberal thought [Hayek, Friedman] took political ideals of human dignity and individual freedom as fundamental, as "the central values of civilization".'[42] According to the neoliberal mode of conception, these values are realized by a political-economic order of robust private property rights and the free market. The state produces this order by providing a strong police force, enforcing social relations in the form of legal structures, particularly contracts, and guaranteeing the integrity of money.[43] This should not be confused with a minimalist state. In addition to perpetuating existing markets, the state is also creating new ones, say in pollution credits and the securitization of pensions.[44] Neoliberal mental conceptions make of the entire world standardized commodities circulated in markets. The state form is integral to this process of colonizing all aspects of life with the commodity form.

The neoliberal state form is also central to the process of producing societies that share a neoliberal rationality; of 'extending and disseminating market values to all institutions and social action.'[45] For the past forty-five years, how people think about the entirety of the social and natural worlds has been revolutionized. Increasingly, 'all dimensions of human life are cast in terms of a market rationality.'[46] Rational thought is more and more closely equated with profitable thought. What is right and good is what is expedient and/or what results from a cost–benefit calculation. This kind of thought is not epistemologically given, but instead has been constructed as the dominant norm. Citizens are made, through a system of rewards and punishments, to think and behave in all spheres as self-interested, utility-maximizing entrepreneurs. The neoliberal mode of conception is essentially Benthamite.[47] The idea of freedom functions in this mode to control atomized citizens as they are made solely responsible for the consequences of their exercise of freedom.[48] The unemployed are not unemployed because of the logic of capitalist production but because they freely chose not to secure the skills and/or education required by employers, for example.

Not only has the state form helped produce this economic rationality, but, dialectically, it has also been reconstituted by it. The legitimate state is no longer the state that builds parks for children's recreation or reduces instances of domestic violence, but is the state that produces growth.[49] This shift is obvious in the deployment of the bourgeois value of efficiency to assess forms of government. Efficiency makes sense in terms of economic rationality. An efficiently produced commodity can more readily be sold in a manner that enables capital to accumulate more (relative) surplus-value. Concomitantly, efficiency is antithetical to the values of democratic governance, traditionally understood. Separating powers, considering a range of perspectives, compromising and reconciling competing interests – these are not processes that economize on time and resources. Democracy is not efficient. Authoritarian and fascistic governing arrangements are efficient. This does *not* mean, however, that the neoliberal conception of politics is opposed to democracy. It cannot be because the idea that people should be governed by the rules they or their representatives author is still very powerful. Instead, neoliberal thinking has, as it has done with the notion of freedom, redefined the idea of democracy. Democracy is reduced to its bare institutional requirements, namely elections that can be efficiently executed, and those in elected positions are expected to be practical, in other words work within the limits imposed by the Benthamite rationality. In good Orwellian fashion, neoliberal thinking even defines as democratic the rule of undemocratic, technocratic governments and unelected and insulated institutions such as judiciaries and central banks.[50]

The shorthand for this mode of thought on the global level is the (post-)Washington Consensus. As the name implies, this is a shared idea of how to organize and govern political and economic systems; shared by neoliberal states representing the interests of finance capital. The institutions primarily responsible for materially realizing the ideas in the form of conditionalities and structural adjustment programs have been the International Monetary Fund, the World Bank and the World Trade Organization. Societies and state forms are transformed in line with the neoliberal utopia of unlimited growth by freeing trade and the movement of capital in the form of commodities, freeing interest rate adjustment and freeing money capital from state regulation.

In the lead-up to the eruption of the crisis of global capital in Egyptian society in 2011, the ruling mode of conceptualization in the social formation was neoliberal. The neoliberal ideal of democratic governance was hegemonic, shared across a number of disparate groups. The National *Democratic* Party (NDP) reformed the state of the Arab *Republic* of Egypt, through the processes of liberalization and privatization, to make it more efficient and realize growth and economic opportunity.[51] It also realized some women's rights and openness in terms of the media.[52] The Ikhwan repeatedly 'supported the idea of parliamentary democracy.' In 2004, for example, the group announced that it spoke the constitutional language of democracy and supported the division and rotation of powers.[53] And groups such as Kifaya sought to build in Egypt a 'homeland of democracy.'[54] According to the Pew Research Center's Global Attitudes Project, in 2010 '60% of Egyptians said that democracy is preferable to any other type of government.'[55]

The conceptualization of democracy made it synonymous with elections. Democracy in Egypt meant a freely elected executive and legislature. To this end, in 2005, and as a result of the NDP's reforms, Egypt had its first multiparty presidential elections.[56] Before, the president was endorsed through a referendum. Ten candidates contested the elections. The runner-up and leader of Hizb al-Ghad (the Tomorrow Party), Ayman Nour, was jailed on trumped-up charges for having the temerity to challenge Mubarak.[57] Five years later, and in anticipation of the scheduled 2011 president elections, Mohamed ElBaradei returned to Egypt after leading the International Atomic Energy Agency (IAEA) and proceeded to form the National Association for Change (NAC). The emphasis of ElBaradei and the NAC was free elections. Elections were to be supervised by the judiciary, monitored domestically and internationally, permit expatriates to vote and require national identity cards rather than registration.[58] In another mark of the ideal hegemony of democracy defined as elections, prominent Ikhwan members participated in the NAC.

Groups not directly involved in the political apparatuses also put heavy emphasis on core neoliberal values. Kifaya saw its homeland for democracy being built on individual freedoms, free media and free and fair elections.[59] Similarly, the group 'We Are All Khalid Said,' while focused on the issue of police brutality, also took the position that 'Egyptians are aspiring to the day when Egypt has its *freedom* and *dignity* back, the day when the current thirty-year-long emergency martial law ends and when Egyptians can *freely* elect their true representatives.'[60]

Ultimately, the neoliberal conceptualization of Egyptian society was hegemonic, commonsensical because the working class reproduced it. Workers' actions in the early twenty-first century bear this out. In keeping with Benthamite rationality, in many cases, 'rather than demonstrating confrontational class consciousness, signs and slogans at strikes and protests called on President Hosni Mubarak or some other government official to come and investigate workers' grievances.'[61] Even when workers escalated their actions – for example, when they were subject to state violence for striking to have bonuses paid and previous contractual agreements honored – they were still, at most, realizing new paths to the same neoliberal conceptualization of democracy.[62] In a telling example, when the real estate tax collectors' strike demands for wage increases were realized they pushed their actions farther because, according to the chair of the strike committee and president of the first union independent of the state form's Egyptian Trade Union Federation (ETUF) since 1957, '[e]ven though people had gotten their financial demands that we initially went on strike for, we wanted more. We wanted our freedom.'[63]

In the neoliberal moment, Egyptian society, in general, conceived of the world in neoliberal terms. The use-values of these ideas for capital are numerous. Rational, practical thought is restricted within parameters established by capital. Bourgeois democratism is about denying class antagonisms under cover of the doctrine of the harmony of interests, not dialectically overcoming them. Elections are mechanisms by which control over the growth-realizing state form is legitimized. They are not about smashing the bourgeois state form or transferring class power. Opposition to police brutality is not opposition to capital's repressive state apparatuses, but rather about improving the functioning of the police and legal structures. Ensuring the rule of law is really about respecting private property relations, including the contracts under which the working class sells its labor-power commodity. All of these ideas, in addition to the widespread interest in being more equitably integrated into the relations and processes of global commodity society, amounted to a reform of the neoliberal vision; reform in the sense of changes *within* the neoliberal view of life, not a change *from* the neoliberal view. Neoliberal mental conceptions were not rejected by the Egyptian working class. They were modified to be made better. It is a standard neoliberal trope that the ideas are good, it is the implementation of the ideas that is problematic. An obvious expression of this is the complaining about 'corrupt' privatization. Ultimately, there was no widespread mental production of a new Egyptian society. And moreover, if, as Marx says, '[t]he existence of revolutionary ideas in a particular period presupposes the existence of a revolutionary class,'[64] then the hegemony of neoliberal reformism in Egyptian society relates dialectically to the absence of a revolutionary class in the period preceding the eruption of crisis in 2011.

Production processes

Extraction of the social relation of value, rather than the oil commodity, is one of the defining processes of the neoliberal moment of the capitalist mode of production. During the Keynesian moment, capital accumulated through the expanded reproduction circuit of $M - C - M + \Delta M - C - M + \Delta M$, in which money (M) is advanced to produce commodities (C) that objectify the original money advanced in addition to more money $(M + \Delta M)$, which is constantly reintroduced into production, after the sale of the commodity, on an ever larger scale. In the neoliberal moment, on the other hand, capital increasingly accumulates through extraction. In place of growth and the (re)production of more value, existing value is taken out of one form, often forcibly under cover of bourgeois law, and transferred to another, say from a bankrupted worker's house to a bank's balance sheet. Marx calls this primitive accumulation. Harvey calls it accumulation by dispossession. The processes of this mode include:

> the commodification and privatization of land and the forceful expulsion of peasant populations; the conversion of various forms of property rights (common, collective, state, etc.) into exclusive property rights; the suppression of rights to the commons; the commodification of labour power and the suppression of alternative (indigenous) forms of production and consumption; colonial, neo-colonial, and imperial processes of appropriation of assets (including natural resources); the monetarization of exchange and taxation, particularly of land; the slave trade; and usury, the national debt, and ultimately the credit system as radical means of primitive accumulation.[65]

This kind of 'accumulation through force, fraud, predation and the looting of assets' is not exclusive to the antediluvian history of capitalism.[66] These extractive processes of accumulation are realized the world over in the contemporary moment. The invasion and occupation of Iraq in 2003 are a glaring example; more commonplace is foreclosure following on from predatory lending by finance capital, the devaluation of commodities, particularly that of labor-power, realized by the World Trade Organization (WTO) under cover of trade liberalization, and debt financing realized by the International Monetary Fund (IMF), the World Bank and, increasingly, the European Central Bank (ECB).

The restorative aspect of the neoliberal political project dovetails with this process of redistribution. Power and value are increasingly taken from workers by capital. The faction of capital hegemonic in the neoliberal moment is not, however, the same faction as was hegemonic in the Keynesian moment. As Harvey observes, '[w]hile neoliberalization may have been about the restoration of class power, it has not necessarily meant the restoration of economic power to the same people.'[67] Since the early 1970s, finance capital has eclipsed productive capital in the intra-class balance of forces in global capitalism. This is patently obvious in the prioritizing of the interests of banks and other financial institutions at the expense of commodity producers, to say nothing of workers. It follows that dispossession characterizes finance capital's moment because finance capital accumulates only through extraction via the interest mechanism. Finance capital does not directly produce surplus-value. Nor does it have to metamorphosize through the production process or run the risks associated with the commodity form (i.e. having the value objectified in the commodity lost because it cannot be sold). The formula of interest-bearing capital is $M–M+\Delta M$, and finance capital's ΔM is the form of expression of the value it extracts from the working class, as indebted consumers, as well as productive and commercial capital.

Capital's neoliberal goal of restoring to it power and value was realized in Egyptian society through the debt mechanism. By the early 1990s, Egypt was the fourth-most indebted state in the global political economy. 'Total external debt stood at $US49 billion, and the total external debt to GDP [gross domestic product] ratio had reached 150 percent.'[68] In return for Egypt's participation against Iraq in the 1990/91 Gulf War and acceptance of the imposition of structural adjustment policies authored by the IMF and the World Bank, what became the Economic Reform and Structural Adjustment Program (ERSAP), the foreign debt was reduced by US$20 billion.[69] In addition to having value extracted in the form of interest on the remaining debt, value in Egyptian society was notably redistributed by Law 96 and extensive privatization. Law 96 was promulgated in 1992 as part of a movement for agrarian reform. 'After 1992 rents [on agricultural plots] increased from seven times the land tax to [at] least twenty-two times the tax. After 1997 landowners could retake "their" land and charge tenants a market based rent, so that rents increased by as much as 400 per cent.'[70] The land could be 'retaken' because Law 96 abolished the inheritance of rent contracts. 'Before 1992, the average rent for agricultural land was LE200 per feddan per year and increased to an average of LE600 in the transition period between 1992 and 1997 and again to an average of LE3,000–4,000 after 1997.'[71] Law 96 had huge social implications. It affected a third of all the agricultural land in Egypt and more than 900,000 tenants supporting at least five million family members.[72] Ostensibly, Law 96 was to help reduce Egypt's balance of payments deficit by increasing crop production and exportation through the consolidation of landholdings. In actuality, Law 96 dispossessed peasant families and dramatically increased the power of the landowning aristocracy.[73]

A more general point about agricultural reform in Egypt: Egypt's current status as a major food importer and the society's condition of food vulnerability have a material history. In the 1960s, Egyptian society was self-sufficient in almost all basic food commodities. The notable exception was wheat, of which the society grew 70 per cent of what it consumed.[74] It even produced agricultural surpluses that it exported to the tune of US$300 million in 1970.[75] This food self-sufficiency was transformed into food dependency and vulnerability through processes of neoliberalization initiated with the *infitah* policy of the early 1970s. By the end of the 1980s, Egypt was only 20 percent self-sufficient in wheat.[76] The promulgation of Law 96 domestically is only the most blatant in a long line of measures that have provided capital with an important use-value in its war on Egyptian workers. The society's food dependency and vulnerability mean that even if its working class wanted, it could not challenge or defect from the global neoliberal order for fear of being unable to feed itself. The process of agricultural liberalization in the interests of capital has transformed Egyptian agricultural workers from feeders of the world to hostages easily threatened with starvation.

Privatization was another weapon used to dispossess Egyptian workers of value. In essence, privatization is a process whereby social goods serving social purposes are commodified and then transferred to private ownership for the purposes of individual accumulation. From just after the implementation of the ERSAP to 2003, 197 state-owned enterprises were privatized.[77] In the dialectic of accumulation and exploitation, the process was intensified after 2004 as more enterprises had to be privatized to provide profitable investment opportunities for the capital recently extracted from the commons. Between 2004 and 2010, 379 state-owned enterprises were privatized.[78] Capital accumulated doubly in this process. First, it took from the commons the value objectified in the industries. Had the industries been sold for their value this process still would have provided capital more opportunities to accumulate at the expense of the working class. However, the industries were *not* sold for their value. Capital also accumulated through the transfer of the value at 'nominal prices.' In one of the examples Farah provides, the Ammoun Hotel was sold for less than the price of the land on which it sat.[79] In the neoliberal moment of global capitalist relations and processes, capital in Egyptian society, too, restored its class power and accumulated value by expelling workers from agricultural land and dispossessing the commons.

The preceding reference to the dialectic between accumulation and exploitation is bound up with the surplus capital problem of commodity society, particularly acute in the neoliberal moment. Accumulation by dispossession works well from capital's perspective. Of course, in good contradictory fashion, the fact the techniques work actually causes capital more problems. The capital extracted from the commons and through debt must be constantly thrown back into motion lest it lie fallow and be devalued. The successful realization of accumulation by dispossession does not satiate capital, but rather drives it to demand production of ever more profitable opportunities. However, the more workers are dispossessed of value in the sphere of production, the more ineffectual they are as consumers in the sphere of circulation (assuming their consumption is not debt financed). Applications of surplus capital must have the value objectified in the commodity realized, in other words see successful transformations through sales, if they are to be profitable. 'Crises arise when the ever-increasing quantities of surplus-value that capitalists produce [and redistribute] cannot profitably be absorbed.'[80]

One of the processes used to try and check the eruption of such crises of overaccumulation, and what guarantees that each eruption is bigger than the last, has been financialization. Financialization is, in essence, a temporal displacement of the contradiction between capital paying labor-power its value and labor-power producing surplus-value for capital. In algebraic terms, the value capital advances to produce a commodity is $c+v$ while the total value capital realizes from the produced commodity is $c+v+s$. Given the exchange of equivalents assumed by the labor theory of value, there is insufficient demand within the producing society to consume the surplus. There are no consumers for s. This is the problem of effective demand. Financial instruments such as debt pull yet-to-be-produced future value into the present moment. Deficit financing makes up the difference between the value paid and the surplus-value produced, thereby allowing for the completion of the circuit and the expansion of production (i.e. $M-C-M+\Delta M-C-M+\Delta M \ldots$). When a worker takes a mortgage from a bank, what (s)he in effect does is promise her/his future exchange-value for the use-value of the house in the present. Of course, for enabling this immediate use finance capital extracts interest from the worker long into the future. It also means that productive capital does not have to wait to realize the value objectified in the house and can immediately reintroduce it into the circuit of expanded reproduction.

Technology

Central to the process of financialization has been the technology of derivatives, particularly futures (aptly named for an analytical framework that understands temporality as the essence of capitalist relations and processes). Admittedly, while technology is probably the biggest fetishistic illusion of recent Egyptian history, these are not the technologies most readily referenced. Instead, scholars such as Lynch, Achcar and Henry mistakenly make much of the role of satellite television, the internet, including so-called social media, and cheap mobile phones. What is lost on these authors is that all of this technology is means by which capital accumulates. Every show transmitted, every email sent, every post 'liked,' every phone call made produces surplus-value. By way of example, according to the ecommerce firm Ever Merchant, Facebook achieves US$5,483 in sales and Twitter US$4,308 *every thirty seconds*.[81] If it did not produce surplus-value, the technology would not have been developed. It persists because by accelerating the movement of ideals this technology raises the rate of profit for capital.

In 'Reconsidering the robustness of authoritarianism in the Middle East: lessons from the Arab Spring,' Bellin correctly notes that some technology can function as an effective means of mobilizing workers.[82] Centuries ago, workers developed a stronger sense of class consciousness, solidarity and institutions such as unions because production was organized in the factory. Of course, they were brought together in the first place to serve the interests of capital, and their ideas and innovations drove capital to develop machine technology. Bellin, like all the others, is blind to the contradictions of technology. It can empower the working class in its struggle and it is one of capital's weapons in its war against the working class. Technology replaces the worker and is used to dictate the pace and intensity of workers' labors. Cox explains that '[t]echnology is the means of solving the practical problems of societies, but what problems are to be solved and which kinds of solutions are acceptable are determined by those who hold social power.'[83] This is precisely why, today, capital can be moved around the planet in microseconds and yet people still die for want of potable water.[84] The much-vaunted Facebook phenomenon in Egypt is a window on the profoundly unequal power relations between classes in the society. Facebook was inescapable during the period around 25 January 2011, even after Egypt's internet connections had been severed. Wael Ghonim's 'We Are Khalid Said' page was famous. Walls, corrugated fencing and a police truck were emblazoned with 'Facebook.' A couple even named their daughter 'Facebook.' Now Facebook appears to be a social networking site. In actuality, Facebook is technology by which workers' unwaged labor-time is consumed to produce information in the form of user profiles and updates, expressions of preference, shared photos and videos and common-interest groups. Facebook commodifies this information and sells it to advertisers. Beneath the façade, Facebook is the further colonization of workers' free time by the commodity form. If, as Cleaver contends, how the commodity form is realized in society depends on capital's power in relation to the working class, then the fact that Facebook is voluntarily and so widely produced by the Egyptian working class is evidence of just how weakened it is in relation to capital.[85] The Egyptian working class produces vast quantities of the data commodity in exchange for a paltry profile page and some 'likes.'

The class in control of the production process determines the technology developed in any moment. It is no surprise, then, that the information technology developed during the hegemony of finance capital 'facilitates financialization rather than production.'[86] Central to the process of financialization has been the technology of derivatives.

Invented in the 1970s, a derivative is 'a financial instrument whose value depends on (or derives from) the values of other, more basic underlying variables.'[87] Different types of derivatives include forward contracts, futures contracts, swaps and options. The first two are very similar and most germane to my analysis. In keeping with the temporality Marx saw at the heart of bourgeois society, both are contracted relations 'to buy or sell an asset at a certain future time for a certain price [agreed to in the present moment].'[88] The difference is that while forward contracts are private relations traded in over-the-counter markets, meaning over telephone and computer networks, futures contracts are standardized relations traded on an exchange, say the Chicago Board of Trade. Henceforth, I use the term 'futures.' Where a futures contract involves a transaction in the future, a spot contract is an immediate transaction at today's price. Capital takes what are called long and short positions on futures contracts. Taking a long position means agreeing to buy the asset on which the derivative depends on a specified future date for a price set by the contract in the present.[89] Taking a short position means agreeing to sell the underlying asset on a specified future date for a price set in the present moment.[90] Capital taking a long position is betting that between the date the contractual relation is agreed and the date it matures the price of the asset will rise; that the spot price on the day of maturity (Mp) will be higher than the agreed-to contract price (Cp). Capital taking a short position, on the other hand, is betting that the price of the asset will fall between the date the contractual relation is agreed and the date it matures; that the contract price (Cp) will be higher than the future spot price (Mp). Capital profits from buying long-position futures contracts when Mp>Cp. Capital profits from selling short-position futures contracts when Cp>Mp. If more capital wants to go long than short, meaning there is more buying of futures contracts, then the price of the contract is inflated. If more capital wants to go short than long, meaning there is more selling of futures contracts, then the price of the contract is deflated.[91] Because futures contracts only require capital to advance a percentage of the overall price of the derivative in a margin account, the futures market enables speculative capital to obtain considerable leverage.[92] With this leverage capital can create a self-fulfilling prophecy of sorts with futures contracts. Capital can take a long position and then with a relatively small outlay drive up the price of the asset by buying up more futures contracts. Or, in a process captured by Marx's mobilization of the idea of '*Apres moi, le deluge,*'[93] capital also profits by buying contracts to sell them again at higher prices before that moment at which a higher price cannot again be realized.[94] Capital bets the price will rise and raises the price by placing more and more bets.

Legal and governmental arrangements

At first blush, it is reasonable to see Egypt's crisis of early 2011 being connected with the fraudulent parliamentary elections of late 2010.

While the charge that the elections were rigged is essentially worthless in its obviousness, the results – the particular outcome of the rigging – are certainly an interesting appearance of the intra-capitalist class struggle in the society at that moment. Almost completely unexamined, however, is how legal and governmental arrangements authored years before in Washington impacted Egyptian society in 2011. I am speaking specifically of how the Commodities Futures Modernization Act (CFMA) of 2000, the Troubled Assets Relief Program (TARP) of 2008 and the Federal Reserve Bank's policy of quantitative easing of 2008 contributed to the Egyptian working class being unable to reproduce its life and, thereby, endangered commodity relations in the Egyptian social formation.

As one of capital's neoliberal attacks on the working class, the Commodities Futures Modernization Act of 2000 deregulated and financialized the global trade in food commodities. It ended the regulating of food commodity derivatives by the Commodity Exchange Act, and, *inter alia*, reduced the capital requirements involved in the commodity trading, thereby eliminating, to all intents and purposes, the cap on the number of commodity futures contracts capital could hold. Derivatives originally functioned to mitigate risk and provide a form of insurance. For example, a farmer agreeing to sell wheat in a futures contract got the security of a guaranteed price in the present for the yet-to-be-produced wheat. A clearing house purchasing the yet-to-be-produced wheat assumed some risk with the futures contract in that it might have to pay a higher guaranteed price than the market would determine in the future in the case of a bumper harvest and oversupply of wheat, but it also enjoyed the reliability of supply. This reliability was particularly important because inevitably the clearing house had other futures contracts to sell the wheat to another buyer, say a bakery. The act's deregulation of agricultural commodity derivatives transformed them from means of mitigating risks between buyers and sellers to mechanisms of the aforementioned speculative accumulation. The CFMA allowed financial capital in the form of banks, hedge funds and pension funds to inundate food-based derivatives. This capital has no intention of possessing the agricultural commodity. 'The vast majority of futures contracts do not lead to delivery. The reason is that most traders close out [enter into the opposite type of trade] prior to the delivery period specified in the contract.'[95] Finance capital is not interested in the food, or whether the working class can afford to access it, for that matter. It profits from price differences between its long and short futures contracts. In 1996, this speculative capital constituted 12 percent of the holdings in agricultural futures markets. By 2011, speculative capital constituted 60 percent of the agricultural commodity contracts.[96] A derivative is a fetishism of a fetishism and the effect of the CFMA deregulation was to facilitate 'speculation on speculation.'[97]

TARP was created by the Emergency Economic Stabilization Act of 2008 in response to the financial crisis that erupted in 2007. It authorized the US 'Secretary of the Treasury to purchase or insure up to US$700 billion in troubled assets owned by financial firms.'[98] The 'troubled assets' that could be purchased or insured were derivatives dependent on mortgages. As the crisis deluged the American working class and houses were foreclosed upon and ended up 'underwater' (the mortgage balance was more than the price at which the house could be sold), these derivatives were exposed as worthless. Notably, the Capital Purchase Program of the Bank Support Program, which was the centerpiece of TARP and responsible for the disbursement of the majority of the TARP funds, 'did not purchase the mortgage-backed securities that were seen as toxic to the system, but instead purchased preferred shares in banks. The resulting addition of capital, it was hoped, would allow banks to overcome the effect of the toxic assets while the assets remained on the bank balance sheets.'[99] Leaving aside the glaring contradiction that is 'toxic asset,' TARP *added* money to the global economy via the institutions of finance capital while it allowed this capital to escape the devaluation of its derivatives. That devaluation was deferred in time.

Quantitative easing must be understood as a complement to TARP. It was a monetary policy initiated by the US Federal Reserve Bank in late 2008 to increase the quantity of money in the global economy. Additional money could not be pumped into circulation by traditional bourgeois means because monetary policy could not be loosened further; the interest rate was already zeroed.[100] The state fabricated money, as it did to realize TARP, and used it to buy from finance capital government bonds and the worthless derivatives that had been left as 'assets.' The chairman of the Federal Reserve Bank, Ben Bernanke, emphasized that the program was more accurately one of 'credit easing' because it was interested in the composition of purchases from finance capital, not necessarily the size of the purchases. Bernanke was right – the composition of the purchases *is* key here. According to the International Monetary Fund, the state exchanged the newly minted money for much more fictitious capital in derivatives rather than in government bonds.[101] The use-value of this for finance capital was that it got to unload onto the central bank the otherwise worthless derivatives that it had not yet had to devalue because of TARP while it kept the government bonds representing capital still guaranteed by the state form. By 2014, the Federal Reserve Bank had, through quantitative easing, monetarized and socialized US$4.5 trillion in what otherwise would have been losses to finance capital.[102] Together the state policies of TARP and quantitative easing set free the capital locked in the derivatives *before* it was devalued, and thereby enabled finance capital to search out new profitable opportunities for it.

Reproduction of daily life

Between the beginning of 2007 and early 2008, the global working class suffered a food price crisis. The prices of food commodities such as dairy products, edible oils and soybeans were pushed to record levels. The United Nations Food and Agricultural Organization food index rose 71 percent, with the price of rice and cereals rising a devastating 126 percent.[103] Parenthetically, it is a curious lacuna from all of the literature on Egypt's 2011 crisis which historicizes it with references to the protests in Mahalla in 2008 that no thoroughgoing connections are made with that moment's global food price crisis. According to Olivier De Schutter, the United Nations Special Rapporteur on the Right to Food, these 'changes in food prices reflected not so much movements in supply and/or demand of food, but were driven to a significant extent by speculation.'[104] Finance capital flooded into futures contracts for commodities such as wheat and maize and drove the prices higher 'because other financial markets had dried up.'[105] Says De Schutter: 'the reason for [the flood of capital into food commodities derivatives] was simply because other markets dried up one by one: the dotcoms vanished at the end of 2001, the stock market soon after, and the U.S. housing market in August 2007.'[106] This is not surprising because 'speculators make it a rule, when such sudden changes in value occur, to speculate in the raw material in its least worked-up form.'[107] Without expressing it as such, De Schutter describes the 2008 food price crisis as a mode of appearance of the surplus capital problem. This is Panitch and Gindin's analysis, too: 'as the financial crisis hit in the summer of 2007, financial investors not content with the low returns entailed in the safety of US Treasuries turned to commodities.'[108] In another interesting parallel, De Schutter says '[c]ommodity index speculation was the gift that was designed to keep on giving.'[109] This echoes Marx's observation that '[b]y virtue of being value, [the money form] has acquired the occult ability to add value to itself. It brings forth living offspring, or at least lays golden eggs.'[110] Speculation on food commodities that is not really speculation because capital is inflating the price by hoarding futures contracts is the financial equivalent of the goose that lays the golden eggs.

Panitch and Gindin make the salient point that the resolution of crisis changes the terrain for the development of future crises.[111] While the 2007/08 food price crisis involved the technology of derivatives, it appeared before TARP and quantitative easing were initiated. In turn, TARP and quantitative easing contributed to the reappearance of a global food price crisis in 2010/11.[112] Figure 2.1 shows how rapid food price inflation in the second half of 2010 tracks with the second phase of quantitative easing. Food prices shot up as the Federal Reserve Bank was freeing capital from worthless derivatives (prior to devaluation) and financial institutions were again casting around for profitable uses for it. Quantitative easing is not the whole story, but there is clearly a connection between the pumping of hundreds of millions of fabricated dollars into the global economy, the exacerbation of the surplus capital problem and its quick reappearance in the form of another food price crisis.

Figure 2.1 Quantitative easing and the commodity food price index

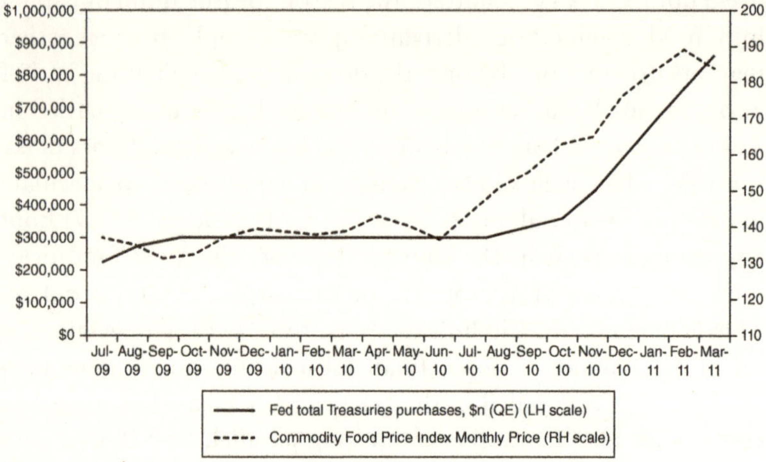

Source: Andrew Lilico, 'How the Fed triggered the Arab Spring in two easy graphs,' *The Telegraph*, 4 May 2011

By 2010/11, '[t]he conditions that created the 2007–08 price hike and food riots [had] not changed.'[113] Surplus capital was still looking for opportunities to accumulate, and while other such opportunities had not (re-)emerged the working class still had to eat. Capital again flooded into food commodity futures and drove the United Nations Food and Agriculture Organization's food price index to its highest-ever level (Table 2.1).[114]

From the first quarter of 2010 to the first quarter of 2011, the price of wheat was increased by 69 percent.[115] In the last quarter of 2010 alone, the World Bank food price index rose 15 percent, with a 20 percent increase in the price of sugar, a 22 percent increase in the price of fats and oils and a 12 percent increase in the price of maize.[116] Between June 2010 and January 2011 wheat prices were more than doubled, with 20 percent of that increase produced in the last quarter.[117] The price of a metric ton of wheat was bid up from US$194.54 in February 2010 to US$348.15 in February 2011 (Table 2.2). In global terms, the food price inflation in the second half of 2010 pushed 44 million more people into extreme poverty.[118]

The 2010/11 food price inflation developed through the dialectal inneraction of capitalism's destruction of our biosphere, neoliberal

Table 2.1 Food and Agriculture Organization of the United Nations' food price index

Year	Food price index
2000	91.1
2001	94.6
2002	89.6
2003	97.7
2004	112.7
2005	118.0
2006	127.2
2007	161.4
2008	201.4
2009	160.3
2010	188.0
2011	229.9
2012	213.3
2013	209.8
2014	201.8

Source: United Nations Food and Agriculture Organization

mental conceptions, deregulation and financialization, relations of derivatives technology and arrangements such as CFMA and quantitative easing. It flooded across Egyptian society in particular via a tripartite relation between the Egyptian working class mediated by the state form, Russian capital represented by the Russian state form and an institution of finance capital unknown to most Egyptians, certainly not a name as familiar as Mubarak or Obama.

Capitalism's destruction of the environment took the form of drought and fires in Russia in 2010. On 3 August, the grain unit representative of Glencore, one of the world's largest financial capital speculators in commodities, suggested that the Russian state impose a ban on wheat sales in the face of the extreme weather.

Table 2.2 Wheat price per metric ton

Year (2010) to year (2011)	Price (US$) of metric ton of wheat, No. 1, Hard Red Winter
February	194.54
March	191.07
April	192.82
May	181.88
June	157.67
July	195.82
August	246.25
September	271.69
October	270.23
November	274.08
December	306.53
January	326.55
February	348.15

Source: Index Mundi, www.indexmundi.com/commodities/?commodity=wheat&months=60

Two days later, on 5 August, Russia did just that. Russia imposed the ban despite having sufficient wheat stocks to make up for the lost harvest.[119]

Glencore's suggestion of a ban and Russia's realization of the ban make sense according to the speculative logic of derivatives. The extraordinary rise in wheat prices in 2010 'hurt suppliers such as Glencore because they likely had signed contracts to supply wheat at much lower prices.'[120] Not expecting the price of wheat to reach record levels, Glencore's short position in futures contracts surely specified prices that were lower than the spot price of wheat in the summer of 2010.[121] Stated simply, Glencore would have lost profit had it had to honor its promises to sell because Mp>Cp. Glencore was not the only party interested in voiding its derivatives contracts. Russian capital, too, did not want to honor its short position and sell its wheat below the market price that was exploding upwards.

Whatever price it had negotiated in early 2010 it was surely below the August spot price. The ban was the panacea for both parties because '[a] government-imposed ban on exports is considered as a "force majeure," which effectively voids the contract and frees both parties from liability in the event of circumstances beyond their control.'[122] The export ban imposed under cover of environmental catastrophe nullified Glencore's profit-losing speculation. This was not all, however. At the same time that Glencore was working to annul its profit-losing bets by realizing the export ban in August, it was betting again on a rise in wheat prices.[123] Incredibly, it was placing new bets in the form of new future contracts that were dependent on a policy it had recommended, while simultaneously using that policy to wipe out its older, losing bets. These new bets paid off as the price of wheat increased 15 percent in two days as a result of the ban.[124]

Glencore is the largest speculator in Russian wheat. Egyptian society is the largest importer of Russian wheat.[125] The Russian state's ban on wheat exports benefitted the finance capital represented by Glencore and Russian capital and cost the Egyptian working class. While Glencore's and Russian capital's short positions were rendered unprofitable by the record rise in wheat prices, the Egyptian state form's long position taken to feed its working class was particularly advantageous because its wheat derivatives were contracted below the market spot price. The declaration of *force majeure* enabled Glencore and Russian capital to void the insurance the Egyptian state form had purchased against just such a rise in wheat prices. The export ban meant more exchange-value for the capital of Glencore and Russian capital while '[c]ountries like Egypt really got screwed.'[126]

All together, the increase in food prices in 2010 was devastating for Egyptian society. It produced 19 percent food price inflation between February 2010 and February 2011, with a full 16 percent of this coming in the last six months of 2010.[127] Such inflation ravages any society, but it is particularly damaging for a society in which 45 percent of the population subsists on less than US$2 a day and in which food claims almost 50 percent of household income, more than housing and utilities, healthcare and education combined.[128]

The damage is not much blunted by the state's bread subsidy. The subsidy is not targeted to deliver relief to those most in need of it. It is biased to urban areas.[129] And it does not fully insulate the Egyptian working class from food price inflation as the prices of nonsubsidized wheat products and other staples still rise.[130]

In the singular, the exchange-value stolen from the Egyptian working class in the form of inflated food prices enabled Glencore to relatively accumulate capital. In more general terms, capital absolutely accumulated power through the food price inflation. It is, of course, not surprising that the American state form and its Federal Reserve Bank were central to the latter process. Glencore profited from the wheat export ban while other finance capital lost money. According to the *Financial Times*, '[o]ther top trading houses, including Cargill, benefited from the supply disruption in Russian wheat, but some, such as Archer Daniels Midland, suffered.'[131] In global neoliberal capitalist relations and processes, finance capital is a price-maker for food commodities. As Miller explained on the Global Research website, with the CFMA's deregulation and removal of 'a limit to the number of commodity futures contracts that could be held, investors [are] able to withhold huge amounts of food from entering the market.'[132] Instead of hoarding the actual commodity, say wheat or maize, speculators now hoard or bid up futures contracts derived from the commodities. The effect is the same – prices of food are driven ever higher for profit and the working class's access to nutrition is further restricted. It is the Bengal famine all over again on a global scale, the same destruction of productive forces and corresponding extraction of massive exchange-values, realized with the new technology of derivatives.[133]

In reality, it is a misnomer to label this process 'speculation.' It is not 'speculation' when capital can dictate the price changes it requires in order to accumulate because of its monopoly power born of leverage. 'Bets [on future price rises] can become self-fulfilling if you are big enough to affect the market,' and finance capital is.[134] The CFMA created a situation, which was exaggerated by TARP and quantitative easing, in which finance capital can guarantee its own accumulation of capital. All it has to do is throw millions more working people into poverty and hunger or starvation by hoarding commodities futures and inflating their price. Clearly, this is a cost finance capital is willing to pay.

The original demand of the 25 January protests was *'aish* – bread. The demand was leveled because bread, the staff of life, had been made too expensive for the Egyptian working class. The surplus value contradiction of global neoliberal capital in crisis, produced and intensified by consumption of natural power, neoliberal mental conceptions and governmental arrangements such as TARP and quantitative easing, was transmitted to Egyptian society via derivatives technology and took the form of inflated food prices.

A number of texts reference rising food prices in connection with the appearance of crisis in Egypt in 2011. Springborg's 'The political economy of the Arab Spring' says, citing *Al-Ahram*, that '[i]nflation in the vital food component of the cost of living index was running at 20 per cent in the early summer.'[135] Bush's 'Marginality or abjection? The political economy of poverty production in Egypt' notes that 'food price *rises* triggered political and social unrest in Yemen and North Africa in general, and foregrounded the Egyptian revolution.'[136] In *Lineages of Revolt: Issues of Contemporary Capitalism in the Middle East*, Hanieh sees food price inflation as a proximate root of the uprising, but by no means the single cause.[137] Vulgar, fetishistic and dialectical studies all broach the issue of food price inflation. None of them, however, makes the essential connection between food price inflation and the crisis of reproduction, of working class life and by extension capital. Springborg's statement concludes a paragraph and receives no elaboration. Bush's note is made parenthetically. In his commitment to dialectical reasoning Hanieh seems unwilling to acknowledge that at one moment one process, in this instance the inflation of food prices, can have a greater effect on other processes than they do on it.[138] Our species has been consuming nature and producing pollutants at unsustainable rates for centuries. Capital's neoliberal attack on the working class, Benthamite rationality, the governmental and legal arrangements of Law 96 and the CFMA and the technology of derivatives are all decades old. While dialectically related, of course, the extent of food price inflation was what was new and originally exploitative in 2010/11. All the relations of global capitalist production and circulation were in severe disequilibrium, but the food price increase in Egypt was a particular appearance of the most acute contradiction. There are historical precedents for this line of analysis. In 1977, the '*intifada* of bread' exploded when the Egyptian state form, at the instruction of the IMF and the World Bank, tried to effectively inflate the price of basic foodstuffs and reduce real wages by drastically cutting subsidies. In 2007, some 10,000 workers in Mahalla waved loaves of bread in demonstration against the rising price of basic foodstuffs[139] as they were ascending toward their then record highs in 2008 (Table 2.1). It is not coincidental that what Beinin characterizes as 'the largest and most sustained social movement in Egypt since the campaign to oust the British occupiers following the end of World War II'[140] emerged at the same moment that the global food price index was being relentlessly driven to its record highs.[141] Lest this analysis be engulfed in the economic and political froth, it must be remembered that it is not about food prices per se, but how the inflating of food prices attacks the wages of the working class and devalues its sole commodity, thereby eroding the class's power.

Food price inflation endangers the reproduction of workers' lives; and more than in the relatively short-term sense of starvation. Where the aforementioned destruction of our species' metabolic relation with nature produces diseases such as asthma and dysentery, food price inflation relates to obesity and malnutrition, which are, in turn, linked to other diseases. The quality of the working class's diet relates inversely to the price of food. As the price of food rises, workers' nutrition deteriorates, presuming there has been no commensurate increase in wages, because they economize by consuming higher-fat and higher-sugar foods.[142] The poor diet that follows on from workers economizing to perpetuate their subsistence malnourishes children and makes adults obese. As the *Arab Human Development Report 2009* observes: 'the cheap, low-grade and processed foods that starve children of absolutely crucial nutrients also make adults fat.'[143] Workers whose reproduction is endangered by food price inflation, and who can, labor longer and have more of their labor-time expropriated by capital so as to earn more wages in an attempt to again have access to the same quality of nutrition. This means they have less free time which often entails them purchasing (more of) the processed foods which are less nutritious, further intensifying the dialectic between malnutrition, obesity and food price. They are weakened in relation to capital, and they are weakened physically. Before the two record price spikes, in 2006, 66 per cent of Egyptian society measured overweight or obese.[144] Obesity 'contributes to diabetes, high blood pressure, coronary arterial diseases, degenerative joint diseases, and some types of cancer.'[145] The World Health Organization estimates that 7 million Egyptians will suffer from diabetes by 2030.[146] The public health epidemic born of the Egyptian working class having to consume less nutritious food because capital was accumulating more value by inflating food prices was another dimension of the crisis that exploded in early 2011. Of course, the food price inflation injurious to the health and reproduction of the working class is another opportunity for capital to accumulate. As Marx says: '[c]apital . . . takes no account of the health and length of life of the worker, unless society forces it to do so.'[147] In 2011, the Egyptian working class was so imperiled that capital was forced to take account.

Social relations

Much has been made of the 'youth' in the appearance of the global capitalist crisis in Egyptian society.[148] This entire discourse is wrong-headed. It is not sufficient, however, to recognize that conducting studies on the grounds that people share the same interests because they are born at approximately the same time is the scientific equivalent of studying people because they are born under the same constellation of stars. El-Mahdi moves us some way away from this nonsense by recognizing in the heuristic device of 'youth' a 'new imaginary homogenous construct' that reduces the class composition of the 25 January protests.[149] Achcar exposes the material interests behind this instrument of knowledge production when he explains that the Youth Bulge theory was '[f]ormulated in Central Intelligence Agency (CIA) circles' and then disseminated by, among others, Samuel Huntington.[150]

What appeared as 'youth' in Cairo, Alexandria and Suez was, in essence, the unwaged surplus population flooding the streets. They are unwaged because they are unemployed (or under-waged because they are underemployed). In other words, they are unable to sell their labor-time to capital. 'Every worker belongs to [the surplus population] during the time he is only partially employed or wholly unemployed.'[151] They are unemployed because capital has made them superfluous to the requirements of production. They are unable to sell their labor-time because their abstract labor has been replaced by machines; they are variable capital displaced by constant capital. The unwaged are particularly weak in relation to capital because they do not possess the power of the wage weapon. They are also instrumentalized by capital as they are used to increase productivity (capital appropriating more unpaid labor-time from variable capital) and deflate the wages of those able to sell their labor-time. Explains Marx:

> [b]ut if a surplus population of workers is a necessary product of accumulation or of the development of wealth on a capitalist basis, this surplus population becomes, conversely, the lever of capitalist accumulation, indeed it becomes a condition for the existence of the capitalist mode of production. It forms a disposable industrial reserve army, which belongs to capital just as absolutely as if the latter had bred it at its own cost.[152]

Just as capital cannot exist without labor, it cannot exist without labor in the form of surplus population. As capital expands and the demand for labor-power increases, and with it wage demands that reduce capital's accumulation, the surplus population is drawn upon to blunt the wage demands. And when capital contracts in moments of crisis, value is destroyed in the form of workers set free to expand the ranks of the industrial reserve army.

Just because a segment of the working class is unwaged does *not* mean it is somehow outside capitalist relations and processes, and it is certainly not grounds to understand it in other than class terms. The unwaged and superfluous are integral to the capitalist totality. Accumulation of capital means the accumulation of surplus population.[153] In the particular case of Egyptian society, Law 96 and privatization accumulated massive amounts of value for capital and increased markedly the quantity of the surplus population through such processes as dispossession and downsizing. While talk of the 'youth' is fetishistic, the conceptual strength of this ideal in Egyptian society is a mark of working-class weakness. When the unemployed and underemployed see themselves in the contrived terms of the doctrine of the harmony of interests they clearly do not have a robust sense of class consciousness. The unwaged surplus population is part of the working class in itself, and it must identify as a class for itself.

Of course, this working-class weakness in relation to capital has a material history that antedates 25 January 2011. In keeping with the old adage, the Egyptian working class was weaker because of the food it ate. More specifically, the Egyptian working class, like the global working class of which it is a particular part, has been increasingly disempowered in relation to capital by the long-running inflation of food prices. In the *Grundrisse*, Marx explains that 'the increase in the wheat price by a factor of [x] would be the expression of an equivalent depreciation of all other products.'[154] These other products include the working class's labor-power commodity. For the sake of ease, round numbers are used to illustrate this point. In one year a society produces 1 bushel of wheat that commands the same price that 100 bushels of wheat did the year before. If it is postulated that the working day necessary to produce one bushel is A, then the society exchanged $A \times 100$ working days for $A \times 1$ working days. The value of the working day has been diminished by a factor of 100, and so too have all the other values in the society. All capital would represent 1 percent of its earlier value.[155] What must be remembered is that the labor-power commodity is exchange-value only in relation to another commodity, in this case wheat.[156] Expressed differently, if five hours of labor-time produce a metric ton of wheat that is sold for US$200 in 2009/10, then when the price is inflated 19 percent to US$238 in 2010/11 it is the equivalent of consuming 5.95 hours of labor-time to produce the same ton of wheat. Inflation has the appearance of increasing the socially necessary labor-time objectified in the commodity. It is tantamount to diminishing productivity. Instructively, in this discussion Marx notes that any distinction between foreign and domestic on the issue of increased food prices is altogether illusory; this applies to a society that sees prices rise because it suffers a crop failure, or a society purchasing food at inflated prices.[157] By early 2011, the inflation of food prices by 19 percent depreciated the Egyptian working class's labor-power commodity by 19 percent.[158]

'[F]ood is a moment of class struggle.'[159] Again, the food commodity has a use-value and an exchange-value for the working class and capital. The use-value of food for the working class is nutrition so it can go on selling its labor-time again tomorrow. The exchange-value of food determines the nutrition the working class can access; the lower the price, the more nutrition. For capital, on the other hand, the use-value of food is that the working class has to work for capital in order to be able to eat. The historical fact that people can no longer feed themselves is what drives workers to continue to produce surplus-value for capital. The exchange-value of food for capital determines profit. What becomes obvious, particularly from the perspective of capital, is that there is a wealth aspect to the food commodity, and also a power aspect. The food commodity is at least as much about the balance of forces in the class struggle as it is about accumulation.

The long-running inflation of wheat prices, particularly pronounced in 2010, decreased the real wages of the Egyptian working class. First, this reduced the claims the working class could make on value objectified in other commodities, such as school books and shoes. Second, it meant the disempowerment of the working class. 'From the standpoint of workers the wage is first and foremost a weapon and a measure of working-class power.'[160] When the real wage is increased, for example when the prices of consumer goods are reduced by productivity gains, the working class is empowered relative to capital. The money can, in turn, be used to free time from capital production and even turned to activities that challenge capitalist relations of production. When the real wage is reduced, as it was most sharply in Egyptian society in 2010, the working class is disempowered in relation to capital. The working class loses the free time and money necessary to effectively contest its own exploitation. Increasing the price of food commodities by 19 percent eroded working-class income and power and gave capital *more* wealth and control in the Egyptian social formation.[161] It also weakened the Egyptian working class in the totality of global capital. In comparison to the 19 percent food price inflation realized in Egypt in 2010, China experienced only 8 percent.[162] Now, commodities produced with value in Egyptian society are in particularly heated global competition with commodities produced with value in Chinese society. Because of the relative values, wages in Egyptian production are forced downward. The difference between national food price inflations meant that if Egyptian workers were going to have the same access to nutrition in 2010/11 as they did in 2009, their wages would have to increase more than those of Chinese workers. In order to be able to enjoy the same quality of nutrition, Egyptian workers would become less productive, and thereby less competitive, in relation to other members of the global working class divided into duplicate bourgeois state forms. Alternatively, in order to remain productively competitive with the working class in China, the working class in Egypt would have to access less nutrition. Table 2.3 shows the relative effective reductions of productivity given the different food price inflations in the Egyptian and Chinese social formations, assuming they are equally productive to start (note: the numbers were selected for ease of calculation, the ratio is what matters). To produce the metric ton of wheat represented by the inflated price in 2010/11 required less than half an additional hour of labor-time in Chinese society compared to 2009/10. In Egyptian society, it required almost a full additional hour of labor-time to produce the value equivalent of the wheat. The inflating of food prices did not diminish productivity in the already more productive Chinese social formation as much as it

Table 2.3 Relative reductions in productivity born of food price inflation

	Egypt	China
2009/10	5hrs = 1 = US$200	5hrs = 1 = US$200
2010/11	5.95hrs = 1 = US$238	5.4hrs = 1 = US$216

did in the Egyptian. More food price inflation in Egyptian society *in relation* to that in Chinese society meant either a less productive working class (if wages were increased) or a more poorly fed one. The Egyptian working class was doubly disempowered – in relation to capital and other members of the global working class.

The 2010/11 inflation of food prices negatively affected the Egyptian working class in the spheres of circulation *and* production. In the market, rising food prices devalued the wage of the working class. In the factory, inflated food prices devalued labor-power and increased the rate at which capital exploited labor. The effects are contradictory. In the sphere of circulation, the effect of food prices being bet up was to reduce productivity, really reduce wages. In the sphere of production, the effect of the inflation of food prices was the same as increasing productivity, namely increasing accumulation. In both instances, capital benefitted.

Inflation reduces the value of the working class's only commodity: labor-power.[163] Recall that 'the value of the labor-power commodity is the value of the means of subsistence necessary for the maintenance of its owner.'[164] Assuming there is no equivalent rise in wages, an increase in the price of food reduces the working class's consumption of food, which, in turn, reduces the value of labor-power because it has been reproduced by less value objectified in food commodities.[165] Phrased differently, the more food costs, the less food the working class consumes, and the less food the working class consumes, the less the value of its labor-power commodity.

Ceteris paribus, the devaluing of labor-power increases the rate of surplus-value accumulation by changing the ratio of necessary labor-time to surplus labor-time in favor of capital. Inflating food prices and devaluing labor-power by further restricting the working class's consumption of food has the effect of reducing the amount of time the laborer must work for himself and increasing that which (s)he works for capital, without the extent of the working period having to be increased. Assume line A--------------------C represents the length of the work day in Egyptian society. Line A-----B represents the labor-time necessary for labor-power to reproduce itself. And line B-----C represents the surplus labor-time worked for capital for which the working class receives no value equivalent in wage form. Working day 1 represents the ratio of necessary labor-time to surplus labor-time before the inflating of food prices. Working day 2 represents the ratio of necessary labor-time to surplus labor-time after the inflating of food prices. Working day 3 represents how the length of working day 1 would have had to be extended for capital to realize the same ratio of necessary labor-time to surplus labor-time of working day 2 in the absence of the food price inflation.

```
Working day 1    A--------B---------C
Working day 2    A----B-------------C
Working day 3    A--------B----------------------C
```

From working day 1 to working day 2 line A-----B is shortened relative to line B-----C. Every commodity produced during working day 2 objectifies relatively more surplus labor-time for capital and less necessary labor-time for the working class. In terms of surplus-value production, inflating the price of food has the same effect for capital as extending the length of the working day at the same food prices. Of course, done in small increments reducing the value of labor-power by inflating the price of wage goods to reduce consumption is politically more expedient than extending the work day.

The manner in which the rate of exploitation was increased by the devaluing of Egyptian labor-power occasioned by the inflating of food price commodities can also be expressed algebraically. Again, the value of a commodity is equal to surplus-value plus the constant capital plus the variable capital: $C = s + c + v$. The rate of exploitation (E) objectified in the commodity is equal to the surplus-value (s) produced divided by the value of the variable capital (v) consumed in production: $E = s/v$. Before the inflating of food prices, let us say that the value of a commodity produced in Egyptian society was US$200, with s = US$50, c = US$100 and v = US$50. Then, the rate of exploitation was 50/50, or 100 percent. As food prices were increased 19 percent, the rate of exploitation was also increased: with s still = 50, but v reduced 19 percent to 40.5 (50–9.5), then $E = 50/40.5$, or 123 percent. In the absence of an equivalent wage increase for labor, an increase in the price of food has the same effect for capital as introducing labor-saving machinery into production – it increases the rate at which capital accumulates surplus-value. The more the price of food is inflated, the larger the difference, pocketed by capital, between the value labor creates and the value it receives.

Reducing the amount of labor-time necessary to produce a commodity by inflating the price of food and reducing consumption transfers value to capital in the sphere of production, all other things held equal. The transfer of value is the transfer of power.[166] At the same time, reducing real wages in the sphere of circulation by inflating the price of food deprives the working class of the wage weapon in its class struggle. The balance of power between the classes is further tilted in capital's favor. Food price inflation is a boon for capital in value terms and in money terms, and it disempowers the working class in both spheres of the class war.

Cleaver's statement of thirty-five years ago is just as pertinent today: '[w]hen, as in the current crisis, [capital] undertakes to engineer a global rise in the exchange value of food, it is not only increasing its profits but also increasing its power vis-à-vis the working class.'[167] The extreme food price inflation realized in 2010/11 was the extreme weaponization of food by capital in the global class war. It is not accidental. It is not a singular event. It is part and parcel, along with the hyper-exploitation of natural power, neoliberal conceptualizing, privatization, governmental arrangements including the CFMA and technology such as derivatives, of capital's neoliberal counter-attack against the working class. This extreme could be realized because of the critical imbalance of forces between the classes in our contemporary moment. The working class, globally and in Egypt, was more nutritiously fed in the Keynesian moment because of the struggles it had fought, not the least of which involved many of its members perishing in capital's world wars. The working class's nutrition continues to deteriorate because it has been losing battles for forty-five years. It continues to lose battles, in Canada, Egypt, Japan, because it is increasingly taken in, by among other things, bourgeois ideals such as nationalism and religion. The crisis that appeared in the Egyptian social formation in 2011 was not produced by an empowered working class, but rather a capital so empowered that it could realize extreme measures that tipped social relations into a disequilibrium that endangered reproduction of commodity society.

Conclusion

Global neoliberal capital was in crisis in 2010/11. Its contradictions were exploding everywhere in different forms, in American society, Greek society, Syrian society. When the contradictions sharpened and the crisis appeared in Egyptian society in 2011 the first demand was *'aish*. The life of the Egyptian working class was under attack on every front. Its environment was toxic. Dominant ways of thinking offered it no real conceptual alternative. It was being dispossessed so capital could accumulate ever more value. Capitalist technology exploited its vulnerability. Governmental and legal arrangements foisted the costs of devaluation onto its back. The inflating of food prices made it sick and threatened its ability to reproduce. And while it was getting sicker and starved, it was more intensely exploited.

The Egyptian working class is not *sui generis*. Like the working class everywhere, it has been weakened in relation to capital. For forty-five years, the class's power has been unrelentingly attacked through the inner relations and interpenetrated processes of global neoliberal capital. Capital increasingly replaces human labor-power with natural sources of power, and poisons the working class's environment. Thinking in terms of class and history, any ideas that develop senses of social solidarity and class consciousness are assailed by a Benthamite mentality and/or the opiates of religion and nationalism. Assumption of debt, privatization and financialization defer the surplus capital contradiction to the future at the expense of workers' value in the present. Finance capital accumulates exchange-value and throws more workers into poverty and starvation by inflating food prices. Governmental arrangements such as TARP and quantitative easing ensure that the value destroyed in crisis is that of the working class' wage and labor-power commodity and not that of finance capital's derivatives. The devaluing of wages and the labor-power commodity starves and sickens the working class while it accumulates more surplus-value for capital. In Egyptian society, this onslaught endangered the reproduction of working-class life. Given the dialectic between labor and capital, this endangering of the working class endangered capital in Egyptian society.

This devastation of the working class is not determined. It is the product of the balance of power between the working class and capital. While the capitalist totality was in extreme disequilibrium at the beginning of 2011, the food price inflation's threat to the reproduction of daily life tipped the totality into crisis. The imbalance was too much in capital's favor; capital accumulated too much exchange-value and too much power for Egyptian society to bear. An empowered Egyptian working class did not realize a revolution in Egyptian society in 2011. Instead, productive capital intervened to restore, momentarily as always, society to a more moderate disequilibrium and perpetuate capitalist relations.

CHAPTER 3

Fetishisms and factions

The crisis of global neoliberal capital erupted in Egyptian society in late January 2011. The protests that started on 25 January were an expression of the capital–labor contradiction. In a reform, meaning readjustment,[1] of this contradiction the military intervened to save itself by rescuing the working class. The appearance of the disposition of President Hosni Mubarak was, in actuality, the military protecting capitalist relations in Egyptian society.

In this chapter, I descend below the surface appearances of Egyptian society and expose the ruling ideas and relations in their essence. First, I pierce the fetishistic veil shrouding the eruption of crisis in Egyptian society. Second, I conceptualize Egyptian society in terms of factions of capital. What is commonly understood as the Mubarak regime is predatory capital. The Ikhwan is commercial capital. The military is productive capital. And third, I use this demystified understanding to start to make sense of the dependent and antagonistic relations of Egyptian society's expression of neoliberal crisis.

Fetishisms

In *Capital*, volume III, Marx states that:

> the analysis of the real, inner connections of the capitalist production process is a very intricate thing and a work of great detail; it is one of the tasks of science to reduce the visible and merely apparent movement to the actual inner movement. Accordingly, it will be completely self-evident that, in the heads of agents of capitalist production and circulation, ideas must necessarily form about the laws of production that diverge completely from these laws and are merely the expression

in consciousness of the apparent movement. The ideas of a merchant, a stock-jobber or a banker are necessarily quite upside-down.[2]

In explaining this, Harvey says that '[t]he self-presentations, self-perceptions and ideas of the agents of finance (as well as of capitalists in general) are delusional, not in the sense that they are crazy . . . but *necessarily* deluded';[3] necessarily delusional in that the surface appearances conceal the real content of our social relations. The same assessment of delusional could be made of the surplus population that flooded the streets of Cairo, Alexandria and Suez in January and February 2011, as well as the vulgar and fetishistic studies of the events. Just like the agents of capitalist production in Marx's quote, the members of the surplus population were 'prisoners of their own mystifications and fetishistic understandings.'[4]

The original expression of the crisis of global neoliberal capital in Egyptian society was *'aish, horreya* (freedom), *adala egtema'eya* (social justice). *Karama* (dignity) was another prominent expression. *'Aish* – that which was made unaffordable and threatened in early 2011 – is the essence of materialism. Again, life is the wellspring of consciousness. All the other expressions are fetishistic illusions. These fetishisms were compounded by even more, including *feloul* (remnants of the old regime), *el-geesh* (the military) and *eslamayeen* (Islamists).

Freedom and dignity are core neoliberal values.[5] Freedom, and by extension dignity, are also fetishistic illusions.[6] They are, in fact, absolutely crucial masks of capitalist relations. In all commodity societies, the worker is free in the double sense that 'as a free individual he can dispose of his labour-power as his own commodity, and that, on the other hand, he has no other commodity for sale, i.e. he is rid of them, he is free of all the objects needed for the realization of his labour-power.'[7] Freedom is integral to the capitalist *market*. Without a working class free of the means of production and free to contract for and sell its labor-time, there would be no capitalist production.

The sphere of circulation or commodity exchange, within whose boundaries the sale and purchase of labour-power goes on, is in fact a very Eden of the innate rights of man. It is the exclusive realm of Freedom, Equality, Property and Bentham. Freedom, because both buyer and seller of a commodity, let us say of labour-power, are determined only by their own free will. They contract as free persons, who are equal before the law. Their contract is the final result in which their joint will finds a common legal expression.[8]

Freedom exists in the sphere where value circulates, not in the sphere where it is produced. Contradictorily, in the free act of negotiating a contract the worker, who must sell his/her labor-time because (s)he does not have the means of production necessary to produce value, bargains away his/her freedom. Once contracted, once the relation moves from the market into the factory, the worker's labor-time is no longer his/her own, but is disposed of according to the unilateral designs of capital. Wage slavery, not freedom, is the reality of production. The bourgeois ideal of freedom actually enslaves labor to capital. Dialectically, it is in their freedom that workers submit to the tyranny of capital.

To demand freedom and dignity as workers in Egyptian society did in 2011 is to demand values of the free market. In making these demands the working class demanded the antithesis of revolutionary goals. Neoliberal thought is our historic moment from the perspective, and according to the limits, of capital. It is the negation of the working class's view of the world. Benthamite rationality crushes working-class dreams and aspirations. It does not spur them. The working class in Egypt was weak in relation to capital. It is not surprising, then, that the working class expressed neoliberal bourgeois fetishisms that perpetuate capital's exploitation rather than revolutionary ideals that would end it.

The ideal of social justice, too, is a fetishism. Conceived of in terms of equality and rights, it exists exclusively in the sphere of money. There is no equality in production. The worker and the capitalist encounter each other in the market as equal owners of commodities – the worker with value in the form of the labor-power commodity and the capitalist with the money form of value. Contracting for the labor-time moves the relation from the market to the factory and transforms it into a despotic one. The inequality of power that defines capitalist production can also appear in the sphere of circulation. In his discussion of the struggle to fix the length of the working day Marx makes the point that as the purchaser of labor-time the capitalist has the right to extend the working day as long as possible. Concomitantly, the worker, as the seller of labor-time, has the right to reduce the length of the working day. In such cases, the balance of power is what decides which right prevails.[9] More contemporarily, the same analysis can be made of the battle between the right of creditors to Detroit or Argentina or Greece to get paid and the right of municipal and national pensioners to receive their deferred wages. In all cases of equal and contradictory rights, the balance of power in the class relation determines the outcome. In 2011, the Egyptian working class demanded an illusion when it called for social justice. Social justice is a ruse under capitalist relations of production, and the class was too weak in relation to capital to realize it as a limited bourgeois value in the sphere of circulation.

Bound up with the demand for social justice was the call of *silmiyya*, that the protests be peaceful. This was an extension of the fetishism. Even the truncated social justice of the market is not realized by the goodness of hearts or the quality of arguments. It is realized by a preponderance of power. The more socially just world is the world in which the working class is more empowered – say, because of better real wages – in relation to capital in the class war. This political understanding is anathema to the bourgeois value of peace, which is, in turn, the ethical form of the doctrine of the harmony of interests. This doctrine, too, was expressed shortly after the appearance of crisis in Egyptian society as *el-geesh wa el-shaeb eid wahdah* (the military and the people are one hand). The doctrine of the harmony of interests and its attendant value of social peace was developed in part, and unsurprisingly, by Bentham and popularized by Adam Smith's bourgeois political economy.[10] These ideas are crucial to capital because they mask the antagonisms that define capitalist relations. Society is not seen as a formation of class relations, but is atomized to become nothing more than the sum of its individual parts. It is because of this idea that Margaret Thatcher could declare '[t]here is no such thing as society.'[11] The good of the community is made identical with what is good for its most competitive individual members because these individuals drive the infinite expansion, 'growth' in contemporary fetishistic terms, of the market. These individuals are able to expand the market in the interests of all under conditions of peace. Those who disrupt the peace and endanger the interests of the most competitive members, and thereby all members, are immoral and irrational.[12] Peaceful perpetuation of the harmony of interests is not a universal good in any commodity society. It is good for capital. For the working class, peaceful perpetuation of the harmony of interests really means perpetuating exploitative, antagonistic relations at relatively little cost to capital. The value of peace and the doctrine of the harmony of interests hide from the working class the imperative of class war. They mask from workers the reality that ultimately, in the last instance, 'no ruling class ever abdicates of its own accord.'[13] The calls for peace and social harmony made by workers in Egyptian society in 2011 were not negations of bourgeois ideals. They were expressions of the reigning neoliberal, Benthamite rationality and morality.

Finally, the demand for social justice is illusory because it imagines the renegotiation of a productivity deal tied to another historic moment. In effect, it seeks the impossible reversal of the progress of capitalist society. In Egyptian society, social justice is a value still readily associated with what is commonsensically understood as the Nasser period of Egyptian history. In actuality, this period of social justice in Egyptian society was the particular governmental product of the dialectical interaction of our species' relation with nature, mental conceptions, technology, production processes, reproduction of daily life and class relations of the Keynesian historic moment. It was the same moment that produced the welfare state in Canadian and French society. Capitalist relations have moved on from that moment, and along with them the distribution of exchange-value and gains in productivity between the classes, and there is no going back. As Samir Amin says so wonderfully, 'history has no reverse gear.'[14] Trying to re-realize a bygone social justice is a Sisyphean task. Worse still, it distracts the working class from again being inventive and producing new means of empowering itself in the spheres of circulation and production, and moving society to a post-capitalist moment.

In 1999, Mitchell said neoliberal ways of thinking defined Egypt in the 1990s.[15] The conceptual hold of these ideas and values only became more powerful and more limiting in the twenty-first century. Analyses such as Dabashi's that claim the protests in late January were a post-ideological revolution are as upside-down as the ideas of Marx's stock-jobbers and bankers.[16] It was not a revolution because the working class was disempowered in relation to the capitalist class. As for being post-ideological, as anyone who spent time in Tahrir Square, or Cairo more generally, knows, the mood in Egyptian society was highly nationalistic. More importantly, the form of expression given to the crisis was neoliberal. The weak working class in Egypt was so thoroughly deluded by Benthamite rationality that it actually thought its interests would be served by the bourgeois fetishisms of freedom and social justice.

The working class must, in detailed ways, demystify ideals and understand their use-values for the bourgeoisie. It must also unmask social forces and see them in their material essence. It is to this task that I now turn.

Factions of capital

The capitalist class is not a monolith. It takes three forms corresponding to the different phases of the circuit of value: finance capital, commercial capital and productive capital. The different factions all seek to accumulate surplus-value. However, because they accumulate differently through different processes, the factions have different interests and interrelate through a constant struggle over the division of the surplus-value. Contentions such as Huws' that '[i]t is increasingly difficult, if not impossible, to separate "finance capital" from productive capital either analytically or empirically'[17] miss the point, certainly in the Egyptian case. In mature commodity society, the different factions have never been separate. In contemporary Egyptian society in particular, the factions exist in dialectical relations *and* can be identified with their preponderant interests and processes.

Predatory capital

The faction of the capitalist class that most blatantly used the Egyptian state form to accumulate capital is commonly represented as 'crony capitalists' or 'corrupt businessmen.'[18] This is a powerful fetishism. While this faction appeared to amass large(r) fortunes through the liberalization and privatization of the Egyptian economy, it was really accumulating capital by dispossessing the working class of value in the form of factories and land.

This fetishism assigns primary importance to Gamal Mubarak, Hosni Mubarak's son, head of the Policies Secretariat and a deputy secretary-general of the ruling National Democratic Party, and heir apparent to the presidency. In social formations individuals matter only to the extent that they personify particular class interests. In this case, Gamal Mubarak does not matter in his individuality but rather as the bearer of the interests of predatory capital.

Gamal Mubarak is a banker who founded an investment advisory firm, MED Invest Partners, after his stint at Bank of America and before his political ascendancy. MED Invest Partners accumulated surplus-value by advising finance capital on the purchase of Egyptian companies and stocks. Gamal Mubarak also owned an 18 percent stake in the largest investment bank in Egypt, EFG-Private Equity, which is a subsidiary of EFG-Hermes.[19] *Egypt Independent* reports that according to EFG-Hermes statements, Gamal Mubarak accumulated LE77.5 million in exchange-value in 2010. In the previous three years he accumulated another LE112.3 million.[20] Lesch notes that '[i]t was not coincidental that the government designated EFG-Hermes to create a LE2.5 million fund (about $425,000) to manage public–private investment in transport, energy, education, healthcare, and infrastructure under the Public–Private Partnership Central Unit established in May 2010.'[21] Surely this use of the state form to accumulate private wealth by transforming the property relation from public to private was not coincidental, but neither was it isolated to the person of Gamal Mubarak.

It seems clear there was a whole faction that used the state form to accumulate by dispossessing the Egyptian working class in the years prior to the appearance of crisis. Ahmed Ezz accumulated his wealth and acquired monopoly power in the Egyptian steel market by buying several privatized companies, draining them of their value and absorbing it into his Ezz Steel.[22] Ezz received illegal production licenses from Rachid Mohamed Rachid, who privately accumulated from his relation with Gamal Mubarak's EFG-Hermes and at public expense as minister of foreign trade and industry.[23] The former minister of transport and owner of the distribution rights for General Motors products in Egyptian society, Mohamed Mansour, is said to have illegally gained ownership of land and refused to repay LE2 billion in loans he had assumed. Mansour's cousin, co-owner of a controlling share of the Egyptian subsidiary of Credit Agricole Bank, and real estate speculator, Ahmed El-Maghraby, profited from the illegal sale of public land as minister of housing. Amina Abaza, Egypt's largest cotton trader, is alleged to have profited from the illegal sale of state-owned land orchestrated while minister of agriculture. Zuhair Garana, a cousin to both El-Maghrabi and Mansour, profited from the illegal sale of public land and issuing of licenses to tourism companies while and after being minister of tourism. Mohamed Ibrahim Suleiman is accused of having sold state-owned land at below market prices to his family members while minister of housing. The former minister of information, Anas El-Feki, gifted broadcast rights to private satellite channels for which he surely received some value as compensation. The former prime minister Atef Ebeid illegally sold state-owned land. Sameh Fahmy, the former minister of petroleum, is accused of profiting from the plundering of Egypt's gas reserves. And Youssef Boutros-Ghali stole cars as finance minister.[24]

Whether looting public assets, as Ezz did, or changing the property relation, particularly of land, from public to private, as so many others did, or privately commodifying licenses, broadcasts, gas and cars, as still others did, this faction accumulated capital through predation rather than production. The faction was the equivalent of unproductive finance capital. The fetishism of the corrupt Mubarak regime was, in actuality, predatory capital accumulating as predatory capital does in the neoliberal moment of global capital.

Neoliberal reform is the fetishistic appearance of accumulation by dispossession. As with so many other societies, it was under the cover of crisis that this predatory reform was realized in Egyptian society post-1991. The predation did not, however, occur in a vacuum. It was not a 'national' phenomenon. The Egyptian equivalent of unproductive finance capital pillaged the Egyptian working class of value *in conjunction with* finance capital represented by the state forms of the Gulf Cooperation Council (GCC). At the time Gamal Mubarak and Rachid Mohamed Rachid were profiting from EFG-Hermes it was dominated by, and accumulating for, two banks based in the United Arab Emirates (UAE), the Dubai Group and the Abu Dhabi Investment Authority.[25] Former prime minister Ebeid has been connected with Citadel Capital, which brings together representatives of the capital of the Olayan and Abanumay families of Saudi Arabia, the Emirates' International Investment Company and a member of the Qatari royal family.[26] Similarly, Beltone Capital, run by the former Nazif-appointed chairman of the Egyptian stock exchange, merges Emirati, Saudi and Egyptian capital.[27] The confluence of capitals was not limited to the circuit of money capital, however. GCC finance capital also flowed into the circuit of productive capital. This transformation of finance capital into productive capital was realized through the process of privatization. '[P]rivatization acted to facilitate the displacement or merging of Egyptian capital with that of the Gulf.'[28] EFG-Hermes was not only a vehicle for the accumulation of advising fees, some of which it collected for advising the Egyptian state form on what value in the form of production facilities to privatize, it also took control of and appropriated this value in the form of, *inter alia*, desalination plants, construction companies and power generation plants.[29] The liberalization of agricultural production realized in no small measure by Law 96 (discussed in the previous chapter) allowed for the swamping of Egyptian food production by capital of the GCC states. GCC capital represented by Citadel Capital consumed much of the production of dairy, juice and poultry in Egyptian society. Capital in the form of Kuwait's Americana Group inundated the markets for starch and glucose as well as fruits and vegetables. And capital in the form of Saudi Savola flooded into pasta and edible oils.[30] 'The privatization of state-owned land that occurred under Mubarak through the 2000s was a[nother] principal route for inflows of Gulf capital into Egypt.'[31] The aqueducts connecting capital flowing into the land commodity from the predatory Egyptian faction and the Gulf finance faction are varied and obscured. The Talaat Mustafa Group is the largest real estate company in Egyptian society. Gamal Mubarak received land from it at below market prices. It also gifted the former housing minister, Mohamed Ibrahim Suleiman, US$7 million. The Talaat Mustafa Group is jointly controlled by the Saudi Binladen Group. The Sixth of October Development and Investment Company (SODIC) is another large private landowner in Egyptian society. SODIC is controlled by EFG-Hermes. Another 22 percent of it is owned by Beltone Financial, representing the capital of the Saudi Olayan and Abanumany families. Not to be outdone, Palm Hills Development, the youngest of these three real estate companies, was founded by Mansour and El-Maghraby Investment and Development Company by the brother of the former minister of transport (Mohamed Mansour is the executive vice-chairman) and the former minister of housing; the co-chief executive officer worked at both EFG-Hermes and Beltone and 5 percent of the company was recently purchased by UAE-based Aabar Investments.

Land was not the only source of surplus-value privatized by Egypt's predatory faction into which GCC capital flowed. Two examples will suffice. The Arab Cotton Ginning Company was privatized in 1996. Presumably it was one of the 260 out of 314 non-financial state-owned enterprises that were profitable on the eve of the 1990 ERSAP reforms.[32] In 2007, capital in the form of Saudi Amwal Al Khaleej bought the Arab Cotton Ginning Company, and with it acquired ownership of the Upper Egypt Flour Mill. The Arab Cotton Ginning Company was the 'largest textile firm by market value in Egypt' and the Upper Egypt Flour Mill was 'the largest publicly listed flour mill in the country.'[33] Also in 2007, capital in the form of the UAE-based Abraaj Capital purchased the previously privatized Egyptian Fertilizer Company, 'one of the largest private sector fertilizer companies in the country.'[34]

Finally, the process of trade liberalization opened the locks for GCC capital to wash into Egyptian society through the circuit of commercial capital. In 2002, UAE-based Majid Al Futtaim Group introduced the French Carrefour franchise into Egyptian society with leave from the predatory faction. And in 2007, Abraaj Capital was at it again, opening the Spinneys Supermarket chain in Cairo with license from the fetishized 'cronies.'

Commercial capital

In their disguises, Gamal Mubarak's cadre were reformers, modernizers and/or corrupt cronies and businessmen, and the Ikhwan are Islamists. In essential terms, Gamal Mubarak, Ezz, El-Maghraby and the rest represented the faction of predatory capital in Egyptian society and the Ikhwan represents the interests of commercial capital. In interrelated circulatory terms, predatory capital flows through the $M-C \ldots P \ldots C'-M+\Delta M$ circuit and commercial capital through the $C'-M+\Delta M-C \ldots P \ldots C'$ circuit, where M is the money form of value, C is the commodity form of value, $\ldots$ P $\ldots$ is the production process consuming the commodities of labor-power and means of production and creating value, C' is the bearer of the value consumed in production as well as the surplus-value added by the labor-power and $M+\Delta M$ is the money form of value of the money originally advanced plus the surplus-value created in production.

Surplus-value is created in the sphere of production. It is distributed in the sphere of circulation. Money and commercial capital receive distributive shares of the surplus-value for the functions they perform for productive capital. Recall that the total value of a commodity is equal to the constant capital plus variable capital (consumed in production) plus the surplus-value it embodies; $C=c+v+s$. The s is distributed between productive, finance and commercial capital depending on the balance of power between the factions. In the neoliberal moment in which finance capital is relatively empowered, it takes a larger share of the surplus-value. Commercial capital performs two notable functions for its share of the surplus-value: it accelerates the turnover time of productive capital, and it assumes risk. First, by accelerating the flow of value through the production circuit, $P \ldots C'-M+\Delta M-C \ldots P$, commercial capital reduces the amount of capital that must be hoarded to realize production, and by throwing more capital into the active production of surplus-value it increases the rate of surplus-value accumulation. In short, because commodity capital exchanges money with productive capital for the commodity en masse, productive capital is able to transform the money back into means of production and labor-power and expand production faster than if productive capital had to wait to sell the commodities to individual consumers on its own. In exchange for accelerating the flow of value from means of production and labor-power through the commodity, where it could otherwise be arrested, then money and back into means of production and labor-power again, commercial capital receives some surplus-value. Second, commercial capital receives a portion of the surplus-value because by exchanging money for the commodity en masse it assumes the risk of being unable to sell the commodity individually and realize the value objectified in the commodity. It gets a share of the surplus-value because it assumes the risk of the flow of value being interrupted while the value is still objectified in the commodity. Fruit spoilage offers a good example of this relation. Productive capital produces apples objectifying surplus-value. If productive capital takes the relatively longer turnover time to transform each individual apple into money representing surplus-value, some of the apples may spoil; meaning they objectify no value because they cannot be sold. Instead, in exchange for money representing the total value of the apples minus a portion of the surplus-value, commercial capital willingly assumes the transfer of this risk to its capital. Commercial capital does not profit by adding surplus-value to the product. Commercial capital's profit is the difference between the total surplus-value created in production and the price productive capital pays to accelerate its turnover time and free itself of the risk of devaluation.

Critical characterizations of the Ikhwan in material terms remain, by and large, superficial. Beinin likes to cite what he calls Mitchell's 'classic study of the Muslim Brotherhood.' In both *Political Islam: Essays from Middle East Report* and his more recent 'Neo-liberal structural adjustment, political demobilization and neo-authoritarianism in Egypt' Beinin speaks of the Ikhwan membership as being educated and urban.[35] He also notes that the Ikhwan's 'leadership is linked to old money and the educated middle classes.'[36] Achcar offers a similar assessment: '[The Muslim Brotherhood] has its base among the traditional middle classes and also among intellectuals both traditional (especially religious) and organic (students, teachers, the lower and middle ranks of the liberal professions).'[37] In an earlier text he explains:

In terms of the nature of their program and ideology, their social composition, and even the social origins of their founders, Islamic fundamentalist movements are petty bourgeois . . . Petty bourgeois Islamic reaction finds its ideologues and leading elements among the 'traditional intellectuals' of Muslim societies, ulemas and the like, as well as among the lower echelons of the bourgeoisie's 'organic intellectuals,' those coming from the petty bourgeoisie and condemned to stay there: teachers and office workers in particular.[38]

Amin says the Ikhwan 'are in reality a component of the comprador bourgeoisie.'[39] Beinin and Achcar's descriptions of the constitution of the Ikhwan leave hanging the question: what objective interests do the Ikhwan represent? Similarly, Amin's characterization leaves unanswered the query: which component of the comprador bourgeoisie is the Ikhwan?

It is famously difficult to secure detailed information about capital associated with the Ikhwan. The organization files no financial statements. The capital of the organization and its wealthiest members have increasingly flowed together. And its wealthiest members obscure their capital under the names of sons, daughters and sons-in-law. This being said, it is still clear that while the Ikhwan appeals to educated, urban professionals, and its constituency is the most oppressed members of the working class, the organization is involved in the processes of commercial capital in Egyptian society.

In 2011, Khairat El-Shater was deputy chairman of the Ikhwan, and its de facto leader. '[I]t is El-Shater, and not the Supreme Guide Mohamed Badie, who really runs the Muslim Brotherhood.'[40] El-Shater exercised so much power – enough power to determine the organization's policies and expel opponents – because he was the organization's chief financier. El-Shater primarily accumulated money as the personification of commercial capital and its interests. He is the son and grandson of prosperous merchants. While El-Shater's holding company, Egyptian Company for Renaissance and Integrated Development, includes capital in the form of Al-Shehab for Bus Manufacturing and Contact Centre Egypt, which operates call centers, and he has sat on bank boards, most of El-Shater's capital circulates through the commercial circuit. His Salsabil was an importer of computer technology and even counted the Egyptian military as one of its clients until 1991, when the enterprise was raided and its commodity capital confiscated by the state form. El-Shater's Hayah trades in pharmaceuticals. His Zad supermarket chain was set up to compete with, among others, Carrefour and Spinneys, as well as the Seoudi market chain owned by the Seoudi Group. Abdelrahman El-Seoudi is another personification of commodity capital related to the Ikhwan. El-Shater's Rawag (Egyptian International Trading and Trade Agencies Company) sells furniture. His Sarar sells men's clothing. And his Istikbal also trades in furniture.

Hassan Malek is another wealthy and powerful member of the Ikhwan. He, too, is a bearer of the interests of commercial capital, as indicated by the name of his Malek Trade. He is head of the Malek Group through which he has contracted ten international import/export agreements.[41] Malek also established the Egyptian Business Development Association, which 'signed 20 economic agreements with foreign traders and embassies.'[42] Further to the point that the Ikhwan, as a group, represents the interests of commercial capital, Malek's Egyptian Business Development Association included, among others, El-Seoudi of the Seoudi Group trading company. Moreover, Malek and El-Shater are partners in a number of ventures. Malek co-owned Salsabil with El-Shater. His capital also co-owns the clothing retailer Sarar and the furniture retailer Istikbal.

Hassan forcefully makes the point that the Ikhwan represents commercial capital. According to Hassan, '[m]ost of the Muslim Brothers' capital power is not dedicated to developmental purposes [in the sense of producing commodities objectifying surplus-value]. As top Muslim Brotherhood officials will tell you, citing a saying ascribed to the Prophetic *hadith*, "Nine-tenths of livelihood is in trade".'[43] The economic hierarchy of the Ikhwan serves the function of circulating capital for those at the zenith, the likes of El-Shater and Malek. Hassan explains that

> [t]he Muslim Brotherhood's top business magnates are sur-rounded by a second class of small merchants whom those that hold the purse strings in the Muslim Brotherhood have helped to found small and mid-sized enterprises such as shops, restau-rants and workshops. In so doing, the Muslim Brotherhood's economic upper crust was not being entirely altruistic. These smaller ventures helped them circulate their capital, which would otherwise gradually lose value or purchasing power under the prevailing inflationary conditions.[44]

Commercial capital washes down to subsidiary commercial capitals through which it circulates to return back to the apex in the money form. Ultimately, says Hassan, 'the lion's share of the Muslim Brotherhood's economic energies are involved in "trade and commerce".'[45]

It is imperative that the Ikhwan be understood in its material essence because this explains the organization's politics, broadly defined. The Ikhwan is not reactionary because it is Muslim. It is reactionary because it represents the interests of merchant capital. Commercial capital is a historical precondition for the development of capitalist production, but in dialectical fashion, the advancement of capitalist production reduces the power and wealth of commercial capital. Commercial capital is functionally 'demoted' by the development of production for the sake of exchange-value, and sees its rate of profit reduced.[46] The relation between merchant capital and commodity society is such that 'the independent development of commodity capital stands in inverse proportion to the level of development of capitalist production.'[47] '[W]here commercial capital predominates, obsolete conditions obtain';[48] and advanced capitalist production requires the subduing of merchant capital. As Harvey explains, a 'hegemonic merchant class would attempt to suppress the rise of the industrial form of capital, since its capacity to extract ultra-profits by exploiting weak and vulnerable producers would be curbed.'[49]

In order to retain its control and rate of accumulation, commercial capital wants to 'preserve and retain old and backward forms of production organized on traditional lines.'[50] It is this relation that makes commercial capital the reactionary faction of capital. Merchant capital opposes productive capital's revolutionizing of social relations because the changes weaken it in relation to the other factions of capital. Commercial capital is reactionary; the Ikhwan represents the interests of commercial capital; the Ikhwan is reactionary because it represents the interests of commercial capital.

The vulgar representation of the Ikhwan being locked in an intractable battle with the Egyptian state form is simply wrong. The factions of capital are in a tripartite battle of forces with each other, and, concomitantly, depend on each other. Certainly, the Ikhwan has struggled with the state form serving, primarily, the interests of predatory and productive capital in Egyptian society. More regularly, certainly since the early 1970s, the Ikhwan has worked hand in glove with the state form in capital's common war against the Egyptian working class. The neoliberal project that enabled the predatory capital faction to extend and intensify its accumulation of surplus-value was supported by the Ikhwan. Predatory capital relied heavily on the neoliberal tactic of privatization. The neoliberal tactic preferred by commercial capital was liberalization. Parenthetically, it is instructive to note that the Ikhwan did not condemn the deployment of the privatization weapon. Its critique, such as it was, mobilized a populist rhetoric only against how the process was realized.[51] The Ikhwan supported the liberalizations of the early 1970s *infitah* (open door) policy. Naguib surmises that 'the Brotherhood was generally supportive of the liberalization policies of the Sadat regime and continued through the 1980s to call for more extensive market reforms.'[52] The Ikhwan supported the tactics because they enriched and empowered the interests the group represented. Citing Saiid, Naguib explains that a decade or so after the launch of the neoliberal counter-offensive 'the private sector of the economy was controlled by eighteen families, of which eight were connected to the Brotherhood: some 40 per cent of all private economic ventures, she suggests, were connected to Brotherhood interests.'[53] According to Amin,

[o]n the terrain of real social issues political Islam aligns itself with the camp of dependent capitalism and dominant imperialism. It defends the principle of the sacred character of private property and legitimized inequality and all the requirements of capitalist reproduction. The support of the Muslim Brotherhood in the Egyptian parliament for the recent reactionary laws that reinforce the rights of property owners to the detriment of the rights of tenant farmers (the majority of the small peasantry) is but one example among hundreds of others.[54]

As representative of the interests of commercial capital, the Ikhwan has long made common cause with representatives of the other factions of capital in their collective war on the Egyptian working class.

The Ikhwan benefitted materially from the extension and intensification of neoliberal processes, and it also benefited ideally. The rise of 'Islamism' is dialectically related to the increasing aggressiveness of capital's neoliberal project. The reconcentration of wealth and power realized by the project comes at the expense of the working class. The contradictory relation is such that the more wealth and power accumulated by capital, the more misery is accumulated by the working class. The fetishism of religion is increasingly interpolated into the ever growing social breach to condition the proletariat to its constantly degraded condition. The most glaring example of this is the rise of evangelicalism in American society. The more the waves of liberalization and privatization crashed onto the heads of workers in Egyptian society, and the more entrepreneurial freedoms constrained them, the more working people turned to the social services and ideals provided by the Ikhwan. The social services included hospitals and schools, and most prominent among the ideals was that 'Islam is the solution.' Of course, never communicated in word or deed was that workers needed solutions to Ikhwan-supported policies; that the Ikhwan was part of the immiserating problem. The same policies that profited the commercial capital interests represented by the Ikhwan also increased the interests' social power. The Ikhwan was a powerful social force in early 2011 because it had been benefitting twofold from neoliberal attacks on workers for forty years.

Productive capital

What appears as the military is, in essence, productive capital in Egyptian society. The failure to penetrate beneath this surface illusion is, arguably, the biggest analytical misstep in studies of the Egyptian social formation. The vulgar literature perpetrates it. Eskandar mistakenly sees the military as one of the 'traditional bureaucratic powers inside the Egyptian state.'[55] Harb similarly misconceives of the military as an institution and an 'interest group.'[56] Hashim confuses the matter the most by speaking of 'the military-industrial-business-commercial complex.'[57] Fetishistic studies commit the same misstep. Achcar, for example, speaks of both the 'military component of the power elite' and the Egyptian 'military-industrial complex.'[58] The error of this misstep is compounded by attempts to determine the military's economic 'footprint,'[59] gauge its 'intervention into the civilian industry'[60] and assess the size of the military's segment of the economy.[61] Estimates that range from 5 to 60 percent of the economy belonging to the military are speculative to begin with, and are made all the more tentative because, as Marshall and Stacher correctly note, the military's capital has increasingly mixed together with finance capital represented by the state forms of the GCC, among others.[62] Attempts to quantify the extent of the military's interests tell us little about the qualitative nature of the interests. In order to understand the military's interests, we must, as with the interests of the 'corrupt cronies' and the 'Islamists' before them, understand them in objective terms; understand through what processes the military creates and accumulates surplus-value. To this end, all the non-scientific scholars evidently need to be reminded of the importance of naming. Field Marshal Tantawi, the man who deposed Mubarak in 2011, was the minister of defense and military *production*.

Two points must be made immediately. First, the Egyptian military is not a war-making force in the traditional sense. The Arab militaries in general, and the Egyptian military in particular, are incapable of effectively waging a war. The Egyptian military's training 'is desultory [and] maintenance of its equipment is profoundly inadequate.'[63] Its tactical and operational readiness has been degraded over the course of more than thirty years.[64] As a result, 'U.S. officers and officials familiar with the military assistance programs to Egypt describe the Egyptian Armed Forces as no longer capable of combat.'[65] Second, the Egyptian military is not a revolutionary force. Militaries are never revolutionary forces. Gramsci explains this best: 'it is not true that armies are constitutionally barred from making politics; the army's duty is precisely to defend the constitution – in other words the legal form of the State together with its related institutions. Hence so-called neutrality only means support for the reactionary side.'[66] The Egyptian military would be ineffectual in a war over territory against, say, Israel, but it is capable of tyrannizing the proletariat in the class war and perpetuating the status quo of Egyptian society and its production and distribution of surplus-value.

Producing department I and department II commodities

The military produces surplus-value objectified in department I and department II commodities. In other words, the military produces commodities that enter productive consumption, i.e. are means of production, as well as commodities that are individually consumed by the working and capitalist classes. Department I commodities remain in circulation expanding production: $C \ldots P \ldots C' - M + \Delta M - C \ldots P \ldots$ Department II commodities fall out of the circuit of capital as their use-values are realized. Table 3.1 provides an abridged list of productive capital's commodities.

The department I and department II commodities are produced by 1) the Ministry of Military Production, 2) the Arab Organization for Industrialization (AOI) and 3) the National Services Project Organization (NSPO). The capital of the Ministry of Military Production is in the form of between eight fend fifteen manufacturing plants, including the Heliopolis Company for Chemical Industries and the Abu Zaabal Company for Specialty Chemicals.[67] The capital of the AOI is objectified in eleven factories and companies, including the Helwan Engine Factory and the Arab Company for Organic Fertilizers. The NSPO organizes capital in another ten

Table 3.1 Commodities produced by the Egyptian military

Department I commodities	Department II commodities
cement	foodstuffs
chemicals	mineral water
petroleum	electronics
oil and gas piping	home appliances
infant incubators	jeeps
fertilizer	sports equipment
merchant vessels	voting booths
	stationery
	pharmaceuticals
	clothes
	heaters
	doors and windows

companies, including the Queen Macaroni Company and ElArish Company for Cement. Recognizing the military's actual, objective interests immediately makes sense of the destruction of the Egyptian working class's metabolic relation with nature discussed in the previous chapter. The air, water and soil are polluted by the military because, like all bearers of capital, it seeks to produce commodities embodying as little value as possible. This means socializing the costs of production to the environmental commons. Moreover, the more polluted the commons and the more degraded the natural factors of production, the more of the military-produced fertilizer farmers will consume. The military doubly benefits, through production and consumption, from polluting the Nile and its delta.

The most important department II commodity of the military *qua* productive capital is food, and 'food production [is] the single most important NSPO activity.'[68] The NSPO's Food Security Division (FSD) produces food with 'dairy farms and milk processing facilities, integrated poultry complexes, fish farms and cattle feed lots' as well as fruit and vegetable farms and packaging plants.[69] Ostensibly, the FSD ensures 'food security' for the Egyptian military and sells its surplus product to Egyptian workers at subsidized prices. The dialectical reality, however, is that food is a department II commodity necessary for the reproduction of working-class life through which the military accumulates surplus-value at the expense of the Egyptian working class. Every FSD-produced tomato, chicken and loaf of bread sold circulates back to productive capital, in the money form, the unpaid labor-time expropriated from workers in the form of conscripts. In terms of the capitalist totality, capital is in a company store relation with the working class. The capitalist class gives the working class claims to value in the form of money, and the working class gives the drafts right back to capital to obtain a share of the product it has produced.[70] The space of this relation in Egyptian society is the military installation. The only commodities available for individual consumption on military installations are commodities produced in the military's factories. Safi water exemplifies this relation. The only bottled water available to conscripts on bases, say in the deserts of the Sinai or Upper Egypt, is Safi water. Safi water is produced by the NSPO, and named after the daughter of the organization's former director, *General* Sayed Mishaal.[71] Military installations do not protect Egyptians. They are, in actuality, a network of factories and monopolized markets for the production and realization of capital. Commodities objectifying labor-time stolen from workers by productive capital are produced, and in their circulation to workers via the money form the surplus-value crystallizes out to productive capital.

The military is party to a wide range of joint ventures precisely because it is productive capital. The military is partnered with Moeller-Maersk and Cosco Pacific in the Suez Canal Container Company, with Hutchison Port Holdings and a UAE-based private equity fund in Alexandria International Container Terminals, with China's Sinopec and the Italian firms Breda and Eni in Tharwa Petroleum, and with capital represented by the state forms of China, Germany, Denmark and Canada to reduce and reverse the damage it is has done to the working class's environment through solar and wind energy and environmental cleanup projects.[72] The AOI is involved in some of these projects and was partnered with DaimlerChrysler through its Arab American Vehicles Company, and Rolls-Royce through the joint venture of the Arab British Engine Company. It is through partnerships with General Electric, Lockheed Martin and Mitsubishi that the military produces such department II commodities as television sets, jeeps and tablet computers.[73] The military is sought out as partner for these ventures because it contributes means of production in Egyptian society that create surplus-value, most notably the labor-power commodity and transportation.

Unsurprisingly, the vulgar politics get matters backwards, upside down. The military is not the protector of the regime.[74] As always, the state form serves and protects the interests of capital. The state form is one of capital's instruments of surplus-value accumulation, just as a lathe, mobile phone and road are. How much surplus-value is accumulated through the state form, and to which capitalist faction's benefit, is determined by the balance of power between factions and classes within the society. As the neoliberal moment of global capital was extended, predatory and commercial capital in Egypt increasingly accumulated through the processes of privatization and liberalization. The extent and intensity of these processes were determined in relation with the military as productive capital and the most powerful faction in Egyptian society. This is precisely why military enterprises were not privatized. It also explains the military's acquisitions. In addition to the neoliberal public–private partnerships just discussed, productive capital acquired value and the means of producing more surplus-value through the privatization process. By way of example, 'Alexandria Shipyard . . . was turned over to the Ministry of Defense in August 2007. It now produces large merchant vessels and warships and offers its repair services to private shipping companies. Likewise, the army-controlled AOI now owns 100 percent of the General Egyptian Company for Railway Wagons and Coaches, initially offered up for privatization in 2002.'[75] Productive capital also acquired many of the holding companies that were created to privatize state-owned enterprises in the 2000s. According to Abul-Magd, '[m]ilitary generals installed themselves in almost every holding company and their subsidiaries,' heading, among others, the 'Water and Sewage, Egypt Tourism, Food Industries, and National Cement holding companies in Cairo and their provincial branches.'[76] Abul-Magd's individual ontology makes much of the fact that the generals are ostensibly retired. In reality, what matters in the general-cum-chief executive officer transformation is not the individual's title but rather the material relations, interests and processes the individual personifies. Retired generals are of and for productive capital. Finally, productive capital in Egyptian society has progressively colonized the governing apparatus. In addition to a president always produced by the military, by 2011 'twenty-one of the twenty-nine appointed governors [were] retired army generals.'[77] Subsidiary to the level of governor are deputy governors, heads of cities, boroughs, village heads, mayors, and local councils with secretaries-general and assistant secretaries-general. All of these positions, too, are appointed, and 'the entire edifice is extensively staffed by former officers.'[78] Sayigh provides a telling example:

> [o]n February 22, 2012, the minister of military production, Major General Ali Ibrahim Sabri, signed an agreement to develop the Giza governorate's wholesale market. Signing for the other side was the wholesale market's executive head, Major General Mohammed Sami Abdul-Rahim. In attendance were the deputy governor of Giza, Major General Usama Shama'ah; the secretary-general of the local council, Major General Mohammad al-Sheikh; and his assistant secretary-general, Major General Ahmad Hani.[79]

This synthesizes the ideas that the military is productive capital, retired generals remain bearers of the interests of productive capital and the state apparatus is instrumentalized by these interests. In American society, the neoliberal counter-attack against the working class has been executed by representatives of the interests of finance capital, the Volkers, Greenspans and Paulsons, through the state form. In Egyptian society, representatives of productive capital, many with the title major general, similarly use the state to accumulate surplus-value and power at the expense of workers.

Extracting land

In addition to creating surplus-value objectified in department I and II commodities produced by exploited workers in the form of conscripts, and selling access to its exploited working class through the joint venture mechanism, the military also extracts land in Egyptian society. This only stands to reason. After all, land and labor-power are the original sources of all wealth.[80]

The military has long been reclaiming land, 'turning unused desert or waste land into valuable land for agriculture or urban development.'[81] This land has been transformed into farms, factories and urban centers. The military disposed of some of this land to build satellite cities around Cairo. By 1986, thirteen such cities had been produced, on land sold by the military and by military-owned construction enterprises, each with a population of 150,000 to 250,000.[82] In fact, according to Springborg, '[i]n 1985–86 almost five percent of all housing constructed in the country was built by and for the military.'[83] Of course, the land owned by the military *qua* productive capital was not restricted to the environs of Cairo. The military also owned land in the Nile Delta, the Suez Canal Zone and the western desert. The military has also been known to seize land under the cover of state law that permits it to do so 'for the purpose of "defending the nation".'[84] In 1986, the military forcibly took possession of land on the outskirts of Nasr City in Cairo and beach-front property in Sidi Krayr near Alexandria.[85] A decade later, '[a] 1997 presidential decree made the military the manager of all undeveloped nonagricultural land' in Egyptian society. This formally granted the military ownership of an estimated 87 percent of the space of the country.[86]

On the surface, land is a target of speculative capital because it is a superior store of wealth against inflation. In societies such as Egypt with perennially high rates of inflation, the insulating value of land is correspondingly high. The speculative allure of land is compounded further because of Egypt's increasing population coupled with a limited supply of urban land.[87] For example, the military's land in the Nile Delta was near growing urban areas and the prices of these properties, predictably, skyrocketed.[88]

In essence, land in Egypt is like oil in Saudi Arabia – it is a means of production that has no value. No human labor-power was consumed to produce the land. Furthermore, land 'helps to create use-values without contributing to the formation of exchange-value.'[89] Land helps to produce commodities without increasing the price of the commodities. The land on which a factory or home is built transfers no value to the factory or home, and consequently no value to the cement produced in the factory or the labor-power produced in the home. Because land has no value, its price is determined exclusively by supply and demand. The 1997 decree formally gave productive capital a monopoly on land and transformed it into a price-maker. Productive capital could inflate the price of land simply by refusing to release it on to the market. The longer time productive capital withheld the land, the more surplus capital would be accumulating, and the stronger the pressure would be for capital to flood into the property once it was released. Productive capital's monopoly of land in Egyptian society explains, *inter alia*, building codes governing construction around Cairo. All of the buildings lining Road 90 in the New Cairo neighborhood are a maximum of seven stories high. This makes little sense in terms of public infrastructure investment, temporal efficiency, and the environment. Height restrictions mean urban sprawl and the corresponding extension of power, water and sewerage networks and roads, more time spent in vehicles moving between places, and increased pollution. The building code makes perfect sense in material terms. Productive capital controls the supply of land by virtue of its monopoly, and it regulates the demand for the land through construction codes that restrict the height of buildings. The less the volume of space the fixed capital of a building can produce vertically, the more land it will consume to produce the volume horizontally. Ultimately, productive capital meets the increased horizontal demand.

The 1997 presidential decree was Egyptian society's equivalent of the Enclosure Act. It was an act of legalized theft in which a common source of wealth was privatized. The state form controlled, though not exclusively, by productive capital granted all the public land in Egypt to productive capital. While of no value in itself, as soon as the land is instrumentalized by productive capital through such processes as subdivision and production of residential homes, it creates surplus-value for productive capital. A number of the NSPO's companies are involved in this process of land instrumentalization – for example, the National Company for

Reclamation and Cultivation of Desert Lands and the Upper Egypt Company for the Manufacture of Agricultural Land Reclamation. The Armed Forces' Land Project creates surplus-value on land owned by productive capital by objectifying labor-power on it. In 2011, the Armed Forces' Land Project was producing residential units for the neighborhood of Nasr City and a tourist resort on the seized Mediterranean beach-front property of Sidi Krayr.[90] The involvement of the NSPO's National Company for Services and Maintenance (Queen Services) in provision of security and guards, hotel management, and facilities and equipment cleaning, disinfecting and maintenance also means it captures a distributional share of the surplus-value created through hotel construction.

Producing value through transportation and communication

In Egyptian society the military as productive capital accumulates surplus-value using department I and department II commodities, land and transportation and communication. Transportation and communication are processes that produce surplus-value that appear in the circulation process. They are independent branches of production and particular spheres of investment of productive capital that appear in the market.[91] The processes appear in circulation because they do not produce new products and their useful effect is consumed as soon as it is produced (usually the two processes are separated in time and space).[92] They are spoken of together because they both sell the same useful effect of spatial movement. Transportation changes the place of the material. Communication changes the place of the ideal. The useful effect 'does not exist as a thing of use distinct from [the production] process.'[93] The communication of utility for a commodity and/or a change in location of the commodity may be necessary for the consumption of its use-value and the realization of the surplus-value objectified in it. Additionally, the acceleration of this communication and/or the location change, say with faster networks or overpasses replacing intersections, shortens the turnover time of capital and, thereby, raises the rate of profit.

The limited observations on the military's production of transportation and communication are fetishistic. Mitchell is a case in point: 'the military also played a leading role in the construction of bridges, roads, power lines, telephone systems, and other civilian infrastructure projects. All these activities provided plentiful opportunities for patronage and personal profit making'[94] Certainly there are appearances of patronage and personal profit, but they are not the essential reason for the construction.

Productive capital has built an extensive transportation network connecting capital throughout Egyptian society. According to the ministry of defense's website, productive capital has built the regional ring road (64 kms), the Cairo–Ain Sukhna road (91 kms to what Cairenes see as a beach destination, but what capital knows is a significant port), the Beni Suef–Assiut road (209 kms), the Shalateen Suheen Road (210 kms), Suhag road near the Red Sea (11 kms), a number of streets in Luxor, the Saad El-Shazly interchange, including a road, tunnel and bridge (5 kms), the Joseph Tito interchange (4 kms), the Al-Ahram interchange (4.5 kms), and further developed the Cairo–Ismailia road (30 kms) and the Cairo–Suez road (7.5 kms).[95] Productive capital also built vehicle bridges in Zagazig and at Martyr interchange and pedestrian bridges in Minia governorate. Because not all transportation is by ground, productive capital has also built Suhag Airport and Almaza Airport in Cairo, as well as the Hurghada seaport, including the port authority and passenger terminal. And, of course, the military has controlled the Suez Canal since 1956 through the Suez Canal Authority and recently realized the much-celebrated Suez Canal Development Project.

The military *qua* productive capital has its representatives in positions of power in holding companies involving transportation, and is partnered in joint ventures involving transportation. 'Officers head or sit on the boards of the holding companies for aviation and airports, maritime and land transport (including all seaport authorities [Alexandria, Port Said, Damietta and the Red Sea]).'[96] In the specific case of maritime transportation, productive capital acquired value and means of creating surplus-value in Egyptian maritime companies 'through the state-owned Holding Company for Maritime and Land Transport, the various port authorities and the Ministry of Maritime Transport, all of which are staffed by naval and other officers.'[97] It also accumulates through other means of maritime transportation through the Arab Federation of Chambers of Shipping. Productive capital's joint ventures in transportation include the Suez Canal Container Terminal Company and the Alexandria International Container Terminals.[98] Nassif cites Rabi' in saying that 'maritime transport in Egypt has fallen under "military occupation".'[99]

Telecommunication, too, is militarily occupied in Egyptian society.[100] In good subsidiary fashion, where the air force controls transportation by air, the navy controls transportation by sea, including the Suez Canal, and the army controls transportation by land, it is the Signal Corps that controls communications for productive capital.[101] The 2011 change of directors at Telecom Egypt is a case in point. In March, Ahmed Fathy El Kassass, formerly the Chief of Staff of the Signal Corps, left Telecom Egypt's board of directors and was replaced by Mohamed Nabil El Maadawy Youssef, Chief of Staff of the Signal Corps.[102] Telecom Egypt is the state-owned joint stock company with a monopoly on fixed telephone lines and a near-monopoly on fiber-optics lines connecting Egyptian society. It fully owns TEData and through it controls more than 60 percent of internet service provision. It also owns 45 percent of Vodafone Egypt, controlling the most mobile phone connections in the society. It was Telecom Egypt's near-monopoly on fiber-optic lines that enabled it to stop all internet communication between Egyptian society and other social formations as crisis erupted in 2011.[103]

To properly understand the dynamism of Egyptian society it is imperative to penetrate the froth of vulgar commentary and fetishistic illusions, and see social forces for what they really are based on how they accumulate surplus-value. The 'crony capitalists' and 'corrupt businessmen' are, in actuality, the predatory faction of capital accumulating through dispossession. This faction steals value, produced by the working class, and objectified in the form of factories under cover of neoliberal reform. The Ikhwan represents the interests of commercial capital. This faction accumulates by circulating commodities in the market. It has the reactionary values of the merchant. Finally, the military *qua* productive capital accumulates by creating surplus-value in the form of department I and department II commodities, extracting and working land and moving commodities and ideals. In all of these processes, labor-time is stolen from workers in the form of conscripts. The factions are not separate. They interconnect, and so do some of their techniques of accumulation. Predatory capital flows into productive enterprises. Commercial and productive capital accumulate through dispossession. All three factions appear in the sphere of circulation. The factions also struggle against each other. Each faction of capital fights to exercise more power relative to the other factions so as to accumulate a larger share of the surplus-value. And the three factions all share the common interest of accumulating at the expense of the working class in Egypt – the only source of surplus-value.

Egypt's social war

Having demystified the neoliberal crisis in Egyptian society in 2011 and unmasked the society's factions of capital, I now start to make sense of the social formation in terms of its dependent and antagonistic relations.

Relation between productive capital and commercial capital

My materialist dialectics analysis produces one notable insight into the productive capital–commercial capital relation in Egyptian society. The military and Ikhwan need each other, and neither can extirpate the other any more than it can extirpate itself. 'Circulation is just as necessary for commodity production as is production itself, and thus agents of circulation are just as necessary as agents of production.'[104] Surplus-value is created in the sphere of production. It is realized in the sphere of circulation. Commercial capital is dependent on productive capital for the creation of surplus-value and productive capital is dependent on commercial capital for the realization of surplus-value. The dependence is absolute; the relative magnitude of the dependence between the factions changes with the balance of forces.

In addition to being dependent, the relation between the military and the Ikhwan is also conflictual. The factions struggle because the more empowered the social force, the larger the share of the surplus-value and power it commands in Egyptian society. During the Keynesian moment, what the vulgar and fetishistic studies conceive of as the Nasser regime, productive capital was dominant, and had relatively little need for commercial capital because surplus-value was being easily realized. In this balance, the military violently repressed the Ikhwan. In the neoliberal moment, productive capital must share more surplus-value and power with the more mobile factions of capital. As much as is made of the Sadat regime's encouragement of the Ikhwan as a supposed counterbalance to the power of the workers' and students' movements, it was really a reflection of the global neoliberal balance of forces. Productive capital in the form of the military and commercial capital in the form of the Ikhwan are locked in constant struggle, the ebb and flow of which changes Egyptian society. When crisis erupted in the society in early 2011, the Ikhwan was at its high-water mark.

The dialectical relation between the factions does not stop the military from trying to reduce its dependence on the Ikhwan. The military, *inter alia*, builds roads and ports as means of transportation towards this end. Circumstances that develop the means of transportation shorten the turnover time of capital and thereby reduce the need for commercial capital.[105] Transporting commodities to Cairo from the port of Ain Sukhna on the military-built Cairo–Ain Sukhna road, for example, reduces the amount of time capital is objectified in the commodity form in relation to transporting the same commodities to Cairo from Alexandria or Port Said. The less time capital stays in the commodity form, the less need productive capital has for commercial capital and the less surplus-value and power productive capital must share with it. The neoliberal moment in which predatory/finance and commercial capital take larger distributive shares of surplus-value and power on the world scale was produced through class and factional conflict. Like productive capital everywhere, the military in Egyptian society has struggled to disempower the merchant class so as to reduce its claims. One technique used by the military has been to control the flow of capital through *both* the production and circulation processes. The department II commodities produced by the military are circulated through retail stores owned by the military. Productive capital creates and realizes surplus-value in such a way as to retain as much of it as possible. Department I commodities producing department II commodities that are then sold for individual consumption in military stores constitute an entirely closed circuit (save for that capital originally exchanged to obtain the department I means of production) with no 'seepage' of surplus-value to commercial capital. The same goes for the military transforming land through the processes of subdivision and construction into fixed capital installations and housing. There is no redistribution of the surplus-value expropriated from conscripted workers to, in this case, finance capital.

The military and the Ikhwan provide essential use-values to each other. Even in moments of severe imbalance in productive capital's favor, at those times of most intense struggle with productive capital on the offensive, the military cannot put the Ikhwan out of existence lest it also reduce itself to non-existence. This is why, after raiding El-Shater and Malek's Salsabil in 1991 and claiming to have 'uncovered information on a Muslim Brotherhood scheme to topple the regime,' the charges against a large number of Ikhwan members were eventually dropped and the case closed.[106] This is why each time El-Shater has been jailed he has been permitted to continue to function as a commercial capitalist from prison. And this is why the death sentences handed to more than a hundred Ikhwan members, including Supreme Guide Badie and former president Morsi, in early 2015 will not be executed or capitalist relations in Egyptian society will dissolve further. The mutual dependence and usefulness of productive capital and commercial capital vividly appeared in the political realm as crisis erupted in Egyptian society in early 2011. The military and the Ikhwan found in each other a social force antagonistic to the working class, and interested in reducing the power of predatory capital. One had the means to deliver the neoliberal state form and the other to cover it with a democratic fig-leaf.

Relation between productive capital and predatory capital

My conceptualization of Egyptian society in objective terms reveals two important aspects of the productive capital–predatory capital relation as crisis erupted. First, the military and Gamal Mubarak's 'corrupt businessmen' clashed because of their competing factional interests. Whether the military despised 'Gamal Mubarak [because he] never completed military service' is irrelevant.[107] So, too, are any supposed senses of national duty and shame, disgust at corruption and desire to restore military honor serving as motivations for the military's involvement in the political realm.[108] And it is not the case that 'the Egyptian military establishment does not believe in US-style neoliberalism or free market policies, particularly those that would result in the army's loss of its valued companies and assets.'[109] Empty psychologizing cannot be allowed to stand in for materialist dialectics analysis. Moreover, productive capital's position on neoliberal processes is not one of simple, categorical opposition. Productive capital in Egyptian society is like productive capital everywhere – it supports privatization, trade liberalization and commodification *provided* they reduce the value of its means of production and labor-power commodity and enable it to accumulate more surplus-value. The military had no problem when neoliberal privatization transferred to it the value of the Alexandria Shipyard. The struggle for productive capital is to find ways to reduce, through neoliberal means, the value consumed in production and increase its rate of exploitation without, in the Egyptian case, losing its monopoly position in its captive national market. The factional conflict intensified, and the military increasingly resisted some of the steps taken by the 'cronies,' because predatory capital was accumulating relatively more surplus-value through the dispossession of the Egyptian commons. The military was not opposed to the processes of the neoliberal counter-attack per se, but rather to policies that primarily served the interests of a rival, and increasingly powerful, faction.

In factional terms, the neoliberal counter-attack on the working class is least advantageous to productive capital because it is the least mobile form of capital. Value objectified in the form of factories is less mobile than value objectified in commodities, which is still less mobile than value objectified in the money form. As Harvey explains, in moments of crisis '[m]oney capital flits away, leaving fixed capital high and dry and subject to savage devaluation.'[110] Productive capital in Egyptian society has tried to overcome, at least in part, its own national limits by flowing its value together with nominally French, Kuwaiti, Chinese, Danish and Emirati finance capital.[111] In its selective opposition to neoliberal tactics and responses to the eruption of crisis, the military mobilized nationalist rhetoric, not because it loves Egypt more than other social forces, but because its value-creating processes are more rooted to the specific space of Egypt than predatory/finance capital. The space of Egypt is integral to productive capital's accumulation, where it is not to predatory/finance capital. The military as bearer of factional interests dependent on a specific space is also the possessor of the means of violence theoretically necessary to retain the space.

One of the contradictions of productive capital is that it is both vulnerable and powerful in relation to the other factions of capital. It is relatively vulnerable because its value is most fixed to a space, and it is relatively powerful because it creates the surplus-value on which the other factions depend for accumulation. Just as one process does not exist on its own, production does not exist without consumption – for example, no one faction governs a society on its own. Taken together, this means that productive capital must govern in conjunction with another faction, and that it choses its junior partner. This is the second important revelation.

When the crisis of global neoliberal capital appeared in Egyptian society in early 2011, the governing coalition was comprised of productive capital and predatory capital. As the crisis intensified, predatory capital transformed from a rival and a partner furnishing productive capital with the use-value of making Egypt a darling of the international financial architecture – the World Bank's *Doing Business* ranked Egypt its top reformer in 2006/07 – into a rival and a handicap.[112] A disadvantageous partner that had been accumulating relative surplus-value against productive capital quickly became an expendable partner. GCC capital was so concerned that the predatory faction would be disposed of by the senior partner that it had then Saudi king Abdullah tell US president Obama, and effectively reassure the productive capital faction, that he would replace US material support if it was withdrawn.[113] The GCC pledged productive capital US$1.3 billion a year to maintain the governing factional configuration because removal of the predatory capital faction threatened the GCC finance capital that had merged with it. The benefits accruing to productive capital, both in terms of surplus-value and power, from sacrificing the predatory faction proved greater than the value of the pledged Saudi material support, and the senior partner chose as its new junior partner the representative of commercial capital. At first, the partnership was more informal. The Ikhwan supported the military-authored constitutional amendments of March 2011, boycotted protests and sit-ins directed at the military, including the Mohamed Mahmoud battles of November 2011, and targeted workers' organizations, and in exchange the military allowed it to be elected into a dominant position in the lower house of parliament in late 2011/early 2012. Once there, the Ikhwan endorsed the military's temporal order for the so-called political transition and condoned the massacre of workers in Port Said Stadium. The two factions were formally partnered in mid-2012 when productive capital awarded commercial capital's representative the presidency after three days of negotiations. The productive capital–commercial capital alignment further rankled capital represented by the GCC because it exposed that value which had washed into the commercial circuit to more intense competition in the Egyptian social formation. As already noted, on 18 July 2012, less than a month after the Ikhwan representative was awarded the presidency, El-Shater inaugurated fifteen branches of the Zad retail chain (associated with capital represented by the Turkish state form) to compete with the Carrefour and Spinneys supermarkets owned, in part, by Emirati capital.

Relation between the working class and productive capital

My value-centric analysis affords two preliminary insights of note into the working class–productive capital relation in Egyptian society in crisis. First, because the threat to the reproduction of working-class life existentially endangered the military *qua* productive capital, the latter had to participate in the crisis in a manner that restored, of necessity only momentarily, society to a less severe disequilibrium, thereby perpetuating capital production. The global inflation of the price of wheat driven by finance capital using the technology of derivatives disempowered the working class in the Egyptian social formation by reducing its real wage and devalued its labor-power commodity by reducing its access to nutrition. Dialectically, capital was empowered relative to the working class and increased its rate of surplus-value accumulation.

The working class has the most immediate and direct relation with the productive faction of capital. The working class's relations with the other factions of capital are mediated by productive capital and reside in the sphere of circulation. The working class, as a class, is not the target of commercial and finance capital. Commercial and finance capital target productive capital because they receive distributional shares of the surplus-value productive capital expropriates from the working class. Commercial and finance capital primarily relate to an atomized working class as consumers in the market. Its own endangerment aside, the threatening of the reproduction of working-class life in Egyptian society most immediately and directly affected the military *qua* productive capital. The military is the biggest consumer of wheat and labor-power in Egyptian society. Within the limits of the sphere of production, the increase in the price of wheat meant that either productive capital could perpetuate the higher rate of exploitation and see the quality of its labor-power commodity further degraded because of reduced nutrition, or it could maintain the value of its labor-power by incurring a reduction to its rate of exploitation (instead of passing on inflated wheat prices in the form of reduced nutrition, productive capital could absorb them against its surplus-value, thereby reducing the ratio between its surplus-value and consumption of variable capital in the form of conscripts). Within the totality of the spheres of production *and* circulation there was, however, another option.

The increase in the rate of exploitation meant, all things being equal, that each of the factions of capital would accumulate more in absolute terms because more surplus-value was being expropriated from the working class in Egyptian society. The increased amount of surplus-value would be distributed between the three factions according to the balance of forces between them. While productive capital's increased accumulation entailed costs in the form of degraded labor-power, commercial and finance capital were relatively insulated from this change. There arose a contradiction such that the faction involved in the relation creating all the surplus-value was the one primarily and adversely affected by the devaluation of the labor-power commodity. The way to blunt the contradiction was to redistribute value, and the redistribution would be executed according to the balance of forces between the factions of capital. In the 2011 moment of struggle, the military could deploy accumulated value, means of violence and the ideal of nationalism; the Ikhwan could deploy accumulated value, its network of social services and the ideal of religion; and Gamal Mubarak's cadre could deploy accumulated value. The loser in this tripartite arrangement is clear.

Redistribution enabled productive capital to temporarily rebalance the severe disequilibrium in Egyptian society *while* maintaining its new, higher rate of accumulation. The rebalancing was realized through a reduction in the theft of value from the working class. Immediately after deposing Mubarak as representative of the interests of predatory capital, the military, *inter alia*, halted privatizations and renegotiated some land contracts (including with capital represented, unsurprisingly, by the Saudi state form). This reduction in the extent and intensity of predation at the expense of the working class was nominal; more apparent than real. Its nationalistic representation, however, ideally reconciled the working class to its newly devalued condition and with it productive capital's increased rate of exploitation.

In early 2011, the dynamism of global neoliberal capital and Egyptian society produced a situation in which working-class weakness aligned the interests of the working class and productive capital in opposition to those of the predatory faction of capital instrumentalizing the state form. The productive faction momentarily arrested the transfer of value from the working class to the predatory faction that was accumulating capital while relatively autonomous from the vicissitudes involving the devaluation of the labor-power commodity. The military did not refrain from an extensive use of direct violence against the demonstrating masses of surplus population because of some psychological nonsense that it lacked the will.[114] It refrained because of its dialectical relation with the working class – to have destroyed the working class would have been to destroy itself, and because it was advantageous to eliminate a competitive faction of capital with which productive capital had to share surplus-value and power. At the same time that productive capital could realize this redistribution because of its power, the working class in Egyptian society celebrated it, and with it the perpetuation of its heightened exploitation at the hands of productive capital, because it was so weak and deluded by neoliberal fetishisms.

Second, the redistribution that attended productive capital's disposal of predatory capital was only ever a deferral of the soon-to-reappear severe disequilibrium in Egyptian society born of the increasingly acute contradiction between labor and capital. Productive capital's organization of surplus-value production and realization in the Egyptian social formation means the rate of exploitation of the working class will again have to be increased. This holds even if global neoliberal capital does *not* again destroy value in the form of Egyptian labor-power. *Ceteris paribus*, Egyptian society will be racked by ever more severe disequilibrium even in the rosiest of futures.

The military *qua* productive capital creates and circulates surplus-value in a manner that requires interminable deficit financing, and the servicing, to say nothing of the reduction or elimination, of this constantly growing outflow of value necessitates the expropriation of ever more surplus-value from the working class. Most of the value in constant capital form consumed by productive capital in the production of department I and II commodities (i.e. machinery producing television sets, wheat producing labor-power, aircraft and bridge-building mobile cranes producing spatial movement) is imported. This value is, in turn, transformed into a department I commodity that is then productively consumed to produce a department II commodity that leaves the circuit of value through individual consumption, or directly into a department II commodity that is individually consumed for its use-value. In either case, most of the value imported into Egyptian society by productive capital in commodity form never again flows out in commodity form.

The breaking of the circuit of capital in the Egyptian social formation means there is a constant outflow of value in the money form. This ending of the movement of capital entails an absolute deficiency. It is not about a difference between value exported and imported because importation is also immediately exportation, and exportation is immediately also importation. Rather, the manner in which productive capital creates and accumulates surplus-value means it must continuously throw value out of the society. No matter how much value the society may seek to send out, because the value productively consumed is brought in and much of it does not leave the society, there is a deficiency that must be financed.

An example proves elucidating, even one based on the ideal assumptions that the exchange process starts balanced and the trade is balanced in value terms. In trade 1, what is understood in fetishistic terms as an import, the equivalent of 100 hours of labor-time comes into the society in the commodity form in exchange for the equivalent of 100 hours of labor-time leaving the society in the money form. As it circulates through Egyptian society, say the equivalent of 80 hours of that labor-time objectified in commodities is individually consumed. This leaves the equivalent of 20 hours of labor-time objectified in commodities to circulate in the circuit of capital. At the same moment trade 1 is realized, so is trade A, a fetishized export. The equivalent of 100 hours of labor-time flows into Egyptian society in money form and the equivalent of 100 hours of labor-time flows out in commodity form. Now, to renew the movement and realize trade 2 in the second moment the society requires the equivalent of 100 hours in money form to obtain the equivalent of 100 hours in commodity form. As a result of trade A, the society has the requisite 100 hours in money form to realize trade 2. It does not, however, have the requisite 100 hours in commodity form to realize trade B. It only has the equivalent of 20 hours. In order to be able to continue the process, the society must borrow the equivalent of 80 hours of labor-time in money form. Of course, this only ensures the exchange of equivalents in the second trade moment. The value that is unproductively consumed by the society in the second circulation means that another 80 hours of labor-time in money form must be borrowed, plus the money equivalent necessary to service the usurious interest, to realize the third trade moment, and so on and so on.

Because productive capital consumes imported value to produce commodities and most of this objectified value leaves the circuit of capital through individual consumption, Egyptian society has less value available to release out than it allowed to flow in in the form of department I and II means of production. There is a structural deficit between the value that flows in in the commodity form and that which flows out in the commodity form. Value in the money form must be used to account for the difference if the capitalist cycle is to be renewed. One way out of this increasingly indebted relation would be for productive capital to produce commodities objectifying predominantly 'domestic' value. This way, more value would leave the society than stays in it through unproductive consumption. The society's dependence on wheat imports makes this impossible. Given the flow of value, importing wheat means a constantly expanding debt relation. Another way to get the money to bridge the deficit without producing commodities using imported value is to sell land. This explains the flurry of contracts for land negotiated since 2011, particularly the massive New Capital project announced in 2015.

So long as productive capital circulates most of the value transferred from imported means of production to Egyptian workers and capitalists who individually consume the value, Egyptian society will have a value shortfall requiring deficit financing. Furthermore, this deficit financing can only be reproduced through the assumption of debt that will require an ever increasing expropriation of value and surplus-value from the working class to produce the money necessary for debt payments.

Conclusion

This chapter was about seeing Egyptian society and its expression of crisis as they really are. I demystified the ideals of freedom, dignity, social justice and peace as fetishistic illusions with use-values for capital. And I unmasked the capitalist factions and social relations producing Egyptian society.

In their essences, Gamal Mubarak and his 'corrupt businessmen' personify the interests of predatory capital, the Ikhwan the interests of commercial capital and the military the interests of productive capital. In the lead-up to the appearance of crisis in early 2011, predatory capital primarily accumulated by dispossessing the Egyptian commons of value. Commercial capital primarily accumulated through trade. Productive capital primarily accumulated by producing department I and II commodities, extracting land and providing transportation and communication. Dialectically, the accumulation of value and surplus-value by and empowerment of the capitalist factions of Egyptian society concentrated misery and disempowerment with the working class.

My detailed analysis of the real, inner relations of Egyptian society in crisis produced five insights. First, the military and the Ikhwan need each other, and neither can extirpate the other without extirpating itself. Second, the military and Gamal Mubarak and his cadre of 'cronies' clashed because of their competing factional interests. Predatory capital was accumulating value and power relative to productive capital through neoliberal tactics. Third, the military must govern in coalition with another capitalist faction, and it chooses its junior partner. Fourth, to save itself the military had to intervene in 2011 to reduce the severe social imbalance endangering the working class. Fifth, the military corrected the severe imbalance by stopping the redistribution of value to predatory capital. The correction was only temporary and severe imbalance is reappearing more and more vividly in Egyptian society, in part because the manner in which the military produces and realizes surplus-value ensures a constant and ever growing outflow of value from the social formation that can only be balanced by deficit financing, the costs of which are being borne by an increasingly exploited working class.

A revolution of fetishisms, shifting factional alignments that further devalue and disempower the working class, and temporal displacement of contradictions is no revolution at all.

CHAPTER 4

Realignments and reform

Egyptian society erupted in crisis in early 2011. The subsequent constitutions, parliamentary elections, presidential elections, mass trials and massacres are modes of appearance of changing class and factional relations particular to the Egyptian social formation. This chapter tells the story of the political moments and forms of expression of these dynamic relations: Moment I – 28 January 2011 to 2 July 2013, and Moment II – 3 July 2013 to the end of 2015. Each moment and its forms of expression are the product of a struggle between different configurations of factions and classes. The start dates mark social realignments. Reform of legal and governmental arrangements has dominated across these moments because, while the senior governing faction has persisted, and extended and intensified the war on the Egyptian working class, the junior faction has twice been replaced.

Of course, the particular circumstances under which Egyptian society erupted were transmitted from the past. A brief historicizing of the social relations and political forms that bequeathed the circumstances is necessary. Table 4.1 presents the *long durée* history of the Egyptian social formation's governing alignment of factions, what Gramsci called historic blocs.

Table 4.1 Factional alignments governing Egyptian society

	1971–2010	2011–13	2013–15
Senior faction	productive capital	productive capital	productive capital
Junior faction	predatory capital	commercial capital	finance capital (GCC state forms)

Historicizing changing relations and their political forms of expression

The neoliberal counter-attack on the working class was realized in Egypt in the same moment it was realized elsewhere around the world. Egyptian society's particular expression of this universal social phenomenon was the *infitah* policy. The Egyptian social formation was 'corrected' and 'opened' in the same moment that, *inter alia*, limits to accumulation were overcome through abandonment of the gold standard in 1971 and capital staged a savage coup in Chile in 1973.

Owen's description represents the dominant view of the *infitah* policy as being 'aimed at increasing the efficiency of the Egyptian public sector, revitalizing the private sector and encouraging foreign investment, particularly from the increasingly wealthy Gulf oil states.'[1] In non-fetishistic terms, the *infitah* policy was about deploying many of the weapons of the neoliberal arsenal against the working class in Egyptian society. Processes such as trade liberalization and privatization were initiated so as to devalue the workers' labor-power commodity and facilitate accumulation through theft from the productive commons. As Beinin offers from a more critical perspective, the *infitah* policy 'reintegrated [Egyptian society] into the transnational political economy on a subordinate basis regulated by a new mode of neo-liberal capital accumulation.'[2] The Egyptian social formation was never outside global capitalist relations and processes, but the way in which it differently related starting in the early 1970s was on terms decidedly disadvantageous to the Egyptian working class.

Egypt's particular mode of appearance of the neoliberal assault on the working class also mobilized and institutionalized the mental conceptions of the moment, namely growth and religion. The growth fetishism was succinctly expressed in Sadat's motto: 'Food for every mouth, a house for every individual, and *prosperity for all*.'[3] In the early 1970s, the Egyptian state form 'encouraged political Islam in its pronouncements. [Sadat's] Vice President Hussein al-Shefei, for example, called for "building a society that could resist and confront Israeli society which claims that it is the Chosen People of God" and claimed that "the only society that could do so is: *the society of there is no God but Allah*" (Islam).'[4] Most notably, in early 1980 the constitution, the fundamental legal arrangement of the society, was amended to make *shar'ia* (Islamic law) the principal source of legislation.

Infitah was a policy of relatively empowered capital in Egyptian society that further empowered capital in relation to the working class. It was not a radical break with the Keynesian form of state associated with Nasser, but rather an updating, for that moment, of the legal and governmental forms expressing always dynamic social relations. As Aoude says, '[t]he die for the *Infitah* was cast before Nasser suffered a heart attack that ended his life on 28 September 1970.'[5] Contrary to upside-down commonsensical 'understandings,' the Keynesian form of state in Egypt was bourgeois. The land reform of 1952 and the nationalizations of 1961 and 1962 never threatened the relations of the commodity form. Concomitantly, the state form executed workers and destroyed autonomous and representative workers' organizations.[6] ElGeziri asserts that the 'Open Door policy created the conditions for the rise of new social groups and the changing class landscape in favor of the rich.'[7] Citing Imam, she goes on to explain:

> [t]he opening up implied a reconfiguration of state policy away from Nasser's concerns with improving the living conditions of the poor towards the interests of the rich. The latter included landed interests, the bureaucratic bourgeoisie of the sixties and the commercial bourgeoisie of *Infitah*, who engaged in financial activities, contracting, import and export and wholesale trading.[8]

Fetishistic as it is, this explanation gets matters backwards; as do all that begin in the political sphere and reduce the reconfiguration of power relations in Egyptian society to Sadat and his struggle with 'leftists.' The change to the policy of the state form developed dialectically through the change of social relations. *Infitah* most assuredly empowered capital, but it could be realized only because capital was already empowered in relation to the working class. The legal and governmental arrangements of the Egyptian form of state came to express an increasingly bourgeois character that facilitated accumulation of greater quantities of capital at the expense of workers because capital was more powerful in relation to labor.

The *infitah* policy also had an intra-class element. Abul-Magd broaches this when she explains that: '[t]hrough his "open door" policy, [Sadat] took steps to privatize parts of the state-owned sector that military leaders had previously dominated. Military leaders then had to share influence with a rising community of crony capitalists.'[9] The privatization process was political because it entailed a transfer of value from the commons to different, dependent and competing, factions of capital. The accumulation through dispossession was universally realized at the expense of disempowered workers, and the particular beneficiaries of the dispossession were determined by the shifting power relations between factions; which, in turn, had their relative positions further improved or degraded by the redistribution of dispossessed value. The legal and governmental arrangements governing Egyptian society changed as they did in the 1970s because the inter-class balance of forces was shifting further in capital's favor, and the intra-class balance of forces between productive capital and predatory capital was being brought closer to level by the latter.

This inter-class and intra-class rebalancing through which capital was empowered in relation to the working class and predatory capital continued for the next three decades and was expressed in, and deployed through, a range of legal and governmental arrangements, including inflation, assumption of debt and fiscal policy. Inflation, particularly punishingly throughout the 1980s and early 1990s, destroyed the real wages of workers – '[t]he real wage per worker declined from US$70 in 1980 to only US$11 in 1991'[10] – devalued their labor-power commodity and had the effect of increasing productivity and surplus-value accumulation for productive capital. After 1991, indebtedness was used to rationalize sustained reductions in social spending. Like inflation, the reductions in social spending reduced real wages, cheapened the renewal of life processes for the Egyptian working class and devalued its labor-power commodity. By way of example, if x is the laborer's wage, and the laborer spends all of her wage on food, clothing and shelter because of social spending on healthcare, the value of her labor-power commodity is C; $C=x$. When social spending on healthcare is reduced by the value of y, with no attendant increase in wages, then the value of the worker's labor-power commodity is reduced because she has less wage with which to buy food, clothing and shelter and consequently must renew herself with less value; $C=x-y$. The shifting of more of the burden of, say, education and healthcare to workers had the value effect of increasing their productivity for productive capital. And early in the twenty-first century, a regressive flat tax of 20 percent disproportionately appropriated value in money form from wage-earning workers.[11]

Law 96 is a notable expression and instrument of the class struggle in Egyptian society. According to Ayeb, 'the counter-revolution to Nasser's reforms was initiated by Anwar Sadat in 1974 and culminated with deposed President Mubarak's Law 96 of 1992.'[12] Law 96/1992 was intended to reverse Egypt's growing trade imbalance by increasing agricultural production. It was a model of neoliberal export-led growth.[13] The law 'established that tenant farming, sharecropping and land markets (sales, purchases and rentals) would be completely liberalized in October 1997. It also stipulated that the price of rent for the period 1992–1997 would immediately increase from seven to twenty-two times the land tax.'[14] This reform of agricultural production increased the fragmentation of small farms and all but eliminated tenant farmers from Egyptian agriculture.[15] Concomitantly, the legal arrangement further concentrated the means of production of land and water in the hands of large-scale capitalist landowners.

The Ahmed Nazif government most spectacularly deployed the process of privatization as the primary mechanism for distributing value to the predatory capital faction. This faction was personified by individuals such as Gamal Mubarak, Ahmed Ezz and Rachid Mohamed Rachid. As Wurzel puts it: 'in many cases privatization "Egyptian style" led to a distribution of former state-owned assets to a limited number of well-connected business cronies of the regime and to friends and relatives of regime members, and allegedly also to the takeover of large parts of attractive state assets by high-ranking regime figures themselves.'[16] The Nazif government used different schemes to privatize socially produced value in the form of state-owned industries, but consistently the process redistributed the value to the predatory and productive capital factions which were part of the state's governing configuration. This process was defended through the mobilization of the ideal of nationalism. The process of privatization was legitimized on the grounds that the value was redistributed to Egyptians, and not foreigners. Privatization enriched factions of capital at the expense of Egyptian workers. Moreover, after the value had been stolen from the commons under cover of legal arrangements, the workers not cast into the surplus population had their wages, both immediate and deferred, and benefits slashed.[17]

The reform of legal and governmental arrangements was an expression and instrument of the factional battle raging in Egyptian society. This factional battle is often misrepresented as the Egyptian military being 'largely disapprov[ing] of the "Washington Consensus"'[18] and opposing the political ascendancy of Gamal Mubarak.[19] Such representations are apolitical. The military as productive capital *selectively* opposed the deployment of neoliberal tactics such as privatization. On one hand, the military did not oppose the privatization of the Alexandria shipyard because the process transferred value and the means of creating surplus-value to productive capital. On the other hand, the military's representative in government opposed the privatization of banks and 'stopped the government giving the contract for a railway connecting Cairo and 10 Ramadan City to a company owned by close associates of the regime.'[20] Productive capital's opposition to predatory capital's neoliberal counter-attack on workers' value was by no means absolute. It is too simple to assert that the military resisted privatization owing to the threat it posed to the military's economic empire.[21] Productive capital supported those arrangements that devalued the labor-power commodity it consumed, i.e. trade liberalization (productive capital was, in political effect, the only governing faction when Egypt became a contracting party to the General Agreement on Tariffs and Trade in 1970), and opposed those that empowered rival factions. Productive capital opposed the privatization of finance capital in the form of banks because it would have empowered its rival, predatory capital, and opposed the privatization of the railway because transportation is productive of value and, as such, its prerogative. Of course, this is not how the factional battle was represented. Nationalism was the mental conception used to disguise the struggle. 'Speaking at a cabinet meeting [in 2008], Field Marshal Hussein Tantawi told former prime minister Ahmed Nazif and his ministers that they were selling off the country [through privatization], "the soil of which we liberated with our blood," and that the army wouldn't allow it.'[22] Productive capital couched its opposition in bourgeois nationalistic, rather than material, terms.

Commercial capital, too, was always a party to these dynamics. It supported the *infitah* policy and Law 96. It accumulated relatively more surplus-value as a result of the devaluation of the workers' labor-power commodity and the realization of the flat tax. Reducing the amount of value transferred to the worker by way of social spending also had an ideal use-value for commercial capital. The process opened space for Islamist charities to provide social services[23] and disseminate their mental conceptions, including 'Islam is the solution.' At the same time, other governmental arrangements, such as the politicization of the extension of credit and selective trade liberalization, asymmetrically exposed commercial capital to competitive pressures from capital outside the Egyptian social formation.[24] As an element of the capitalist class, commercial capital benefitted from legal and governmental arrangements expressing and extending the disempowerment of the working class. As a faction of capital, it was relatively more coerced by the laws of competition because it was not a partner to the governing configuration of social forces.

The most recent mode of appearance in governmental arrangements of these changing factional relations is the parliamentary elections of 2000, 2005 and 2010. In 2000, commercial capital was represented by 17 independent legislators in the People's Assembly. In 2005, commercial capital's representation increased to 88 seats. Obviously, it had been empowered materially and organizationally in relation to the predatory faction of capital because the gain of 71 seats came at considerable expense to NDP representation, which was reduced by 23 seats. Five years later, the Ikhwan's representation was reduced to a single parliamentarian. While surely accurate, charges of voting fraud do not explain why the 444 contested seats were distributed as they were in 2010 (the Ikhwan lost 87 seats and the NDP gained 90 seats). Why this particular fraudulent result and not another? Of the myriad possible distributions of seats, all of the Ikhwan's seats were effectively transferred to the NDP in an expression of factional retrenchment. The state is a form of economic power,[25] and in order for productive capital and predatory capital to continue to use their legal and governing arrangements to accumulate at the same rate when growth rates were falling (the 2010 5.1 percent annual growth rate of gross domestic product (GDP) was up from 4.7 percent in 2009, but down considerably from 7.2 percent in 2008 and 7.1 percent in 2007),[26] commercial capital's position had to be attacked. Productive capital was the senior governing faction by virtue of being the relatively most empowered, and its position was secure. Predatory capital was the junior governing faction because it was disempowered in relation to productive capital and empowered in relation to commercial capital. Commercial capital was the weakest faction of capital, even in spite of its empowerment through earlier decades, and, as a result, its representation was decimated.

From the early 1970s until 2011, the working class in Egypt was disempowered relative to capital, and the predatory faction of capital was empowered relative to productive and commercial capital. The factional alignment governing Egyptian society through the state form came to be more and more defined by its predatory capital faction. What started as productive capital effectively governing alone in 1952 was transformed into a productive capital–predatory capital configuration by the time crisis erupted in 2011. These changing social relations were expressed in, and instrumentalized, reform of legal and governmental arrangements.

In dialectical fashion, just as the relative empowerment of the predatory faction as junior partner was realized through the process of reform, it was also contested through the reform process. In an early expression of what would become recognizable as a structural adjustment program, the Egyptian form of state cut social spending on bread subsidies in early 1977. Workers protesting the draconian devaluation of their labor-power commodity were violently repressed by the productive capital that stood to gain most from the devaluation. The working class's less spectacular, everyday struggles against fiscal policies that further immiserated it were met with coercion through the permanent realization of emergency law after 1980. Commercial capital, too, struggled for surplus-value and power through the reform of legal and governmental arrangements. Relations between commercial capital and the governing configuration of productive and predatory capital expressed in the state form are antagonistic and dependent. This explains both the killing of personifications of the interests of commercial capital and/or their being dispossessed of value, say in police raids, and their being permitted to accumulate and organize. The three factions of capital need each other and are constantly battling. The relations are close, and close relations are turbulent. The Ikhwan supported the *infitah* policy because it accumulated through it. Again, Naguib, citing Saiid, notes that 'by the 1980s the private sector of the economy was controlled by eighteen families, of which eight were connected to the Brotherhood: some 40 per cent of all private economic ventures, [Saiid] suggests, were connected to Brotherhood interests.'[27] Moreover, the Ikhwan did not oppose the privatization process in principle. It was the manner in which the privatization was realized that the faction critiqued.[28] In reality, commercial capital supported legalized theft from the Egyptian working class; it just wanted a share in the distribution of the spoils.

This political transformation had Egyptian particularities, but was by no means uniquely Egyptian. Nor did it occur in a vacuum. Predatory capital empowered itself in Egyptian society concomitant with the universal neoliberal counter-attack on the working class. From 1971 onwards, the increasingly balanced productive capital–predatory capital alignment progressively homogenized Egyptian society's legal and governmental arrangements to the ideals, relations and processes of global neoliberal capitalism. This homogenization made the Egyptian form of state increasingly permissible to capital represented by the international financial institutions and the

American form of state. The apogee of reform of the Egyptian social formation, meaning the most relative empowerment of predatory capital in the governing bloc, was concomitant with the eruption of crisis in American society in 2007 and in Egyptian society in 2011.

Reform through crisis

Social relations

In early 2011, Egyptian society erupted in a particular appearance of the crisis of universal capitalist relations and processes. The first expression of this crisis was *'aish, horreya, adala egetma'eya* – bread, freedom, social justice. Bread was demanded because the labor-power commodity of the Egyptian worker had been so devalued and his/her exploitation so intensified by the inflation of wheat prices by overaccumulated capital on the world market that his/her renewal of life processes was endangered. The demands for freedom and social justice were demands for the reigning bourgeois fetishisms of the neoliberal moment.

The political form of appearance of this crisis was the deposition of President Hosni Mubarak and the NDP by the military, ostensibly in response to protestors' demands, and its subsequent governing of Egyptian society in partnership with the Ikhwan. In a reconfiguration of the governing bloc, productive capital replaced its rival and burdensome junior partner, the predatory capital faction, with commercial capital. This reconfiguration provided productive capital with the political cover it needed to temporarily rebalance a contradiction that had moved too far into disequilibrium and thereby protect commodity relations in Egyptian society, and its accumulation through and dominance in those relations.

The initial mode of appearance of crisis was dubbed the 'Day of Anger' and organized by groups with connections to the Egyptian working class, notably the April 6 Movement. The Ikhwan, which 'never had a strong base in the industrial working class' and even helped break strikes in the past,[29] did not heed the call to participate. The next day, however, after the protests demonstrated the scale of the crisis and the support they had in Egyptian society, the Muslim Brotherhood opportunistically announced that the organization would participate in the Friday 'Day of Rage.' The Brotherhood joined the protests on 28 January and shortly thereafter was fully integrated into the tripartite discussions among the capitalist factions of Egyptian society. Some time after 29 January prominent members of the Ikhwan, including Saad El-Katatny, who would become speaker of the house in 2012, and Mohamed Morsi, who would become president later the same year, met secretly with Vice-President Suleiman. The 'Brotherhood leaders were asked by Suleiman to withdraw from Tahrir . . . in exchange for the release of prominent MB [Muslim Brotherhood] figures Khairat El-Shater and Hassan Malek.'[30] It seems the representatives of commercial capital acceded to the arrangement, and it went unrealized only because they could not convince the organization's rank-and-file members, meaning religiously opiated workers, to vacate Tahrir Square.

Much has been made of the integral role played by the Ikhwan in the infamous 2 February Battle of the Camel in and around Tahrir Square. More important than the objectification of this spectacle, however, is how the Ikhwan's involvement in the expression of crisis changed the expression itself. On 6 February, groups active in the protests, including the April 6 Movement, the Popular Campaign to Support El-Baradei and the Muslim Brotherhood, formed a coalition called the Unified Leadership of the Youth of the Rage Revolution. The Unified Leadership had seven demands:

> the resignation of Mubarak, the immediate lifting of emergency law, release of all political prisoners, the dissolution of both the upper and lower chambers of parliament, the formation of a national unity government to manage the transitional period, investigation by the judiciary of the abuses of the security forces during the revolution, and protection of the protestors by the military.[31]

These demands were a marked change from the original calls for *'aish, horreya, adala egetma'eya*. Between 25 January, when the Ikhwan was not involved, to 6 February, when it was actively participating and coordinating, the expression of crisis was transformed from one prioritizing the increasingly devalued and exploited labor-power commodity to one of bourgeois reformism. The participation of commercial capital reduced the expression of crisis to a (more acceptable) bourgeois scale. This was clearly articulated on the banner that hung across the center of Tahrir Square: 'The People demand removal of the regime.'

Productive capital's actions were dialectically related to the Ikhwan's recasting of the mode of appearance of crisis. The military deployed its means of violence throughout Egyptian society on the same day the Ikhwan involved itself in the protests. The next day Defense Minister and Minister of Military Production Tantawi rejected the president's request that violence be used against protesting workers.[32] Productive capital refused to attack the workers on which its accumulation depended in the interests of its rival predatory faction. On 31 January, the military announced that it was aware of the legitimacy of the protesting workers' demands. Productive capital was able to recognize the legitimacy of the Unified Leadership's demands precisely because commercial capital had reduced them to a scale more acceptable to capital. The changed expression of crisis ensured the perpetuation of commodity relations in Egyptian society at the same time that it opened an opportunity for productive capital to replace an increasingly empowered rival with a relatively disempowered rival that was similarly antagonistic towards predatory capital and the working class.

A crucial and often misunderstood point demands to be made here. On 29 January, the military assured the president of its loyalty and 'that [it] would stay neutral while he dealt with the situation.'[33] Gramsci says of neutrality: 'it is not true that armies are constitutionally barred from making politics; the army's duty is precisely to defend the constitution – in other words the legal form of the State together with its related institutions. Hence so-called neutrality only means support for the reactionary side.'[34] Those millions of working Egyptians who welcomed the tanks into Tahrir Square, shook hands with and hugged soldiers and chanted *el-geesh wa el-shaeb eid wahdah* (The military and the army are one hand) were celebrating *the* institutional form most opposed to genuine, thoroughgoing change of the social formation that would alleviate the crisis conditions. As for the military's loyalty, it certainly stayed loyal to its interests as productive capital, which were increasingly divergent from the interests of predatory capital.

The Battle of the Camel is an ideal mode of appearance of the war being fought in Egyptian society in early 2011: the two social forces not party to the governing bloc, a working class deluded by fetishisms and too weak to effect revolutionary social change, and a relatively empowered commercial capital recently successful in rescaling the crisis as one of political reform, were aligned in the space of Tahrir Square and assailed by an increasingly expendable and desperate predatory capital, while productive capital, securely positioned to continue to accumulate as the senior partner in the governing configuration, waited to see which social force would emerge victorious. Ultimately, predatory capital was bested; the forces of productive capital and commercial capital emerged in an alliance that cast aside the weak working class and the process of reforming the legal and governing arrangements in line with this new factional configuration was initiated.

Legal and governing arrangements, mental conceptions, accumulation and reproduction

The new factional alliance was immediately expressed politically and extended its attack on the Egyptian working class. The Ikhwan supported the constitutional reforms authored by SCAF, the political form of productive capital's executive committee, and put to workers on 19 March 2011. On 23 March 2011, the SCAF-appointed cabinet 'approved a decree-law [Law 34/2011] that criminalize[d] strikes, protests, demonstrations and sit-ins that interrupt[ed] private or state owned business or affect[ed] the economy in anyway.'[35] Five days later, the military issued the Political Parties Law, strictly prohibiting the establishment of class-based parties.[36] The conditions for party formation laid out by the law clearly empowered capital: '[t]he principles, programs, activities, or means of selecting leaders and members must not be founded on the basis of religion, class, geography, or on the basis of race, language, religion or creed.'[37] The law's conditions for publicizing the formation of a political party further extended capital's power vis-à-vis labor: '[n]otifications must include the notarized signatures of at least 5000 of its members, which originate from at least 10 governorates with at least 300 members in each of the governorates' and 'the political party must publish the names of its founding members in two widely circulated daily newspapers.'[38] The Political Parties Law imposed asymmetrical organizational and material obstacles which seriously disadvantaged the working class. This is hardly surprising given the fact that the committee that drafted the junta's decree included an Ikhwan member. The proletariat was even more severely disadvantaged because while the legal arrangement prohibited religious parties, the prohibition was not enforced during the period of this factional configuration.

Throughout 2011, the Ikhwan ceased participation in workers' protests 'demanding retribution for individuals killed by security forces during the 2011 uprising, an end to military trials of civilians, and the bringing to justice members of the former regime.'[39] The Ikhwan also actively criticized the 8 July sit-in targeting the judiciary and pursued its parliamentary campaign rather than condemn the state form's killing of workers in the Mohamed Mahmoud battles of late November.[40] The junior partner was not going to run afoul of the senior partner in the run-up to the parliamentary elections in December.

There are myriad other instances of the new alignment of factions attacking the working class under the guise of reform of legal and governing arrangements. The interim government appointed in 2011 by productive capital and supported by commercial capital was 'full of former board members of Mubarak's Ministerial Privatization Committee. They include[d] [Prime Minister] Ganzouri, Field Marshal Hussein Tantawi, Minister of International Cooperation and Planning Fayza Abouelnaga, and Electricity Minister Hassan Younis.'[41] This government, and then the parliament dominated by the Freedom and Justice Party (FJP) as the political form of expression of commercial capital, refused to recognize the Egyptian Federation of Independent Trade Unions (EFITU), a genuinely representative replacement for the productive capital–predatory capital bloc's Egyptian Trade Union Federation (ETUF). They both also opposed the drafted Trade Union Liberties Law.[42]

Throughout 2012, the productive capital–commercial capital bloc also opposed strikes and other collective actions realized by workers. In response to actions in February, the military released a statement telling Egyptians: '[w]e are facing plots against the nation aiming to undermine the institutions of the Egyptian state, and to topple the state itself so that chaos reigns.'[43] In a similar vein, Mahmoud Hussein, the general secretary of the Muslim Brotherhood, said the strike call was 'a destructive action'[44] and 'very dangerous to the interests of the nation and its future.'[45] In July, the FJP's newspaper characterized a sit-in by Mahalla workers as 'treason.'[46] In August, the Egyptian working class was subjected to even tighter surveillance by the Egyptian state form. It was announced that '[t]he Manpower and Immigration Minister is more closely tracking labor protests under its new [FJP] leadership.' More specifically, that '[m]inistry offices across the country must send in daily reports about labor protests, hunger strikes and sit-ins to an observatory established by the newly appointed Minister Khaled al-Azhary [a member of the aforementioned ETUF].'[47] Finally, in response to strikes by public bus drivers and teachers in September, one member of the FJP claimed the actions were being 'organized by counter-revolutionary forces' while another asserted the bus drivers were 'committing an act of treason'; the state media said the actions 'harmed the country's economy, transportation and education' and the state form's violent apparatus forcibly broke up sit-ins and stormed an organizing center.[48]

As suggested by the preceding statements, the new governing alignment cloaked the extension of its attack on the working class in bourgeois mental conceptions. Unsurprisingly, commercial capital deployed religious rhetoric to, say, support the March constitutional reforms. Much more powerful, however, was the deployment of the doctrine of harmony of interests. After productive capital's executive committee seized the state form it began issuing governing edicts as statements. The SCAF's second statement affirmed 'the need for work to continue at the agencies of the state, and for the restoration of normalcy in order to preserve the interest and properties of our great nation.'[49] Similarly, its fourth statement instructed that 'all agencies of the state, and the private sector must play their noble and patriotic role to drive the economy forward, and the people must fulfill their responsibility towards that goal.'[50] Productive capital posited its, and commercial capital's, bourgeois interests as the interests of all Egyptian society and represented dissenters as troublemakers. In an instance of dialectical negation, these mental conceptions transformed workers contesting their devaluation and exploitation into 'counter-revolutionaries.' Possibly the most obvious expression of the doctrine, certainly the most insulting, is the still-displayed poster depicting an Egyptian soldier holding a small child in his arms punctuated with *el-geesh wa el-shaeb eid wahdah* (The military and the people are one hand). Not only does the representation communicate a social unity without contradictions, it infanticizes Egyptian society such that it needs the military to survive.

The productive capital–commercial capital alliance relied most heavily on a particular expression of the doctrine of harmony of interests, namely nationalism. Immediately after the eruption of crisis subsided, the governing bloc turned to the ideal of nationalism to overcome unresolved class antagonisms calling on 'striking workers to go back to work, claiming that the continuation of protests could lead to economic catastrophe' and having government-run newspapers call on 'strikers to put the "national interest" ahead of their economic demands.'[51] Later in 2011, the Egyptian state form intensified nationalist sentiments by raiding a number of Egyptian, German and American non-governmental organizations (NGOs) on the grounds that they were facilitating illegal foreign interference in Egyptian affairs. In June 2012, a military-authored advertisement aired on Egyptian television 'cautioning Egyptians against relaying sensitive information to foreigners, suggesting that the latter could be foreign spies hungry for information.'[52] Then later that same month, the state form's repressive apparatus tightened 'control over hotels and rented apartments and follow[ed] names of foreigners, especially Palestinians.'[53] The incitement became most acute in December 2012. Almost simultaneously, the Ikhwan blamed the clashes near the presidential palace on conspirators who 'use the money they stole from Egyptians and the funds they receive from corrupt figures *abroad* who had escaped justice.'[54] The Ikhwan's El-Shater 'warned that different forces were trying to create a state of "sabotage" in Egypt.'[55] And former presidential candidates Mohamed ElBaradei, Amr Moussa and Hamdeen Sabahi were accused of being leading figures of espionage.[56] Nationalism and its negation, the idea of *asabe' kharegeya* (foreign fingers), was *the* mental conception of the predatory capital–commercial capital period. The ideal externalizing of responsibility for the destruction of workers' value has considerable use-value for capital.

The productive capital–commercial capital configuration's reforms were endorsed and redoubled by capital represented by the American state. Shortly after the SCAF seized the state form, then US Secretary of State Hillary Clinton announced that the USA was reprogramming US$150 million for Egypt to support the political transition.[57] A month later, Clinton announced a package of capital support: '$90 million in near-term economic assistance, $80 million towards insuring letters of credit, plus a new U.S.–Egypt Enterprise Fund and an increase in special duty-free investment zones.'[58] This was in addition to the US$1.3 billion annual subsidy the American state form channels to Egypt's productive capital faction. In her remarks with Egyptian foreign minister Al-Arabi, then-Secretary Clinton also noted:

> I brought with me the head of our Overseas Private Investment Corporation [OPIC], Elizabeth Littlefield, to discuss the ways that we could support this effort. And we want to see a very specific commitment by OPIC and by [the] U.S. Export-Import Bank to provide letters of credit, to encourage private sector investments, because the long-term economic growth of Egypt depends not on government jobs but on private sector jobs.[59]

In May 2011, President Obama announced that the American form of state would 'relieve a democratic Egypt of up to $1 billion in debt, and work with our Egyptian partners to invest these resources to foster growth and entrepreneurship. We will help Egypt regain access to markets by guaranteeing $1 billion in borrowing that is needed to finance infrastructure and job creation.'[60] Obama also made clear that '[t]he goal must be a model in which protectionism gives way to openness.'[61] To this end he announced that the American form of state would

> launch a comprehensive Trade and Investment Partnership Initiative in the Middle East and North Africa. . . . So we will work with the EU to facilitate more trade within the region, build on existing agreements to promote integration with U.S. and European markets, and open the door for those countries who adopt high standards of reform and trade liberalization to construct a regional trade arrangement.[62]

Increasing the number of special duty-free investment zones, encouraging growth in the private sector and entrepreneurship and liberalizing trade are ideal and material weapons in the neoliberal arsenal. The capital that produced the 2011 expression of crisis in Egyptian society instrumentalized the productive capital–commercial capital alignment's temporary blunting of contradictions to further extend the devaluation of the Egyptian worker's labor-power commodity and intensify his/her exploitation.

Presidential election

The presidential election of 2012 was another political form of expression of the new governing bloc in which productive capital was the senior faction and commercial capital the junior faction. It was also another advance of the neoliberal counter-attack on the Egyptian working class.

All of the candidates in the first round of balloting in May personified reform. For example, Hisham El-Bastawisi of the supposedly socialist Tagumma Party supported privatization of workers' value reified in national industries.[63] Khaled Ali was so deluded by bourgeois fetishisms that he contended that the prerequisite for realizing workers' demands was 'the businessmen giving up the idea of sacrificing workers' rights to make profits.'[64] Amr Moussa was adamant – Egypt had to 'create a healthy business climate – cutting red tape, attracting investment, reforming the financial sector and monetary policy, building infrastructure, and creating a modern labor market that rewards hard-working Egyptians.' In addition to encouraging entrepreneurship and improving competitiveness, Moussa declared: '[w]e must make clear that Egypt's future lies in the free market and sends [*sic*] the signal that Egypt is open for business.'[65] Even the Nasserist (a Keynesian particular to Egyptian society) Hamdeen Sabahi mobilized the doctrine of harmony of interests packaged as a national project and the fetishism of social justice.[66]

Much like the Battle of the Camel, the second round of presidential balloting was an expression of the intra-class struggle being fought in Egyptian society. The second round reduced to two the number of candidates and in so doing pitted a representative of the predatory faction of capital against a representative of the commodity faction of capital. Both Ahmed Shafik and Mohamed Morsi sought to advance the social war on the working class through neoliberal reforms.

Shafik's mental conceptions were unabashedly neoliberal. His rhetoric was heavily nationalistic. He said Egypt had to restore its 'seriousness toward protecting foreign capital as much as we protect Egyptian capital – we have to safeguard our partners.'[67] He depoliticized workers and nonsensically denied their dialectical struggle: '[w]orkers' rights are [primarily] human rights, justice and obtaining your rights without struggling to get them.'[68] Echoing Clinton, he envisioned expanding export processing zones: 'I plan to transform the area of the Suez Canal into the best and biggest free zone for industry in the world.' And, of course, he identified the devalued labor-power commodity in Egyptian society as a use-value for global capital.[69]

Morsi and the Ikhwan's political form of expression in the FJP personified Benthamite rationality. The language is problematic, but Zeinab Abul-Magd referencing Avi Asher-Schapiro makes the point that '[t]he Brotherhood hails free-market capitalism; wealthy businessmen whose economic agenda embraces privatization and foreign investment . . . lead its party. The Brotherhood does not espouse the idea of redistribution of wealth, preferring charity instead as a means of combating poverty.'[70] Abul-Magd herself continues: 'the [FJP's] platform borrows considerably from the principles of American neo-liberalism and free market capitalism.'[71] She also notes that '[t]he party's platform calls for the withdrawal of the state from providing subsidized services to the people and expands the role of businessmen in managing state affairs. Safeguarding the rights of the poor is considered an act of social solidarity rather than a duty to be fulfilled by the state.'[72] Kirkpatrick similarly reports that immediately after the first round of voting in the presidential elections, El-Shater, as the Ikhwan's representative, delivered a speech to the American Chamber of Commerce in Egypt 'so committed to promoting free markets, foreign investment and other business interests that some in the Chamber said it was as if he was reading their own talking points.'[73] Morsi and the FJP were neoliberal reformers with beards and the Quran.

After three days of negotiations, productive capital, which remained the arbiter, awarded the presidential election to the representative of commercial capital on 24 June. In exchange for having Morsi named president, commercial capital acceded to a power-sharing arrangement with productive capital. This agreement divided responsibility for governmental ministries between the Ikhwan and the military. The former took control of such ministries as Education, Finance and Foreign Affairs and the latter retained control of the Ministries of Defense, Interior and Justice. The agreement also stipulated that while the military would not intervene in the constitution-writing process, it would not be subject to budgetary or parliamentary oversight. According to journalistic representations, the agreement amounted to 'a de facto continuation of the old regime which, since 1952, has seen a clear split between so-called service and sovereign ministries.'[74] The real significance of the arrangement was that productive capital retained control over the means of violence and the interpretation and application of the legal form of expression of commodity relations in Egyptian society; the most immediately robust barriers to social change. The arrangement expressed the factional alignment governing through the state, with the senior faction controlling those institutional forms most able to paralyze society's movement in the short term.

Trade, fiscal and monetary policy

The productive capital–commercial capital configuration appeared again in a trade-off, of sorts, of governing arrangements in the fall of 2012. In September, the Egyptian state form sought to amend its free trade agreement with the USA and Israel. The Egyptian, American and Israeli state forms negotiated a Qualified Industrial Zones (QIZ) trade agreement in 2004. According to the agreement, Egyptian products to the US market that contain an Israeli component of 10.5 percent enjoy duty-free access. The new factional alignment sought to reduce the Israeli component to 8 percent.[75] This was productive capital's part of the intra-class exchange. Productive capital would compensate for the reduction of the Israeli component by increasing the contribution from Egyptian production. The increase in Egyptian production would increase the expropriation of surplus-value from workers by productive capital in Egyptian society. In the fall, commercial capital enjoyed its part of the intra-class exchange. During the presidential campaign, the Ikhwan contended that the normal banking sector was incapable of financing the political program – the *Nahda* plan – it proposed for the country. 'Islamic' financial instruments were needed to attract the necessary foreign investment.[76] In October, Prime Minister Qandil announced that his government would issue *sukuk*. *Sukuk* is a financial instrument in 'which the financier becomes a partner in a debt, an asset or an enterprise' and '[p]rofits are shared by the financier and the borrower, while losses are either incurred entirely by the financier or shared by both according to the details of the agreement.'[77] *Sukuk* is a public–private partnership glossed with an Islamic veneer. This was the process of privatization of workers' value for commercial capital.

The productive capital–commodity capital bloc was also served by and used a capital strike to extend its attack on the working class in Egyptian society. In September 2012, the Egyptian Central Bank released figures indicating that the balance of payments deficit stood at US$11.3 billion.[78] Increasingly more value was flowing out in the money form than was flowing in with tourists. As a result, by November Egypt's foreign currency reserves stood at US$15 billion, less than half what they were in February 2011.[79] This meant there were foreign reserves sufficient only to cover a scant three months of imports. A Keynesian redistribution of wealth through progressive taxation would have helped address the balance of payments deficit and the dwindling stocks of foreign currency. Consumption of luxury goods produced in other societies and imported into the Egyptian social formation increases with the growing wealth disparity. A fiscal policy that reduced wealth inequalities would have reduced the balance of payments deficit by reducing the quantity of capital exported in money form in exchange for value imported in the form of, say, Mercedes-Benz automobiles. Concomitantly, a reduction in the quantity of capital exported in money form would have left more in the central bank's vault. In October, Finance Minister Momtaz al-Saeed announced 'that the country's budget deficit had already reached LE170 billion, much larger than the predicted LE135 billion for the 2012–2013 fiscal year.'[80] A redistributive regime would also have increased tax revenues and thereby reduced the difference between state expenditures and revenues, assuming the former remained constant. Such Keynesian redistribution was idealistically anathema to the productive capital–commercial capital bloc, and the working class was too relationally weak to realize it. The president declared that '[t]here are no new taxes that will be imposed on the Egyptian people';[81] the prime minister said, '[t]he government will not raise taxes but will instead rely on foreign investment to remedy the country's cash flow problem';[82] and the finance minister 'allegedly told . . . investors that the government was not planning on raising taxes.'[83] Instead of fiscal redistribution, the productive–commercial capital configuration arranged to raise sales taxes[84] and impose an income tax structure that set a very low exemption limit (only LE9,000) with large brackets and a maximum rate of 25 percent.[85] The governing bloc arranged to take more value from the working class, or, as Samer Atallah put it: 'the government philosophy [was] to tax those whom it can tax, not who can afford to pay tax.'[86]

The governing alignment's Benthamite elimination of redistribution as a fiscal policy meant that the striking capital had to be replaced through the assumption of debt. Debt assumption was a two-pronged process during the period of the productive capital–commodity capital alignment. The first prong involved the state form borrowing heavily from money capital represented by Egyptian banks. By July 2012, the extent of domestic borrowing had driven the average yield on 182-day securities to an effective rate of 12 percent.[87] The second prong involved the Egyptian form of state borrowing capital represented by other state forms and institutions. Between the start of 2011 and the end of 2012, the state form borrowed US$1.5 billion from the Saudi state form, another US$1 billion from the World Bank, plus US$913 million from the EU, US$500 million from the Qatari state form, US$500 million from the African Development Bank and US$330 million from the Islamic Development Bank. During this period the Egyptian state form was also involved in extended negotiations over a US$4.8 billion loan from the IMF.

The introduction of yet to be produced value into the contemporary moment was the only means acceptable to the governing bloc to reduce the intensity of the social conflicts arising from the non-equivalence between the value Egyptian society produces and the value it consumes.[88] The process was universally bad for the working class. First, the assumption of debt concentrated capital and power with capital. This concentration came at workers' expense as the capital advanced had to be repaid *plus* a usurious capital that could only be created by workers having more of their labor-time stolen or their labor-power commodity further devalued. Also, regardless of the capital's representative form, the assumption of debt created a class of creditors with preferential access to society's value. By late 2012, the Saudi and Qatari state forms, among others, enjoyed special advantages in relation to Egyptian workers *in Egyptian society*. Second, the inflation that developed through the increased interest rates associated with the domestic borrowing further devalued the workers' labor-power commodity and increased the rate at which surplus-value was expropriated from them. As already indicated, workers in the Egyptian social formation repeatedly took actions during the productive capital–commercial capital period demanding wage increases to offset their reduced purchasing power. The wage increases adopted by both the interim government in 2011 and the Morsi government in 2012 did not keep pace with the devaluation of the Egyptian labor-power commodity. The 2011 increase to LE700 for workers in the state form, for example, elevated the minimum wage to a level that was still below the LE1,200 demanded by workers in 2009 and 2010 *before* the punishing food price inflation of 2011.[89] And it did not govern the workers exploited by individual capital. In real terms, the workers' labor-power commodity was devalued even with the wage increases.

The reduction in the price of the Egyptian currency in late 2012 further compounded the destruction of workers' value. Egypt's Central Bank propped up the price of the Egyptian pound until December 2012. Then, after limiting its decline to 6 percent over two years by spending US$1 billion a month, it let its price slide 3 percent in just two days.[90] A stronger pound had use-values for capital, but so, too, did a weakened pound. Reducing the price of the Egyptian currency cheapens Egyptian commodities. This served the investment interests of the governing bloc. In August, Morsi said that '[t]he main axis is investment, encouraging investors, tourism, foreign trade, exports.'[91] At the Euromoney conference in October, Prime Minister Qandil stated in no uncertain terms: '[w]e want Egypt to be a Mecca for investors.' And Finance Minister El-Saeed declared: '[a]ll my faith is in the return of investment.'[92] Reducing the price of the currency was a way of realizing that faith by making value in Egyptian society more 'attractive' to capital. The cheapening of commodities was not restricted to land and national industries. Reducing the price of the currency also cheapened the labor-power commodity consumed by capital, including the two governing factions. The reform of the price of the Egyptian currency was another attack by the productive capital–commercial capital alignment on the working class that further endangered renewal of the class's life processes.

Finally, the fiscal arrangements of the Egyptian state form involving subsidization of fuel and food consumption are inextricably bound up with debt assumption and reduction of the price of the currency. Downward reform of the scale of subsidization dominated negotiations for the IMF loan. The downward reform of the price of the Egyptian pound increased the quantity of value flowing through the subsidization process. For all the apolitical bourgeois blather, subsidization was not fundamentally reformed during Moment I because the more powerful faction of capital accumulates through the process.

According to IMF estimates, subsidies constituted more than 8 percent of Egyptian GDP in 2011.[93] 'More than two-thirds of subsidy expenditures [went] to fuel, mainly benefiting transportation and industry, with the rest directed largely toward food subsidies.'[94] The productive capital–commercial capital alignment repeatedly made shows of reforming the subsidization process. In September 2011, the government decreed an end to natural gas subsidization. Two months later, the government announced a new plan for distributing butane canisters used for cooking. Neither was implemented.[95] A year later, the Morsi government stopped subsidizing 95-octane gasoline. This reform was as inconsequential as the uninitiated policies of the previous year because it impacted only that small percentage of drivers of vehicles requiring the highest-grade gasoline while it left unchanged the subsidization of the widely consumed 92-octane fuel and diesel. The subsidization of food produced similarly reforming theatre. Despite a sustained cacophony, the subsidization of wheat, sugar, rice and edible oil persisted unchanged throughout Moment I until March 2013, when, just before productive capital ousted its junior partner from the governing bloc, a trial of a card-driven rationing system was announced.[96] Reform of the subsidization of food is reflexively represented as too socially difficult; as if the process is realized by a working class sufficiently empowered as to be intransigent. Inevitably, the bread riots of 1977 are ahistorically invoked as some sort of an illustrative example.[97] Such unscientific drivel is never struck by the obvious contradiction between a working class too weak to think as a class for itself, realize real wage increases, secure decent education and quality healthcare for itself and its children and stop state brutality being powerful enough to perpetuate subsidization.

Fuel and food are both energy. Fuel is energy for machines and food is energy for the working class. The subsidization of energy reduces the value of the means of production consumed in production. Subsidization of fuel reduces the quantity of constant capital and subsidization of food reduces the quantity of variable capital. If the value of a commodity is $C = c + v + s$, the rate of productivity, also known as the organic composition of capital, is $P = c/v$, the rate of surplus-value accumulation is $E = s/v$, the rate of profit is $Pr = s/c + v$, the value equivalent of the fuel subsidy is k_1 and the value equivalent of the food subsidy is k_2, then the value of a commodity produced with subsidized fuel and food is changed to $C = (c - k_1) + (v - k_2) + s$, the rate of productivity is changed to $P = (c - k_1)/(v - k_2)$, the rate of surplus-value accumulation is changed to $E = s/(v - k_2)$ and the rate of profit is changed to $Pr = s/(c - k_1) + (v - k_2)$. Assuming the same numbers as in Chapter 1, that $c = 100$, $v = 100$ and $s = 50$, and that $k_1 = 20$, $k_2 = 20$, $k_3 = 5$ and $k_4 = 5$, the last two being reduced magnitudes that demonstrate the relation between fuel and food subsidization, Table 4.2 is produced.

The table offers five notable insights. First, the process of subsidization increases capital's rate of profit. Equal subsidization produces the highest rate of profit at a relatively unproductive level. Second, the process of subsidization devalues the commodity. A devalued commodity is a cheapened commodity. A devalued commodity produced through consumption of subsidized means of production should circulate through the market at a lower price than a commodity produced through the consumption of unsubsidized means. A lower-priced commodity, in turn, stands

Table 4.2 Subsidization, value, productivity and accumulation

Type of subsidization	Commodity value	Rate of productivity	Rate of accumulation	Rate of profit
No subsidization	250	1.0	0.5	0.25
Equal subsidization	210	1.0	0.625	0.31
Fuel exclusively	230	0.8	0.5	0.28
Food exclusively	230	1.25	0.625	0.28
More fuel than food	225	0.84	0.53	0.29
More food than fuel	225	1.19	0.625	0.29

a better chance of having its surplus-value realized than does an identical unsubsidized commodity. Third, disproportionate to exclusive subsidization of fuel reduces the rate of productivity in relation to no subsidization and equal subsidization of fuel and food. However, by devaluing the commodity, subsidization of fuel gives the appearance of increased productivity. Subsidization of fuel can make less productive, outdated processes and relations seem more productive because the commodity still appears in the market with a lower price. Fourth, any food subsidy increases the rate of surplus-value accumulation, and food must be subsidized at a rate equal to or more than that of fuel to achieve the highest rate of accumulation. The subsidization of food is qualitatively more important to the working class than is the subsidization of fuel. For capital, reducing the value of, say, the bread consumed by workers reduces the value of the labor-power commodity. A reduction in the value of the labor-power commodity means capital must pay workers less value in the money form of wages. It also means a reduction in the quantity of labor-time necessary to reproduce the labor-power commodity. Subsidization of food changes the relation of necessary labor-time to surplus labor-time in such a way as to reduce the former and increase the latter without having to extend the working period or intensify the labor. Food subsidization increases capital's rate of accumulation. Fifth, a tension exists between equal subsidization of fuel and food and disproportionate to exclusive subsidization of food. Equal subsidization of fuel and food produces the most devalued commodity, and the highest rate of profit, and a relatively reduced rate of productivity. Disproportionate to exclusive subsidization of food makes labor more productive, and does not produce the most cheapened commodity. Capital unconcerned with competitively devaluing commodities, capital in a captive market, for example, reduces fuel subsidies relative to food subsidies. Capital coerced to appear to produce with a high rate of productivity wants equal subsidization of fuel and food. A striking contradiction: the neoliberal weapon of trade liberalization deployed against the working class devalues the commodities consumed by productive capital, and, because capital with relatively lower rates of productivity wants to seem to produce devalued commodities, encourages increased subsidization.

Subsidization is not a process impelled by the Egyptian working class. Egyptian wages chase, are pulled along by, the rate of accumulation of surplus-value. In order to expand accumulation, productive capital must provide the working class its value in wage form. In the absence of subsidization, the working class must still receive its subsistence wage. Subsidization allows productive capital to reduce real wages below the value of the labor-power commodity and still have a working class able to renew its life processes.

The subsidization process was not reformed during Moment I because, contrary to fetishistic 'analyses,' it is a process through which productive capital, as the largest productive consumer of fuel and fed labor-power, accumulates. The subsidization of fuel maintains or increases productive capital's rate of surplus-value accumulation and gives the appearance of an increased rate of productivity in its extensive factory and transportation systems relative to capital in unsubsidized or less subsidized production, and increases the likelihood that productive capital's surplus-value will be realized, and unsubsidized or less subsidized capital's value will be destroyed, in the sphere of circulation. Subsidization of 95-octane gasoline was stopped precisely because it did not adversely affect productive capital's accumulation. Any subsidization of food always increases the rate of surplus-value accumulation for productive capital, and when done to the exclusion of subsidization of fuel, it results in the highest rate of productivity. The highest rate of productivity does not cheapen the commodity as much as equal subsidization of fuel and food, however, and, consequently, does not produce the most competitively priced commodity. This cannot be stated clearly enough: it is not a failing of the process of subsidization that value is not transferred to workers, but instead flows to capital. This is the way capital wants it. Furthermore, it is not because of some imaginary working-class strength that the process persists. The process persists because productive capital accumulates relative surplus-value through it, and, as the dominant faction of the ruling class in Egyptian society, productive capital has the power to perpetuate it.

2012 constitution

In late 2012, productive capital and commercial capital reformed the Egyptian constitution. At one and the same time, the constitution expressed changing class and factional relations. The working class's increased weakness in relation to capital since the previous constitution of 1971 appeared, for example, in the promulgations of bourgeois democracy in Article 1 and that unions were to raise the standard of productivity and safeguard capital's assets in Article 52. For the working class, recognition by Article 63 that the 'right to peaceful strike is regulated by law' was a valueless sop, particularly given the fact that workers who struck in productive capital's extensive factory system would be tried in military courts.[98]

The intra-class rebalancing was also written into the constitution. Four exemplary legal forms suffice to make this point. First, with no precedent in the 1971 constitution, Article 219 of the 2012 constitution read that the 'principles of Islamic Sharia include general evidence, foundational rules, rules of jurisprudence, and credible sources accepted in Sunni doctrines and by the larger community.'[99] In this instance, the expression and ideal instrument over which commercial capital had relative power was more deeply entrenched in the arrangements of the state. *Shar'ia* was introduced into the 1971 constitution because commercial capital had empowered itself, and its legality was made more robust in 2012 because commercial capital was further empowered. Second, in contrast with Article 5 of the 1971 constitution, which said 'no political activity shall be exercised nor political parties established on a religious referential authority, on a religious basis or on discrimination on grounds of gender or origin,' Article 6 of the 2012 constitution stated that '[n]o political party shall be formed that discriminates on the basis of gender, origin or religion.'[100] A prohibition on religious political forms was transformed into a prohibition against the process of religious discrimination. Its increased power enabled commercial capital to legalize the political form expressing its interests, provided it did not actively discriminate against other religionists. Third, Article 53 of the 2012 constitution allowed for only one syndicate per profession. This prohibition on union plurality expressed commodity capital's historical dominance of Egyptian syndicates, particularly those of doctors and engineers, at the same time that it forestalled the emergence of alternative centers of social power and provided the faction the opportunity to extend its power over workers' unions.[101] Fourth, Article 9 of the 2012 constitution stated that the 'State shall ensure safety, security and equal opportunities for all citizens without discrimination.' This marked an expansion, of sorts, on Article 8 of the 1971 constitution that declared the 'State shall guarantee equality of opportunity to all citizens.' The value of security expressed in the 2012 constitution is a reactionary one. It is rooted in prior claims about 'the possibility of politics.'[102] To value security is to accept and seek to project into the future today's classist relations and processes.[103] Commercial capital is the reactionary faction of capital. Recall that commodity capital is demoted, in terms of value and power, through productive capital's progressive revolutionizing of society. The dialectic is such that the rise of productive capital is the decline of commodity capital. This is why commodity capital seeks to 'preserve and retain old and backward forms of production organized on traditional lines.'[104] The emphasis on the reactionary value of security in the 2012 constitution was an expression of the relative empowerment of the reactionary faction of capital in the Egyptian social formation.

While commercial capital's relative empowerment in the governing alignment was expressed in the 2012 constitution, so, too, was productive capital's dominant position in the factional alignment. Article 146 of the 2012 constitution stated that '[t]he President is not to declare war, or send the Armed Forces outside State territory, except after consultation with the National Defense Council and the approval of the House of Representatives with a majority of its members.' This was in contrast to Article 150 of the 1971 constitution, which said: '[t]he President of the Republic . . . shall be the authority to declare war, subject to approval by the People's Assembly.'[105] Fetishistically, this article seems to represent a democratizing of the process of war-making. In actuality, Article 146 ensured that productive capital enjoyed a veto over the destruction of value in Egyptian society through war. Article 229 of the 2012 constitution was another democratic appearance masking productive capital's intra-class dominance. Much like Article 87 of the 1971 constitution, Article 229 declared a minimum of 50 percent representation for farmers and workers in the House of Representatives. This representation was opposed by a number of ostensibly Islamist parties during the drafting of the constitution. The FJP called for 'removing the 50 percent quota from the new constitution because it discriminates in favor of a class.'[106] The Salafist Nour Party said that the quota 'is not appropriate for the future.'[107] And the Salafi-oriented Asala Party asserted that 'the quota does not fit with the process of building a state.'[108] As late as October the draft constitution did not include the article.[109] To be clear, the political forms representing commodity capital did *not* oppose this legal arrangement because it provided representation for farmers and workers. The so-called representation for farmers really belonged to the landed aristocracy. The seats reserved for workers actually served as seats for members of the ETUF; the negation of genuine workers' organization and representation. Commodity capital opposed the legal arrangement because it diminished the faction's power in the legislature while it augmented the effective representation of productive capital. Article 229 was realized in the constitution because the instrumentalization of the working class, or in this case its representation, had a use-value for productive capital in its intra-class battle and because productive capital was empowered in the governing configuration relative to commodity capital. At a high level of abstraction, Article 229 of the 2012 constitution was not unlike the power struggle that was expressed in, and realized through, the repeal of the Corn Laws in the mid-nineteenth century.

Finally, nothing produced so many wrong-headed, fetishistic delusions as the 2012 constitution's statements on female workers. For example, Article 10 established that '[t]he State is keen to preserve the genuine character of the Egyptian family, its cohesion and stability and to protect its moral values, all as regulated by law. The State shall . . . enable reconciliation between the duties of a woman toward her family and her work.'[110] This was in contrast with Article 11 of the 1971 constitution, which said, '[t]he State shall guarantee harmonization between the duties of women towards the family and her work in the society, ensuring her equality [sic] status with man in fields of political, social, cultural and economic life without violation of the rules of Islamic jurisprudence.'[111] While it appeared that the patriarchal notions expressed in the constitution were the result of the dominant role played by Islamists in the drafting of the constitution, in essence they were an expression of the contemporary neoliberal moment. In 1971, the guarantee of women's equality had the use-value for capital in that moment of negating inflationary wage pressures. Over thirty years, capital relieved these pressures and women needed to be regulated differently to realize accumulation. In 2012, the use-value women held for capital was to increasingly subsidize capitalist accumulation through unwaged reproduction of the labor-power commodity in the family home. 'The more work done by women in the home, the less value workers must receive from capital to reproduce themselves at a given level.'[112] The wage reductions that attend the technology-induced labor abstraction and multiplication of the surplus population of accumulation by dispossession have returned, extended and intensified the (re)production functions required of the household.[113] Less value in the money form of wages to male workers means increasing amounts of labor-time are required to, say, prepare food purchased in less worked-up form and educate children outside of school. This unwaged labor-time belongs overwhelmingly to women. The 2012 constitution had to legally redomesticate women because accumulation by capital in our neoliberal moment 'rests on the patriarchal family.'[114]

The 2012 constitution was the expression in legal form of two moving and differently intersecting vectors, one inter-class – the relation between a working class weakened in relation to capital – and the other intra-class – the relation between a commercial capital empowered in relation to productive capital but still subordinate to it. It was also the mode of appearance of governing arrangements reformed to realize accumulation in the neoliberal moment.

2013 political transmutation

In early July 2013, change again appeared in Egyptian society. The then minister of defense and military production, Sisi, deposed

President Morsi and established himself as de facto head of state. As in 2011, this removal of the junior faction of the governing bloc by the senior faction was performed under the cloak of realizing protestors' demands. Given the preceding two years of factional cooperation, including over the state form's violence against workers, the mass protests of 2013 were clearly only a convenient pretext for the senior faction. In actuality, productive capital disposed of commercial capital because the former had consumed the latter's use-value.

When crisis erupted in 2011, commodity capital had the use-value of enabling productive capital to replace its junior partner, namely predatory capital, with a faction similarly antagonistic to the working class, but not as powerful in relation to productive capital. In terms of the intra-class dialectic, commodity capital, too, could be counted on to fight the class war against workers while not posing a threat to productive capital's dominance of the historic bloc.

In inter-class terms, commodity capital transformed the 2011 expression of crisis from one prioritizing the increasingly devalued and exploited labor-power commodity to one of limited political reform. This cover of 'democratization,' along with the deployment of the mental conceptions of nationalism and religion, momentarily reconciled workers to their degraded conditions and enabled productive capital to ever so temporarily blunt the contradiction and disequilibrium between labor and capital. The use-value of democratic reform provided by the representatives of commercial capital was degraded considerably by the drafting of a new constitution throughout 2012, and most markedly in November 2012, when Morsi declared all presidential decisions immune from judicial review. Finally, in keeping with their shared bourgeois interest in accumulation, the representatives of commercial capital continued to perpetrate and intensified productive capital's attack on the working class. The Ikhwan gave the valuable appearance of pluralism to, and legitimized, reform of such bourgeois legal and governmental arrangements as the Political Parties Law, opposition to the EFITU and Trade Union Liberties Law, and the tightening of surveillance of workers by the Ministry of Manpower and Immigration.

Commercial capital's reformism limited to the political sphere perpetuated commodity relations in Egyptian society, and with them productive capital's accumulation of surplus-value. This obtained until November 2012, when commercial capital finally accepted the US$4.8 billion IMF loan (the same month the military called for a 'national reconciliation'). The loan condition that the subsidization process in Egyptian society be reformed was unacceptable to productive capital. It was precisely the avoidance of such conditionalities that caused the loan negotiations to drag on for so long in the first place. Productive capital was unwilling to have an international institution representing finance capital reduce its accumulation through subsidization. In accepting the loan, the representatives of commercial capital negated their use-value to productive capital, and had to be discarded. Sisi admitted in an interview with the *Washington Post* that productive capital started telegraphing the disposal of its junior partner to the American state form months before the senior partner realized it.[115] All that was required was the pretense.[116]

In 2011, the eruption of crisis produced a temporary union of necessity between productive capital and commercial capital. In 2013, commercial capital was disposed of as productive capital's junior partner, not because it failed to surrender its value, but because it had successfully realized its value. In getting productive capital out of the crisis of 2011, changing the expression of crisis, rescaling demands, momentarily ideally reconciling workers to devaluation of their labor-power commodity and heightened exploitation, supporting reactionary legislation, imposing tighter surveillance on workers and securing the IMF loan, commodity capital negated its value to productive capital.

Mental conceptions

Productive capital represented its disposal of commercial capital in nationalistic terms, just as it had earlier represented its opposition to the relative empowerment of the predatory capital faction. In announcing the disposal, Sisi, as the personification of the interests of productive capital, said the military had invoked its patriotic role, acted 'in compliance with [its] historic and national duties' and would firmly and decisively meet its national responsibilities.[117] Of course, this was all to the glorious end of national reconciliation. Productive capital also re-enforced the harmony between its interests and those of 'the people.' Productive capital was performing the public service it had been called to perform, and would continue to make 'sacrifices to maintain the safety and security of Egypt and its great people.'[118]

Immediately after the disposal, these unimaginative bourgeois mental conceptions were more specifically reconstructed to the ideal necessities of the new period. What had been an oft-lamented financial crisis of Moment I was transformed into a national crisis in Moment II. The Egyptian nation was endangered, beset by looming catastrophe. Fractious forces were sowing discord within it. Concomitantly, it was surrounded by regional tumult in Libya, Syria, Iraq and Yemen.[119] Only those whose sole loyalty and obedience were to the nation as defined by productive capital were authentic Egyptians and trustworthy members of the community. The seditious domestic forces were passing themselves off as authentic Egyptians, but really had ulterior allegiances. The regional chaos encouraged, depending on the demands of the moment, by HAMAS, Hezbollah, Shiites supported by Iran and/ or Zionists, all manner of terrorists, also threatened the nation of authentic Egyptians. The members of the Ikhwan were excluded from this construction on both counts. As the representative of productive capital said: '[t]hey have an international presence in more than 60 countries – the Muslim Brotherhood. The idea that gathers them together is not nationalism, it's not patriotism – it is an ideology that it totally related to the concept of the organization.'[120] The construction of the Egyptian nation in crisis, in turn, eliminated claims against productive capital as it governed through the state form. A military desperately struggling to avoid the calamity of civil war and keep Egypt from descending into the regional abyss could not be expected to also fight unemployment and build infrastructure. 'Long before his presidential candidacy, al-Sisi was open about how bad things are and how the Egyptian state has "nothing" . . . financially speaking, to offer.'[121] The nation-in-crisis representation conveniently occulted productive capital's opposition to a mildly Keynesian redistribution of value in favor of its concentration and centralization. It also produced the ideal of sacrificial Egyptians.

Members of the Ikhwan are not the only inauthentic Egyptians. All those workers not sharing with productive capital its interest in accumulation are also constructed as threats within the national body politic. The national reconstruction process since the disposition of the representative of commercial capital has intensified the commodity faction's characterization of workers' actions as treason[122] and extended it to equate them with acts of terrorism. In a deservedly rich transformation into its opposite, in Moment II commercial capital is part of the same treasonous social grouping as the working class it helped productive capital to exclude and attack in Moment I.

Productive capital has continued to intensify its reproduction of the mental conceptions of nationalism, the harmony of interests and neoliberal reform since disposing of its junior partner in the governing alignment. In the fall of 2013, the song and music video of *Teslam El-Ayadi*, a heroizing of Sisi and the military, dominated Egyptian society.[123] At the same time massive posters of Sisi in military uniform declaring 'Egypt against terrorism' appeared on walls. In the original 3 July announcement of the disposal of commercial capital, Sisi made reference to '[a] media charter of honour . . . that . . . advances the homeland's top interests.' In October 2014, lemming-like, the '[c]hief editors of 17 state and private daily newspapers' said they would stop publishing 'statements undermining state institutions.'[124] In April 2014 the 6 April Movement was banned on accusations of espionage.[125] Russian president Putin's visit and authorization of the Egyptian form of state in February 2015 was realized with unparalleled pomp and ceremony. Roadways and buildings were plastered with banners welcoming Putin in Arabic, Russian and English. All the while productive capital has also intensified its war on the working class. Since 2013, workers have been rounded up in mass arrests and convicted in mass trials. Labor lawyer Haitham Mohamedein was arrested on charges that 'included "being a member of a secret group which aims to stop the state's authorities . . . incite and empower a certain social class against the entire society . . . and attack citizens and to disrupt societal peace".'[126] Alaa Abdel Fattah was arrested in 2013, received a clearly politicized conviction in 2014 and reconviction in 2015. And productive capital has perpetrated unprecedented violence against workers in the Sinai peninsula.

For all of this, the most spectacular mode of appearance of productive capital's ideals was the inauguration of the 'New Suez Canal' in 2015. This technology's indivisibility from the mental conception of nationalism is immediately evident in the labeling. The new canal was, in actuality, an expansion of the existing canal. A 35-kilometer parallel channel was dug to increase two-way traffic through the canal, and another 37 kilometers of existing canal was dredged to enable passage of larger ships with deeper drafts. The military equates Sisi with Nasser and the canal has a strong connection with Nasser, who nationalized it in 1956. When announced in 2014, the expansion was financed by interest-bearing certificates that Egyptian workers were encouraged to purchase to realize the great national feat. Egyptian workers stampeded to exchange their value in money form for these certificates, with their five-year tax-free yields of 12 percent annually. The certificates were sold out in a nationalist fervor in eight working days.[127] The inauguration of the expansion was saturated with symbols of the nation under reconstruction. Sisi appeared in military uniform. He sailed the expansion aboard *El Mahroosa* – the yacht of former king Farouk and the first to ever sail the canal. Nationalistic songs played along the banks of the canal. In Cairo, banners hung from the Nile bridges announcing the expansion with references to Egypt as *Um El-Dunya* – the mother of the world. This popular reference was similarly made in *Teslam El-Ayadi*. The productive process of transportation was extolled with stickers on city buses and posters greeting workers and capital moving through Cairo International Airport. And despite the protest law, authentic Egyptians were permitted to celebrate the national accomplishment in Tahrir Square.

The statements announcing the expansion were expressions of the post-2013 national reconstruction. Ignoring the contracts awarded to capital represented by the Belgian, Emirati, Dutch and American state forms, the chairman of the Suez Canal Authority, retired admiral Mohab Mamish, said that 'the Egyptian people are rewriting history.'[128] More expansively, Sisi welcomed 'Egypt's loyal friends' to share with its 'great people' the accomplishment that 'forge[s] a prosperous future for humanity as a whole.' Egypt, which 'is taught around the world so that the peoples of the world take inspiration from the values it espoused [sic],' presented 'its gift to the world for the sake of humanity, reconstruction and development.' The realization of the feat was not easy, and our species needs to be thankful for it: 'Egypt and its people confronted the most dangerous, extremist, terrorist thinking, which, had it prevailed, would have set the world ablaze.' The Egyptian people are great and were able to succeed because 'they are united as one entity, standing together hand in hand.' And because Egyptians sacrifice: 'Egypt's fallen heroes . . . made the ultimate sacrifice for their homeland in order to establish stability. Their sacrifice is not only for Egypt, but for all humanity.'[129] By realizing his call to expand the canal in one year rather than the initially planned three years, Sisi said Egyptians 'showed their ability to efficiently make history and leap to the future for the prosperity of humanity.'[130] The same general message was conveyed in a video broadcast on state television that declared '[t]he new Suez canal changes the world map and serves humanity everywhere'[131] and an advertisement in New York's Times Square to celebrate with Egypt its gift to the world that would 'boost the world economy.'

The ideal of Egyptians gifting the world the expansion represents the external dimension of the sacrificial Egyptian motif. This was originally expressed in Sisi's August 2013 interview with the *Washington Post*. Said Sisi: '[the United States] left the Egyptians, you turned your back on the Egyptians and they won't forget that. Now you want to continue turning your backs on Egyptians. The U.S. interest and the popular will of the Egyptians do not have to conflict.'[132] Productive capital is crafting a national identity with a memory, but one that remains altruistic. Furthermore, the identity is so virtuous as to invite, not compel, others to emulate its generosity and selflessness. Where others are egoistic, Egyptians are devoted to others. While others have interests, Egyptians have only good, popular will. The 'New Suez Canal' is a form of expression of that Egyptian virtue.

Clearly, the technology of the Suez Canal expansion had an ideal use-value for productive capital, but it also had a thus far unrecognized exchange-value for productive capital. The technology was most assuredly not only about propaganda and public relations. In contradictory fashion, Egyptians workers' reproduction of productive capital's ideal of nationalism in connection with the Suez Canal technology negated their material interests.

There was no readily evident material need to expand the canal. This is because usage of the canal is not determined so much by the technology's size, as by the quantity of value in commodity form moving through global trade (and the price of fuel powering the container ships transporting the commodities). The same crisis of global capitalist relations and processes that erupted in Egyptian society in 2011 destroyed value in production and with it consumption of transportation through the canal. According to *Bloomberg News*, in 2015 'the number of vessels using the canal remain[ed] 20 percent below its 2008 level and just 2 percent higher than a decade ago.'[133] Not only was the transportation use-value of the existing canal not being fully consumed, the expanded capacity could not be realized unless global traffic increased at an unprecedented rate. With no supporting evidence, Admiral Mamish blindly asserted that canal traffic was expected to double to ninety-seven vessels per day by 2023.[134] The *Financial Times*, citing the consultancy firm Capital Economics, noted that 'to achieve its Suez Canal traffic goals, global trade volumes would need to rise by about 9 per cent year on year. This is higher than the 3 per cent year-on-year average seen over the past four years.'[135] The *Financial Times* also noted that 'the International Monetary Fund predicts that economic growth will remain in the region of 4 per cent in the coming years.'[136] Capital Economics characterized the realization of Mamish's claim as 'unlikely to say the least.'[137]

So what, then, was the exchange-value of the canal expansion for productive capital? It is too quick and easy to simply see in this technology the military accumulating through toll collection. This does not penetrate to the essence of the phenomenon.

There is a dialectic between production time and inflation such that the longer the production time of a commodity, the more upward pressure is exerted on commodity prices in the market. As Marx explains in *Capital*, volume II, '[s]ince elements of productive capital are constantly being withdrawn from the market and all that is put into the market is an equivalent in money, the effective demand rises, without this in itself providing any element of supply. Hence prices rise, both for the means of subsistence and for the material elements of production.'[138] Later he makes much the same point with some examples particularly germane to the present discussion:

> In all branches of industry whose production periods (as distinct from their working periods) extend over a relatively long time, money is constantly cast into circulation by the capitalist producers during this period, partly in payment for the labour-power applied, partly for purchasing the means of production that are to be used. Means of production are therefore withdrawn from the commodity market directly, and means of consumption in part indirectly, by the workers when they spend their wages, and in part also directly by the capitalists themselves, who in no way suspend their consumption, even though they do not cast into the market at the same time an equivalent in commodities . . . This factor becomes very important in developed capitalist production, in connection with long-drawn-out enterprises undertaken by joint-stock companies, etc. such as the building of railways, canals, docks, large municipal buildings, the construction of iron ships, the draining of land on a large scale, etc.[139]

Value flowing into means of production in the money form of wages with no equivalent flow of value out in commodity form produces price inflation. The longer the production period, meaning the more value flowing into means of production in the money form of wages with no equivalent flow out in commodity form, the more price inflation. The more price inflation, assuming no commensurate rise in wages once the long-term production has been initiated, the more devaluation of the labor-power commodity. This is one way capital has 'spent its way out of crisis' – massive, long-term projects producing roads, armories, bridges, buildings, airports and dams 'inflate' the market by consuming degraded value in the labor-power commodity form without increasing the supply of value in other commodities.

This is precisely what happened in Egyptian society through the expansion of the Suez Canal. The *Washington Post* referencing Pharos Holding for Financial Investments noted that 'Egypt's economy grew at over four percent in the nine months to March [2015] for the first time since 2010, mainly due to infrastructure spending related to the canal upgrade.'[140] What appeared as the military's employment of tens of thousands of workers, directly and indirectly through contractors, and 80 percent of the world's dredging machinery for a year was, in actuality, productive capital's extended consumption of variable and constant capital in the sphere of production with no equivalent introduction of value into the sphere of circulation. The money advanced in the market did not represent equivalent value produced in the factory. The workers from all over Egypt, some of whom reportedly received wages of LE3,000–4,000 per month and others considerably less,[141] sold their labor-power commodity for wages which they then converted into individually consumable commodities. These purchases of bread and water from the market were not matched by sales of commodities into the market. In the place of value in commodity form there was only more value in money form. Concomitantly, wages did not rise over this period. The bourgeois 'growth' of 2015 that was spurred by the long-term production of the Suez Canal technology was, in essence, the devaluation of the Egyptian worker's only commodity through the process of inflation. As the largest consumer of the labor-power commodity in Egyptian society, productive capital accumulated relatively more surplus-value as the labor-power commodity was devalued through inflation driven by this long-term production of technology.

Three final points regarding the expansion of the Suez Canal technology. First, the expansion was, in fact, 'Egypt's gift to the *bourgeois* world.' By accelerating transit through the canal and reducing the quantity of time needed to valorize value from the commodity form by some eight hours, the expanded technology increases the general rate of profit. Second, the expanded technology is being talked about as part of a larger, longer-term production called the Suez Canal Development Project. According to the General Authority for the Suez Canal Economic Zone, what amounts to the export processing zones envisioned by Clinton and Shafik will include seaports, productions centers and whole new cities built on hundreds of square kilometers ranging from Ain Sukhna in the south to West Port Said in the north. Most assuredly, much of the land for the project will be purchased from the military and all of the project will be made more 'attractive' to capital by the devalued labor-power commodity readily available for exploitation. Third, the devaluation of the labor-power commodity through the Suez Canal expansion would have been extended further had the project been realized across the three years initially projected, but this would also have further forced up prices on the means necessary to produce the transportation value, notably the dredging machinery. Also, three years would have been too long to satisfy the ideal use-value of the technology. Productive capital was able to dictate the production schedule alone because it has no 'domestic' partner in a governing alignment. The temporality of the Suez Canal expansion was determined by the balance of productive capital's interests, not the balance of forces in Egyptian society.

Social relations, arrangements, accumulation and reproduction

The fact productive capital does not have a governing partner particular to Egyptian society does not mean it has no partner in governing. The military's disposal of Morsi in 2013 was an expression of productive capital's partnering with finance capital represented by the GCC state forms. This was immediately apparent. The Saudi state form publicly announced its support for the coup a scant two hours after it was executed. As it did in 2011 when productive capital was arbitrating between the predatory and commodity factions, the Saudi state form also promised productive capital that it would replace any funding cut by the American state form as a result of the coup. Shortly thereafter, the Saudi state form pledged US$5 billion in capital in the form of grants, loans and commodities. The Emirati state form did much the same, pledging

US$3 billion in the form of grants and loans. The Kuwaiti state form also pledged US$4 billion in money form. Even Qatar, which for vulgar studies was an ally of Morsi and the Ikhwan, supported the coup, congratulating the productive-capital-appointed interim president and praising 'the role of the Egyptian armed forces in defending the country and its security.'[142]

Commercial capital and finance capital are ultimately dependent on the productive capital faction for their distributional shares of surplus-value. In the Egyptian social formation, this meant that while Gamal Mubarak's reformers and the Ikhwan *had* to partner with the military, the military chose its junior faction. In 2011, productive capital had no viable alternative and, so, aligned with commodity capital. By 2013, productive capital chose to partner with finance capital represented by the GCC state forms. Productive capital's 2013 realignment with this money capital faction was possible only because the governing configuration of Moment I had reformed the state, opiated the working class with heavy doses of nationalism and religion and extended and intensified surveillance and violence against workers. While the union of 2011 was necessitated by the eruption of crisis, productive capital chose to align with finance capital represented by the GCC states because, well, it got a better deal. The dumping of the junior partner of predatory capital in 2011 removed an increasingly empowered and burdensome rival from the governing bloc. It also removed what amounted to a middleman between productive capital and the finance capital represented by the GCC state forms. In the social metabolism of the exchange process money always sticks to the hands that mediate its flow.[143] In 2011, productive capital eliminated the friction personified by people such as Alaa Mubarak. This provided productive capital with two options in the market: 1) it could maintain the price of commodities moving through the privatization process, most obviously land, and accumulate, in addition to its portion of the price, what had been predatory capital's share, and 2) it could encourage circulation by reducing the price of the commodities by the amount of predatory capital's share while it still accumulated its portion. Despite these opportunities, and finance capital clearly had a preference for the second option, the flow of money into Egyptian society slowed during the period of the productive capital–commercial capital alignment. This was due in large measure to the antagonisms between the two unproductive factions of capital, i.e. El-Shater's Zad competing with nominally Emirati capital in the form of Spinneys and Carrefour.[144] In 2013, productive capital disposed of another restriction to the flow of value in money form in exchange for value and surplus-value in the form of its commodities.

Two years later there was another wave of expressions of the value relation between productive capital and finance capital; this time at the widely touted economic conference in Sharm El-Sheikh. The Saudi state form pledged Egyptian society another US$4 billion; US$1 billion to augment the reserves of the Egyptian Central Bank and US$3 billion in investment. The Emirati state form similarly pledged US$4 billion, with US$2 billion to the central bank's coffers and US$2 billion in investment. The Kuwaiti state form pledged US$4 billion with no announcement as to the division. And the Omani state form pledged US$500 million divided equally between bank deposits and investment. The organization and performance of the economic conference are instructive as to the factional alignment governing the lives of workers in Egyptian society in Moment II. The conference morphed from a call for a donors' conference originally made by then Saudi king Abdullah. The conference's organizing committee included the Saudi finance minister and the Emirati minister of state. Sisi, as the personification of productive capital, related directly to, among others, the emir of Kuwait and the Saudi crown prince, as representatives of Gulf finance capital (to say nothing of the global representatives of finance capital in the form of American Secretary of State Kerry, International Monetary Fund managing director Lagarde and World Bank president Kim). There was no intervention of middlemen with sticky fingers.

The money pledges productive capital secured from the GCC state forms between 2013 and 2015 were considerably larger than the IMF loan that was negated when it appeared that the military deposed the Ikhwan president. *Inter alia*, this capital enabled productive capital to extend its accumulation-supporting subsidization. Of course, the capital of the GCC state forms was not pledged for nothing. Recall that dispossession is the process that characterizes finance capital's moment, and recall further that the processes associated with such primitive accumulation include assumption of debt and privatization of land. In exchange for receiving finance capital's pledges, productive capital extended and intensified the processes of primitive accumulation throughout Egyptian society. The assumption of billions in debt is obvious in the preceding. Equally obvious, once the fetishism is penetrated, has been, and is, the privatization of land.

Just as the land commodity brought together predatory capital and finance capital represented by the GCC state forms in the pre-2011 period, it brings together productive capital and GCC money capital in Moment II. In 2014, Emaar Misr, a subsidiary of Emirati Emaar Properties, 'signed an agreement with the Ministries of Defense, Housing and Local Development to build a retail development as part of the Uptown Cairo housing project.'[145] In another instance, Emirati Arabtec Holdings joined 'an initiative to build 1 million housing units' around Egypt.[146] While cloaked in the bourgeois rhetoric of solving capital's social problems, such public–private partnerships are, in reality, means of accumulation for both of the factions of the governing bloc. Having acquired the land for free by dispossessing workers of it, productive capital accumulates by exchanging the stolen means of production for value in the money form from, in these instances, the Emirati state form. Furthermore, both factions of capital accumulate surplus-value through the production of commercial and reproductive space on the privatized land.

The New Capital Project was announced at the same economic conference in Sharm El-Sheikh where finance capital pledged its billions. The appearance is of a seven-year production project with a US$45 billion budget that will build a new national capital with some two thousand schools, more than six hundred hospitals and clinics, millions of housing units, a network of public transportation, an expansive park and an airport between New Cairo and the Suez Canal hub. In essence, this is a joint factional venture that, in a process reminiscent of the state-mandated land consumption in New Cairo, first increases the sale price of 700 square kilometers of land expropriated by the productive capital faction that otherwise would have little to no price, and then exchanges the land for value in the money form. The project was initially contracted to nominally Emirati capital. In a potential harbinger of the deterioration of the productive capital–finance capital relation, the Egyptian state form suspended the Arabtec deal in March 2015 and in September 2015 reportedly cancelled the memorandum of understanding with Capital City Partners for the New Capital Project.

The productive capital–finance capital bloc has also realized accumulation by dispossession through extensive reform of the legal arrangements governing Egyptian society; a number of which relate to the privatization of land. Law 32 of 2014 now prohibits third parties from challenging state contracts. This precludes reversals of privatizations of workers' value as happened in 2011 when the sale of Omar Effendi to Saudi capital was annulled. The March 2015 investment law

> not only grants blanket immunity to investors and state officials in dealing with public funds, it also annuls existing procurement procedures, enabling state officials to sell, rent, and dispose of public property for investment purposes by direct order, without resorting to public tenders and bids. What's more, the new investment law allows state officials to hand over public property to investors free of charge, for a period of five years, for 'developmental' purposes.[147]

The recently reformed bankruptcy law ensures safe exit for investors from failing projects. Also in Moment II, the state form has reduced corporate income taxes and increased subsidies for capital's accumulation. Now capital is exempt from the stamp duty, is partially exempt from value-added tax, receives complete tariff exemption on commodities for productive consumption and can regain 5 percent of tariffs on all imports.[148] This is what the war on the working class looks like when it is directed, in part, by the finance capital faction. It is, however, not the full extent of the attack weaponizing the state form.

The price of Egyptian money has been reformed downward and with it the value of the Egyptian workers' labor-power commodity.

In societies that import wage goods, capital can devalue the workers' labor-power commodity by reducing the price of the currency. Reduction in the currency price = increase in price of imported wage goods = reduction in consumption of wage goods by workers = devaluation of the labor-power commodity. In 2008 and again in 2011, food price inflation was the weapon primarily used to devalue the workers' commodity in Egyptian society. Currency deflation, like price inflation, is a process that changes the relation between the exchange-value of the labor-power commodity and the exchange-value of imported wage goods such that the latter rises relative to the former. In Moment II, the weaponized currency is increasingly being deployed. When predatory capital was finally discarded from the governing coalition, the exchange rate was LE5.882/US\$1. When productive capital disposed of commercial capital as its junior partner, the exchange rate was LE7.029/US\$1. And when productive capital and finance capital represented by the GCC state forms celebrated their bloc in Sharm El-Sheikh, the exchange rate was LE7.628/US\$1. This means that the moment Gulf capital pledged to wash billions across Egyptian society, all of the society's commodities had been devalued by 8.5 percent since the disposal of the representative of commodity capital. Moreover, the commodities had been devalued by almost 30 percent from the moment when the predatory capital faction was removed. There is a dialectic of circulation between the assumption of debt, currency reserves and currency price. The Egyptian state form can sell its foreign currency reserves to purchase Egyptian pounds and maintain the price of the currency, and thereby manage the size of its import bill. Of course, the extension of these relations into the future necessitates regularized transfers of capital into the vaults of the Egyptian Central Bank. Alternatively, the Egyptian state form can reduce its dependency on regularized transfers of capital and the pressure on its foreign reserves by reducing the price of the Egyptian pound, but doing so will increase its import bill. While on the surface the GCC deposits in the Egyptian Central Bank appear to be demonstrations of Arab solidarity and/or investments in regional stability, in reality they are modes of appearance of the governing factional alignment destroying value in Egyptian society *in a controlled manner*. The transfers are of sufficient quantity and timed so as to best balance the contradictions following from Egyptian society's consumption of more value than it produces. As long as the disequilibrium does not become too acute, commodities in Egyptian society will retain their use-value for GCC money capital and be available for purchase at crisis-sale prices. The analogy is to throwing someone from an airplane with and without a parachute. The person with the parachute will still fall to earth, but in a measured manner that preserves most of her value at the bottom. The person with no parachute hurtles to her death and has no use-value whatsoever. GCC deposits in the Egyptian Central Bank are finance capital's parachute. And speaking of gravity, there is another equally powerful law the working class in Egypt would do well to learn: if the GCC state forms support the phenomenon, the phenomenon is antagonistic to working-class interests.

If the economic reforms more strongly express the junior partner's role in the governing alignment, reform of more properly 'political' arrangements expresses the senior partner's abiding contradictions with commercial capital and the working class. The military's negation of the 2012 constitution in the summer of 2013 momentarily reverted Egyptian society to the 2011 constitution, which was based on the productive capital–predatory capital text and revised exclusively by productive capital. In 2014, intra-class and inter-class relations were again expressed in constitutional form.

The intra-class realignment appears as exclusions from and inclusions in the new constitution. Commodity capital's Article 219 from the 2012 constitution adumbrating the principles of *shar'ia* has been discarded. Commercial capital's Article 6, which prohibited religious political parties from discriminating, has been negated by Article 74, which, like Article 5 of the 1971 constitution, declares '[n]o political activity may be exercised or political parties formed on the basis of religion.'[149] Fittingly, in August 2014 commercial capital's political form of expression, the FJP, was banned. The disposal of the reactionary faction of capital also means the muting of the conservative value of security. Article 9 of the 2014 constitution now simply declares: '[t]he state ensures equal opportunity for all citizens without discrimination.'[150] Productive capital enjoyed a veto on the destruction of value in Egyptian society in the 2012 constitution because it was relatively empowered in relation to commercial capital. By 2014, it was even more relatively empowered, and this is expressed in the retention of the veto in Article 152. Finally, in contradistinction to the 2012 constitution, the 2014 constitution eliminates the 50 percent representation for workers and farmers. Instead, Article 243 declares: '[t]he state grants workers and farmers appropriate representation in the first House of Representatives to be elected after this Constitution is adopted, in the manner specified by law.'[151] Absent the rival faction of commodity capital, reserved representation had no use-value for productive capital and was eliminated.

The changing inter-class relation between a relatively empowered capital and disempowered working class, too, is expressed in the new constitution. More accurately, the 2014 constitution extends productive capital's attack on workers farther than did the constitution of Moment I. The preamble and Article 1 still declare Egypt a bourgeois democratic republic. Like the 2012 constitution, Article 12 allows for forced labor in 'order to perform a public duty.'[152] Reminiscent of Article 63 from the 2012 constitution, Article 15 of the 2014 constitution guarantees as a right only 'striking peacefully.'[153] Instead of 'raising the standards of productivity among their members and safeguarding their assets,' now unions are to 'contribute to improving the skills of their members, defend their rights and protect their interests.'[154] Phrased differently, unions exist to ensure that workers remain use-values for capital and contest disputes according to capital's laws of exchange in the sphere of circulation. In unprecedented fashion, Article 76 goes so far as to prohibit the establishment of syndicates within governmental bodies.[155] Article 53 of the 2012 constitution is retained in Article 77, which prohibits union plurality and attempts to control workers through parastatal organizations; '[n]o profession may establish more than one syndicate.'[156] Article 204 of the 2014 constitution states: '[c]ivilians cannot stand trial before military courts except for crimes that represent a direct assault against military facilities, military barracks, or whatever falls under their authority; stipulated military or border zones; its equipment, vehicles, weapons, ammunition, documents, military secrets, public funds or military factories.'[157] Between the inclusive exclusion and the state form's October 2014 equating of all public property, including universities and roads, with military facilities, this article effectively means that workers committing any public transgression, and certainly striking workers, will be subject to military tribunals.[158] As acknowledged by the head of the contradictory military justice, Radwan Ghazi, 'civilians could face military courts for arguing with the employees of army-owned gas stations.'[159] Article 204 is more draconian than was Article 198 of the 2012 constitution. And Article 207 creates a new Supreme Police Council, which means, quite simply, that the state form's repressive apparatuses targeting Egyptian workers have been strengthened.

Again, with specific reference to female workers, Article 11 of the 2014 constitution appears less reactionary than Article 10 of the 2012 expression. Article 11 now declares that '[t]he state commits to achieving equality between women and men in all civil, political, economic, social and cultural rights.'[160] It continues: '[t]he state commits to the protection of women against all forms of violence, and ensures women empowerment to reconcile the duties of a woman toward her family and work requirements.'[161] These expressions in no way change the reality that primitive accumulation depends on extending and intensifying the exploitation of women's unwaged labor in the patriarchal family. Furthermore, none of the statements of Article 11 can be taken seriously. The state form that authored them expresses the dominance of the bourgeois faction that committed and defended sexual assaults against female workers under the guise of 'virginity tests.'

Finally, bourgeois parliamentarism has also been an expression of inter-class and intra-class relations in Egyptian society. For two and a half years after productive capital's disposal of commodity capital the state form had no legislature. Vulgar analyses mistakenly attribute this to intra-regime rivalries.[162] In more developed commodity societies, parliamentarism is an expression of a relatively empowered working class, deluded by fetishisms, that does not seek change beyond bourgeois limits. The Egyptian state form went two years without a legislature because the working class is increasingly disempowered in relation to capital. Moreover, having aligned with finance capital represented by the GCC state forms, productive capital did not have an alliance with a force particular to the Egyptian social formation *and* materially invested in the rule of productive capital. Absent such a partner, parliamentarism would not appear.

Parliamentarians were finally elected in two stages in late 2015. The election process was not the product of less unequal class relations, but rather productive capital's necessities. Productive capital needed an institution to weaken class antagonisms by mediating between the dominated working class and the personification of productive capital and bearing responsibility for the increasing immiseration of workers. The For the Love of Egypt Party featured prominently in the election process, being the only party to contest seats across all the governates. It is headed by Sameh Seif El-Yazal, a retired military intelligence officer, and includes in its membership prominent capitalist Naguib Sawiris. The 'Egypt' list also contested the election process. The 'Egypt' list is an alliance between the Egyptian Front Coalition, headed by Ahmed Shafik, and the Independence Current. The 'Egypt' list was formed after the Egyptian Front's negotiations with the For the Love of Egypt Party collapsed. Other parties seeking parliamentary representation included the Knights of Egypt, led by former lieutenant-general Abdel-Rafie Darwish and populated by former members of the military, and the Democratic Current, led by Sabahi. The legislative election process in Moment II pitted personifications of productive capital against neoliberals and harmonizers. Parliamentarism was finally realized when the dictatorship of capital was assured.

The legal and governmental arrangements are appearances of two moving and differently intersecting vectors – the intra-class relation between productive capital and finance capital and the inter-class relation between a weakened working class and capital. In Moment I, the working class was weak in relation to productive capital and commercial capital. The disposal of commodity capital from the governing bloc means that the working class is still relatively weak in relation to productive capital, and now finance capital, in Moment II. These elements are in dialectical relation with mental conceptions and technology. All are being reformed to realize accumulation by dispossession in Egyptian society.

Assumption of debt, extraction through interest, looting of land – all are processes of primitive accumulation. Recall that force is another prominent element of accumulation by dispossession. Violence is internal to this mode of concentrating and centralizing value. The two are organically linked such that the movement of primitive accumulation is written 'in blood and fire.'[163]

The Egyptian state form is intensifying its use of everyday violence against the Egyptian working class. Between January and September 2011, almost twelve thousand workers were subjected to military tribunals. This was more than the total number of workers to face military trials during the entirety of Mubarak's thirty-year rule.[164] Despite much rhetoric, the governing bloc of Moment I did not deintensify or reduce the extent of state violence, and according to Human Rights Watch, '[a]rbitrary and politically motivated arrests have soared since al-Sisi . . . seized power in July 2013.'[165] Reports indicate that workers are also increasingly being subjected to the individualized violence of torture.[166] Much of this force is realized under the reformed anti-terrorism law.

The most spectacular instance of the blood and fire violence of the state form of Moment II was the massacre of workers in El-Rab'a el-Adawiya Square and El-Nahda Square on 19 August 2013. Over the course of a ten-hour assault the state form killed an estimated one thousand workers in what Human Rights Watch characterizes as the worst mass unlawful killing in Egypt's modern history.[167]

Productive capital and finance capital's state form continues to drain even more blood from and direct more fire at workers in the Sinai peninsula. The vulgar and fetishistic representations suggest that workers initiate the violence in Sinai and/or that is it the result of the deposition of Morsi. What nonsense! As Emma Goldman teaches, the classes with the ability to commit more violence are the first social forces to deploy the means of violence.[168] Moreover, workers in the Sinai were being exploited by capital long before 2013. The state form's intensified violence against workers in the Sinai now takes the forms of killings, forced evacuations of workers' homes, some as part of the construction of a 'buffer zone,' house demolitions, and attacks by tanks, helicopter gunships and F-16 fighter planes. The increasing immiseration of workers in Sinai, coupled with the state form's use of the language of 'purification,' ensures that more working-class lives will be ruined and taken.[169]

Accumulation by dispossession is not realized peaceably. Immiseration is a process against which the working class struggles, and immiseration realized by force produces, of necessity, violent struggle. No matter the opiating power of the ideals, there is a level below which the working class cannot, of necessity, allow its labor-power commodity to be devalued because below this socially particular level the working class cannot renew its life processes. Depriving imprisoned workers of their labor-time, deforming and destroying their capacity to sell their labor-time through torture, razing the space of workers' reproduction through home demolitions and ending the lives of wage earners is devaluing the labor-power commodity of more and more workers below this level in Egyptian society. Distressingly, when workers fight the struggle in terms of fetishistic forms of thought, it is taking the reactionary appearance of the Islamic State of Iraq and the Levant (ISIL), or *Daesh*, affiliate in the Sinai. The progressive devaluation of the labor-power commodity by the state form expressing the productive capital–finance capital alignment is extending and intensifying violence in Egyptian society.

The ratcheting up and wider diffusion of violence is increasingly endangering the reproduction of working-class life. The absolute expression of this, of course, is the state form's killing of workers. The violence of primitive accumulation, in relation with the reform of governing arrangements, technology, and mental conceptions, is making more precarious the daily reproduction of working-class life. The violence, the reform, the development, the thinking – every process realized by the productive capital–GCC money capital bloc through the state form has increased surplus-value production and extraction and capital's power and devalued the workers' labor-power commodity and eroded working-class power. The war on the working class being extended and intensified by the governing alignment of factions – an alignment that can and must extend and intensify the war – is making more acute the contradiction that produced crisis in 2011.

Conclusion

Many workers mistakenly think nothing has changed in Egyptian society since 2011. Such wrong-headed thinking is the result of similarities in relations and processes between the governing alignment of bourgeois factions in 2016 and the bloc that ruled through the state form until the eruption of crisis. In actuality, however, the two reconfigurations of the governing bloc express and have realized much change. There has been extensive reform, all of it antagonistic to and disempowering of the working class.

The state, like the commodity, is a form of expression of contradictory class relations. A commodity must be a social use-value and a bearer of exchange-value. The state must unify contradictory, opposing and dependent, class or factional relations. The bourgeois democratic form of state unifies the working class–capital relation. The authoritarian form of state unifies factions of capital, including mobile capital not particular to the society. Furthermore, the authoritarian state is the necessary form of expression of the commodity relation in which labor-power has been devalued below a certain socially acceptable level because of a too severe imbalance between the power of the working class and the power of capital. It is the obverse of bourgeois democracy being the mode of appearance of a more highly valued labor-power commodity; more highly valued as a result of a relatively empowered working class in dialectical relation with capital.

The history of Egyptian society since the early 1970s is the history of increasingly empowered unproductive and mobile factions of capital (commercial and finance) extending and intensifying their challenges to productive, and less mobile, capital, and their attacks on the working class. The Egyptian state forms in Moments I and II were and are undemocratic because they do not embody the dual character of society. Rather than unifying the working class and capital, they unified productive capital first with commodity capital, and then with finance capital represented by the GCC state forms.

In both moments, the intra-class relations were such that productive capital was the relatively empowered senior partner and the other faction the subordinate, junior partner. The governing blocs of Moments I and II could produce the transportation technology, reform legal and governmental arrangements, accumulate through dispossession and realize conceptions because of the increasingly severe imbalance of forces between capital and the working class; and the increasingly severe imbalance in social relations is changing the other elements, notably the violence of the mode of accumulation. El-Mahdi, citing Beinin and Lockman, makes the seminal point that 'the immense strength of the labour movement in the 1940s . . . forced different political forces (including royalty, communists, nationalists, and Islamists) to compete for its allegiance.'[170] Since the eruption of crisis in January 2011 the working class has not been sufficiently powerful to be the object of competition, much less a member of the governing bloc. This dialectic of power is making more acute the threats to the reproduction of working-class life and building to another eruption of crisis in Egyptian society.

CHAPTER 5

. . . .

The coming eruption of crisis

Expressions of war

The vulgar and fetishistic literatures are wrong. Egyptian society did not realize a revolution in 2011. Moreover, the Egyptian revolution was not stolen.[1] It was not betrayed.[2] It was not hijacked.[3] There was no counter-revolution.[4] And there is no revolution to recover.

The appearance of change the vulgar and fetishistic literatures confuse for revolution was the Egyptian social formation's particular expression of the global crisis of neoliberal capitalist relations and processes. Egyptian society's expression of universal capital's contradiction of overaccumulation crystallized out of the particular dialectical inneraction of seven elements: capital's relation with nature, the neoliberal mode of accumulation and its mental conceptions, technology, governmental arrangements, reproduction of daily life and social relations. More specifically, anthropogenic climate change and 'civilizational dependence' on fossil fuels, Benthamite rationality, accumulation by dispossession of value through privatization, derivatives technology and the CFMA, TARP and quantitative easing, produced food price inflation that endangered the Egyptian working class's ability to renew its life processes, and with it the totality of bourgeois society in Egypt. The so-called 'revolution' was the form of capital's transferring, or dumping, of value destruction on the Egyptian working class. Instead of toxic assets being devalued on bank balance sheets in New York in 2007, the capital was preserved and came to inflate the price of life, namely the wheat that produces bread. This inflation of the price of bread devalued the labor-power commodity of the Egyptian working class below its socially acceptable limit. An empowered working class did not rise up in Egypt in early 2011. In point of material fact, the overaccumulation of capital disempowered the

Egyptian working class in relation to capital by devaluing its labor-power commodity and increasing capital's rate of exploitation. The severe disequilibrium was an existential threat to the working class, and by dialectical extension, to capital.

When the crisis appeared in 2011, the first demand was material. The people wanted bread. The ideals demanded – freedom, social justice, dignity, peace – were bourgeois fetishisms. The working class mobilized capital's mental conceptions because it was weak and decidedly not revolutionary.

The apparent 'crony capitalists' of the Mubarak regime were the predatory faction of capital. This faction was the equivalent of unproductive/extractive finance capital particular to Egyptian society, and it accumulated through theft. It stole socialized value from the working class in the form of factories through the process of privatization. It stole land – the source of wealth – too, under the cover of reform. The predatory faction pillaged the Egyptian working class of value in conjunction with money capital represented by the GCC state forms. The Ikhwan represents the interests of commercial capital. The faction is reactionary, *not* because it is Muslim but because it is commodity capital. Commercial capital supported the neoliberal counter-attack on the working class because the tactics benefitted it materially and ideally. Trade liberalization concentrated value with the merchants, and the immiseration of workers drove them to the Ikhwan's social services, which opiated them with 'Islam is the solution.' The military is, in essence, productive capital in Egyptian society. The surplus-value it creates is objectified in department I and department II commodities such as cement, fertilizer, foodstuff, mineral water and clothing. Productive capital, too, accumulates by dispossessing the workers' commons of land. It also accumulates through the productive processes of transportation and communication; changing the place of the material and the ideal.

The dependent and antagonistic intra-capitalist class relations of Egyptian society are such that: 1) the military, as productive capital, and the Ikhwan, as commodity capital, need each other, and while they struggle, they cannot destroy the other lest they destroy themselves; 2) as the eruption of crisis built, productive capital was not opposed to the neoliberal attack on workers' value, per se, but rather those governmental arrangements that primarily served the interests of the rival, and increasingly powerful, predatory faction of capital; and 3) productive capital must govern Egyptian society in conjunction with another faction, and it chooses its junior partner. As regards the primary contradiction of Egyptian commodity society, in 2011 productive capital temporarily reduced the severity of the disequilibrium of a devalued labor-power commodity by redistributing value from the least powerful faction of capital, predatory capital, and reconciled workers to their increased exploitation with the ideal of nationalism.

From the 1970s until early 2011, the working class in Egyptian society was disempowered in relation to capital, and the predatory faction of capital was empowered in relation to productive and commercial capital. For forty years, the factional alignment governing the Egyptian social formation through the state form came to be more and more defined by its predatory capital faction, and its accumulation through neoliberal reform.

In 2011, productive capital disposed of its predatory junior partner and struck a temporary union of necessity with commercial capital. The realignment perpetuated commodity relations in Egyptian society, replaced productive capital's increasingly empowered rival with a relatively disempowered rival that was similarly antagonistic to the working class, and furnished the new bloc with a bourgeois democratic legitimacy. The productive capital–commercial capital configuration mobilized the ideals of religion and nationalism while realizing accumulation through privatization, liberalization, subsidization and currency depreciation, and was expressed in the form of, *inter alia*, the Political Parties Law, tighter surveillance of the working class by the Ministry of Manpower and Immigration, the 2012 power-sharing agreement and the 2012 constitution. In 2013, productive capital, having consumed commercial capital's use-value, again disposed of its junior partner in governing. This time productive capital aligned with money capital represented by the GCC state forms. This bloc, too, mobilized the harmony of interests doctrine, specifically the ideal of nationalism, to reconcile the working class to the devaluation of its labor-power commodity and increased exploitation; a devaluation and exploitation realized, in part, by the technology of the 'New Suez Canal' and the downward reform of the price of the Egyptian currency. The bloc's relations were expressed in such legal arrangements as Law 32 of 2014 pertaining to privatization, the 2014 constitution and the 2015 investment law. The factions realize accumulation through the privatization of land and the assumption of debt. The reproduction of workers' daily life is being made increasingly difficult, not least because the alignment's accumulation by dispossession is, of necessity, violent.

In 2016, when downtown the NDP building has been razed and Tahrir Square remodeled, New Cairo and its surrounding spaces may be the clearest expression of the class war raging in Egyptian society. New Cairo's Road 90, *Shara'a Tis'een*, east of the ring road, connects with El-Musheer Tantawi Road west of Cairo's ring road. El-Musheer Tantawi Road is named for the personification of productive capital that disposed of the predatory capital faction in 2011 and ensured the extension of commodity relations in Egyptian society. At both ends of the road are overpasses – expressions of the productive process of transportation – built by productive capital, and along the length of the road is an objectification of the ideal of religion in the form of the Musheer Tantawi Mosque and a military-owned gas station – again, an expression of the productive process of transportation. From the military-built overpass that transitions El-Musheer Tantawi Road into Road 90 to the American University in Cairo at its other end lies objectification after objectification of finance capital. Representations of money capital along Road 90 include: the National Bank of Egypt, Union National Bank, Ahli United Bank, National Bank of Abu Dhabi, Commercial International Bank (CIB), the Housing and Development Bank, Emirates NBD (Emirates Bank and National Bank of Dubai), National Bank of Kuwait, the Export Development Bank of Egypt and BLOM Bank. Of course, New Cairo is not somehow outside the totality of capital and is also home to objectifications of non-GCC finance capital in the form of Allianz, BNP Paribas, HSBC and Citigroup. Additionally, New Cairo houses the academy of the repressive apparatus of the state form, Cairo Festival City, built by

Al Futtaim, nominally Emirati capital, and the Air Force Specialized Hospital, which was expanded by several floors after the 2011 disposal of the predatory faction. This capital is objectified on land stolen from the Egyptian working class and sold by productive capital to finance capital (and would be west of the New Capital Project and Suez Canal Development Project). The space is also a monument to dead Egyptian labor. Dead labor is objectified in building after building. Overwhelmingly, living labor does not remain in the space. So many of the workers are daily transients. In a supremely representative instance of New Cairo being the space of dead labor, in February 2015 the state form killed twenty-two workers at the Air Defense Stadium, renamed the 30 June Stadium, along El-Musheer Tantawi Road. Workers' lives were ended by the state expression of the productive capital–finance capital alignment at a venue intended to opiate them with sports named for the disposal of the commercial capital faction along a transportation route named for the representative of productive capital. Concomitantly, New Cairo is also an early appearance of the deterioration of the governing alignment of Moment II. The aforementioned contentions surrounding the contracts awarded to Arabtec and Capital City Partners (Emaar Properties) indicate sharpening contradictions between productive capital and finance capital. It was reported, for example, that the memorandum of understanding with Capital City Partners was cancelled because of disagreements over the government's percentage in the project, meaning productive capital's share of the surplus-value produced through the construction.[5] Struggles over distributional shares are not unusual, but the cancelling of agreements signals a raising of the level of antagonism.

Contradictions at a higher stage

The crisis that appeared in Egyptian society in 2011 was a particular expression of the global crisis of overaccumulation. Five years later, the capitalist totality is still awash in surplus capital. In fact, the contradiction is more acute now than it was in 2011. There is even more ΔM sloshing around the totality. Through arrangements such as TARP and quantitative easing, the value of finance capital that would have been destroyed in 2007/08 escaped unscathed and instead the savage devaluation was dumped on the rest of the world, particularly the imperialized world; those societies least able to suffer the destruction. The contradiction of surplus capital has been further compounded by the central banks of other state forms following the lead of the Federal Reserve Bank. Quantitative easing, or large-scale asset purchases as the Federal Reserve Bank calls the process, involves the central bank buying bonds issued by the Department of the Treasury from finance capital. Originally, the Department of the Treasury issues the bonds to fund American society's consumption of more value than it produces and finance capital buys the bonds to extract money in the interest form from the state. The bond-buying process reduces the supply of available bonds, increases the price of the remaining bonds, and lowers the bond yields. The central bank's two-step process of buying the debt of the state form increases the quantity of money flowing through the circuit of finance capital and lowers interest rates. While the Federal Reserve Bank started buying bonds in 2008 and stopped in 2014, the Bank of Japan initiated its most recent monthly bond-purchasing program in April 2013 and increased the extent of it as the Federal Reserve Bank ended its program, and the European Central Bank announced the start of its buying of government bonds in January 2015. Central banks are assuming massive debts of their own state forms to inflate markets. Now, the surplus capital contradiction is appearing in high equity prices, stock buybacks and dividends, mergers and acquisitions and house prices. It is also attacking the workers' deferred wages in pension form. When this speculative bubble bursts, as they all do, maybe because of the contradiction of printing money representing no equivalent value or because interests rates are increased to again steal value in the form of houses and cars from the indebted working class, that capital will again search for profitable investment in the least-worked-up forms of commodity futures. The manner in which the last crisis was addressed is exacerbating the coming crisis.[6]

Our bourgeois civilization continues to destroy our species' metabolic relation with nature and our ability to reproduce our daily lives so as to fuel machines with natural sources of power. Capital's consumption of nature's free gifts, notably oil, so as to produce use-values without increasing exchange-value, is producing pollutants and increases in global temperatures and sea levels. In the case of Egyptian society, these processes will continue to destroy food production and make it even more difficult for the Egyptian working class to reproduce itself on a daily basis. This means Egyptian workers will be even more vulnerable to devaluations of their labor-power commodity by capital's speculation through commodity derivatives and currency deflations.

This destruction is being extended and intensified by the low price of oil. In December 2015, oil was US$37/barrel. The destruction will be extended and intensified further still if the price of oil goes to US$20/barrel, as suggested by Goldman Sachs.[7] This is a global threat to workers as oil is weaponized in production. The lower the price of oil, the more the labor-power commodity must be devalued lest capital replace its variable capital with constant capital.

The low price of oil is also threatening the dependent element of the dialectic between finance capital and productive capital in the Egyptian social formation. Already, the price of oil is curtailing the GCC state forms' expenditures, including their ability to support productive capital. Most assuredly, the GCC state forms will not continue to deposit money in the Egyptian Central Bank if IMF managing director Lagarde is correct, and they will either have to reduce spending or impose taxes in the near future.[8] In order to maintain the class imbalance in Egyptian society in the face of the crisis of 2011, productive capital pulled value from the future into the present in the form of debt, primarily contracted with the GCC state forms. A sustained reduction in the price of oil will mean that the GCC state forms will not advance the capital to slowly devalue Egyptian commodities, and the class disequilibrium will become more severe more quickly.

Concomitantly, productive capital cannot continue to keep finance capital as its junior partner and needs finance capital as its junior partner. The accumulation by dispossession required by finance capital is a predatory and violent process that when realized erodes productive capital's dominance in Egyptian society, and, because the manner in which productive capital creates surplus-value ensures a constant and ever-growing outflow of value from the social formation that can only be balanced through deficit financing, productive capital cannot maintain its social dominance without assuming debt from finance capital. In 1976, finance capital in the form of the Gulf Authority for the Development of Egypt (GADE), in coordination with the Egyptian state form, attacked the working class in Egypt with neoliberal weapons including new legal arrangements and removal of bread subsidies.[9] Shortly thereafter, Egyptian society exploded in the 'bread riots' of 1977. The same devaluation of the labor-power commodity is being realized in Moment II using different weapons, including downward reform of the price of the Egyptian currency, and the working class is similarly contesting its destruction. The use-value of ideals such as nationalism and religion is ultimately diminished in the face of material destruction; the flag does not put food on the table. The state form of Moment II can only further extend and intensify the violence against the working class to realize accumulation by dispossession. This endangers or ends the reproduction of working-class life on which productive capital and finance capital depend to accumulate surplus-value. Of course, more extensive and intensive violence by the state form also begets more violent resistance. Reproduction of commodity society in Egypt is possible only with finance capital as productive capital's junior partner and is impossible with finance capital as productive capital's junior partner. The militarism of the joint Arab Force being pressed by productive capital is an attempt, ultimately futile, to institutionalize and arrest the raising of the contradictory factional relation to a higher stage in a form to which the GCC states will provide value in the money form and the Egyptian state will provide value in the form of the labor-power commodity.

Relatedly, the Egyptian form of state cannot continue to realize the neoliberal counter-attack on the working class while governed by productive capital as the senior faction. The neoliberal state is the form of expression of a governing bloc in which finance capital is the senior faction. Productive capital as the senior governing faction of a neoliberal state form is a building contradiction. A productive capital seeking accumulation will continue to extend and intensify processes and relations such as trade liberalization and commodity devaluation and progressively erode its political power. A productive capital seeking to maintain its political dominance will stop extending and intensifying the processes and relations of the neoliberal mode of accumulation. Productive capital cannot continue to accumulate *and* maintain its political dominance. Productive capital can continue to devalue the means of production and labor-power commodity on which its accumulation depends and be increasingly subordinated to finance capital, or it can maintain its dominance, lose finance capital as its governing partner and arrest the devaluation of its means of production and labor-power commodity necessary for its accumulation. Capital abhors limits, and productive capital will most assuredly try to transcend this limited choice by pursuing a third, short-run option.[10] Productive capital will seek to continue to accumulate and perpetuate its political dominance by socializing the costs of this contradiction to the Egyptian working class. Such socialization will, of necessity, require an extension and intensification of violent destruction of workers and their labor-power commodity. In the long run, however, this is only a raising to a higher stage the contradiction that exploded in 2011, namely the dialectical destruction of productive capital through the destruction of the working class.

These contradictions lead, inexorably, to another contradiction: productive capital needs, and increasingly so, commercial capital, and productive capital is currently unwilling to share surplus-value and political power with commercial capital. Productive capital ended the governing alignment of Moment I when commercial capital's use-value was exhausted by the necessary assumption of debt from the IMF. This political reconfiguration does not change the material fact that commercial capital is necessary for productive capital to realize the surplus-value objectified in commodities, and currently the productive capital–finance capital state form is imprisoning and threatening with death the representatives of commercial capital. The primary antagonism is between the different factions of unproductive capital competing for distributive shares of productive capital's surplus-value; the interests of the finance capital represented by the GCC state forms are inimical to the interests of commercial capital represented by the Ikhwan. No matter the severity of the imbalance in productive capital's favor, no matter how intense productive capital's assault on commodity capital, the military cannot destroy the Ikhwan. Productive capital cannot prosecute absolutely its social war on commercial capital because by doing so it would, dialectically, destroy itself. The fact that El-Shater, Morsi and Badie are still alive suggests that legal conviction and imprisonment are the measured height to which productive capital is willing to allow the antagonism of the unproductive capitals to ascend. The representatives of commodity capital have a use-value for productive capital only so long as they are alive: in this moment they can be demonized as terrorists behind all manner of plots, the combating of which legitimizes the extension and intensification of the violence of the state form, and in a future moment, when the contradictions of the Moment II governing bloc become too acute through accumulation by dispossession, they can be released and rehabilitated as again having the use-value of a (potential) junior partner.

The sharper, the nearer

Capital in Egyptian society is increasingly hard pressed to reproduce the conditions necessary for its own existence. Productive capital cannot reconcile the rising contradictions. The deficit financing demanded by its creation of surplus-value must constantly be borne by the working class. It cannot even stop itself making the contradictions more acute. For example, in May 2015 it was revealed that the Ministries of Defense, Communications, Finance, Electricity and Transportation had developed a new plan to develop Egypt's national telecommunication infrastructure. The military will control 60 percent of the planned productive capital.[11] Also in May 2015, it was announced that two military airports around Cairo would start accepting civilian flights. Productive capital moved to create even more surplus-value by controlling the movement of more capital, in diverse forms, through the Egyptian social formation.[12] The working class in Egypt cannot rebalance the contradictions, either. The weak, deluded class of 2011 has been weakened further in relation to capital by attacks through bourgeois conceptions, inflation and downward reform of the price of the Egyptian currency. The daily lives made difficult to reproduce by the devaluation of the labor-power commodity and increased exploitation are now even more difficult to reproduce.

The irreconcilable and sharpening contradictions promise an increasingly violent future for Egyptian society. The violence of this future is already apparent in the present of Moment II in the form of blast shields lining entire city blocks, the cordoning off of traffic lanes, the laying of spiked belts, sandbagged machine-gun emplacements overlooking major thoroughfares, deployments of heavy weaponry and proliferating checkpoints. The violence consuming ever more of Egyptian society is the danger of the governing alignment's rule, and the more forcefully the governing bloc tries to realize order and security by paralyzing the movement of society, the more it will produce disorder and insecurity. Violence will have a use-value for the working class, however, only when it starts producing revolutionary ideals by thinking and acting in class terms. The longer workers remain deluded by bourgeois appearances, the longer workers will suffer the devastating violence of fetishisms – wars fought for the nation and in the name of God.

The war of Egyptian society is intensifying. The contradictions are becoming more acute. The eruption of crisis is nearing. Crises provide revolutionary opportunities, but so long as the balance of forces in the class struggle so heavily tips in capital's favor, the coming explosion will be even more reactionary than in 2011. Then, capital marched Egyptian workers to their graves with weaponized food. Capital will extend and intensify its use of its military arsenal to send even more workers to their graves through the next eruption of crisis.

NOTES

Chapter 1

1 Bertell Ollman, *Dance of the Dialectic: Steps in Marx's Method* (Chicago: University of Illinois Press, 2003), pp. 4–5.

2 Ibid., p. 18.

3 Ibid., p. 27.

4 Ibid., p. 17.

5 Karl Marx, *Capital*, vol.I: *The Process of Production of Capital* (London: Penguin Books, 1976), p. 929.

6 David Harvey, *A Companion to Marx's* Capital (London: Verso Books, 2010), p. 62.

7 Ibid., p. 12.

8 Marx, *Capital*, vol. I, p. 102.

9 Ibid., p. 103.

10 Karl Marx, *A Contribution to the Critique of Political Economy* (Moscow: Progress Publishers, 1977), pp. 20–1.

11 Marx, *Capital*, vol. I, p. 103.

12 Ibid., p. 103.

13 Harry Cleaver, *Reading* Capital *Politically* (Austin: University of Texas Press, 1979), p. 64.

14 Ibid., p. 92.

15 Ibid., p. 94.

16 Marx, *Capital*, vol. I, p. 800.

17 Ibid., p. 125.

18 Ibid., p. 127.

19 Ibid., p. 129.

20 Raya Dunayevskaya, *Marxism and Freedom: From 1776 until Today* (New York: Humanity Books, 2000), p. 138.

21 Marx, *Capital*, vol. I, p. 274.

22 Ibid., p. 275.

23 Ibid., p. 275.

24 Harvey, *A Companion to Marx's* Capital, p. 104.

25 Marx, *Capital*, vol., p. 317.

26 Harvey, *A Companion to Marx's* Capital, p. 33.

27 Marx, *Capital*, vol. I, p. 131.

28 Ibid., p. 131.

29 Ibid., p. 493.

30 Harvey, *A Companion to Marx's* Capital, pp. 192–3. In his *A Companion to Marx's* Capital, Harvey identifies six moments of what he identifies as the historical materialist method. In his more recent analyses, for example 'The enigma of capital and the crisis this time,' he added the seventh moment of institutional, legal and governmental arrangements. See: davidharvey.org/2010/08/the-enigma-of-capital-and-the-crisis-this-time/

31 Ollman, *Dance of the Dialectic*, p. 71.

32 Ibid., p. 71.

33 Lisa Anderson, 'Demystifying the Arab Spring,' *Foreign Affairs*, 90(3): 2–7; Gregory Gause, 'Why Middle East studies missed the Arab Spring,' *Foreign Affairs*, 90(4): 81–90; Jack Goldstone, 'Understanding the revolutions of 2011,' *Foreign Affairs*, 90(3): 8–16; Rashid Khalidi, 'Reflections on the revolutions in Tunisia and Egypt,' *Foreign Policy*, 24 February 2011, foreignpolicy.com/2011/02/24/reflections-on-the-revolutions-in-tunisia-and-egypt/, accessed 15 February 2015; Dan Tschirgi, Walid Kazziha and Sean F. McMahon, *Egypt's Tahrir Revolution* (Boulder, CO: Lynne Rienner Publishers, 2013); and Marc Lynch, *The Arab Uprising: The Unfinished Revolutions of the New Middle East* (New York: Public Affairs, 2012).

34 Lisa Anderson, '"Early adopters" and "neighborhood effects",' in *The Arab Spring: Will It Lead to Democratic Transitions?*, ed. Clement Henry and Jang Ji-Hyang (Seoul: Asan Institute for Policy Studies, 2012), pp. 27–32; Henry E. Hale, 'Regime change cascades: what we have learned from the 1848 revolutions to the 2011 Arab uprisings,' *Annual Review of Political Science*, 16 (2013): 331–53; and Lynch *The Arab Uprising*.

35 Gause, 'Why Middle East studies missed the Arab spring.'

36 Laurel E. Miller et al., *Democratization in the Arab World: Prospects and Lessons from Around the World* (Santa Monica, CA: RAND Corporation, 2012); Henry and Jang, *The Arab Spring*; Hale, 'Regime change cascades.'

37 Eva Bellin, 'Reconsidering the robustness of authoritarianism in the Middle East: lessons from the Arab Spring,' *Comparative Politics*, 44(2): 127–49; Steven Heydemann and Reinoud Leenders, 'Authoritarian learning and authoritarian resilience: regime responses to the "Arab Awakening,"' *Globalizations*, 8(5): 647–53.

38 Zoltan Barany, 'The role of the military,' *Journal of Democracy*, 22(4): 24–35; Holger Albrecht and Dina Bishara, 'Back on horseback: the military and political transformation in Egypt,' *Middle East Law and Governance*, 3 (2011): 13–23.

39 Robert Springborg, 'The political economy of the Arab Spring,' *Mediterranean Politics*, 16(3): 430; Albrecht and Bishara, 'Back on horseback,' p. 20.

40 Goldstone, 'Understanding the revolutions of 2011.'

41 Hazem Kandil, 'Why did the Egyptian middle class march to Tahrir Square?,' *Mediterranean Politics*, 17(2): 197–215.

42 Clement Henry, 'Political economies of transition,' in *The Arab Spring: Will It Lead to Democratic Transitions?*, ed. Clement Henry and Jang Ji-Hyang (Seoul: Asan Institute for Policy Studies, 2012), pp. 53–75.

43 Koenraad Bogaert, 'Contextualizing the Arab revolts: the politics behind three decades of neoliberalism in the Arab world,' *Middle East Critique*, 22(3): 213–34.

44 *Oxford English Dictionary*, www.oed.com.library.aucegypt.edu:2048/view/Entry/100006?rskey=XekGK2&result=2#eid, accessed 15 February 2015.

45 Hale, 'Regime change cascades,' p. 333; Barany, 'The role of the military.'

46 Harvey, *A Companion to Marx's* Capital, p. 196.

47 Marx, *Capital*, vol. I, p. 617.

48 Karl Marx and Friedrich Engels, *The Communist Manifesto* (London: Penguin Books, 1967), p. 83.

49 Ibid., p. 83.

50 Karl Marx, *Capital*, vol. III: *The Process of Capitalist Production as a Whole* (London: Penguin Books, 1991), p. 634.

51 Karl Marx, 'Marx to Dr. Kugelmann concerning the Paris Commune,' 12 April 1871, www.marxists.org/archive/marx/works/1871/letters/71_04_12.htm, accessed 18 February 2015.

52 E. H. Carr, *The Twenty Years Crisis: 1919–1939* (New York: Palgrave, 2001), p. 192.

53 Nathan J. Brown, 'Egypt's failed transition,' *Journal of Democracy*, 24(4): 45–58.

54 Harvey, *A Companion to Marx's* Capital, p. 240.

55 Marx, *Capital*, vol. I, pp. 165–6.

56 Ibid., p. 1005.

57 Harvey, *A Companion to Marx's* Capital, pp. 83 and 131.

58 Marx, *Capital*, vol. III, p. 428.

59 M. Abdelrahman, 'A hierarchy of struggles? The "economic" and the "political" in Egypt's revolution,' *Review of African Political Economy*, 39(134): 614–28; Rabab El-Mahdi, 'Against marginalization: workers, youth and class in the 25 January revolution,' in *Marginality and Exclusion in Egypt*, ed. Ray Bush and Habib Ayeb (London: Zed Books, 2012), pp. 133–47; Joel Beinin, 'The rise of Egypt's workers,' *The Carnegie Papers* (Beirut: Carnegie Endowment for International Peace, 2012); Samer Soliman, 'The political economy of Mubarak's fall,' in *Arab Spring in Egypt: Revolution and Beyond*, ed. Bahgat Korany and Rabab El-Mahdi (Cairo: The American University in Cairo Press, 2012), pp. 43–62.

60 Vladimir Lenin, *Lenin on Imperialism, the Eve of the Proletarian Social Revolution* (Peking: Foreign Language Press, 1960), p. 18.

61 Rabab El-Mahdi, 'Labour protests in Egypt: causes and meanings,' *Review of African Political Economy*, 38(129): 400.

62 Joel Beinin, 'Workers' struggle under "socialism" and neoliberalism,' in *Egypt: The Moment of Change*, ed. Rabab El-Mahdi and Philip Marfleet (London: Zed Books, 2009), p. 75.

63 Rabab El-Mahdi and Philip Marfleet, 'Introduction,' in *Egypt: The Moment of Change*, ed. Rabab El-Mahdi and Philip Marfleet (London: Zed Books, 2009), p. 2.

64 Harry Cleaver, 'Rupturing the dialectic: the struggle against work, financial crisis and beyond,' la.utexas.edu/users/hcleaver/Rupturing.html, accessed 28 November 2015.

65 David Harvey, *Seventeen Contradictions and the End of Capitalism* (Oxford: Oxford University Press, 2014), p. 4.

66 Anwar Shaikh, 'An introduction to the history of crisis theories,' in *U.S. Capitalism in Crisis* (New York: Union for Radical Political Economics, 1978), p. 219. Available at: www.eco.unibs.it/~palermo/PDF/History%20 of%20crisis%20theories.pdf.

67 Cleaver, *Reading* Capital *Politically*, p. 63.

68 Ibid., p. 62.

69 Leo Panitch and Sam Gindin, 'Capitalist crises and the crisis this time,' in *The Crisis This Time: Socialist Register 2011*, ed. Leo Panitch, Greg Albo and Vivek Chibber (Pontypool: Merlin Press, 2011), p. 13.

70 Harvey, *Seventeen Contradictions and the End of Capitalism*, p. ix.

71 Karl Marx, 'Wage labour and capital,' in *The Marx-Engels Reader*, 2nd edn, ed. Robert Tucker (New York: W. W. Norton & Company, 1978), p. 217.

72 David Harvey, 'The enigma of capital and the crisis this time,' 30 August 2010, davidharvey.org/2010/08/the-enigma-of-capital-and-the-crisis-this-time/, accessed 28 November 2015.

73 Marx, *Capital*, vol. III, p. 615.

74 David Harvey, *The Enigma of Capital and the Crises of Capitalism* (Oxford: Oxford University Press, 2011).

75 Ursula Huws, 'Crisis as capitalist opportunity: the new accumulation through public service commodification,' in *The Crisis and the Left: Socialist Register 2012*, ed. Leo Panitch, Greg Albo and Vivek Chibber (Pontypool, Wales: Merlin Press, 2011), pp. 64–84.

76 Nadia Farah, *Egypt's Political Economy: Power Relations in Development* (Cairo: The American University in Cairo Press, 2009).

77 Ray Bush, 'The land and the people,' in *Egypt: The Moment of Change*, ed. Rabab El-Mahdi and Philip Marfleet (London: Zed Books, 2009), pp. 51–67; Habib Ayeb, 'The marginalization of the small peasantry: Egypt and Tunisia,' in *Marginalization and Exclusion in Egypt*, ed. Ray Bush and Habib Ayeb (London: Zed Books, 2012), pp. 72–96.

78 Beinin, 'The rise of Egypt's workers,' p. 1.

79 Ibid., p. 5.

80 Karl Marx, *The Eighteenth Brumaire of Louis Bonaparte* (New York: International Publishers, 1963), p. 88.

81 Beinin, 'The rise of Egypt's workers,' p. 6.

82 Ibid., pp. 19–20.

83 Abdelrahman, 'A hierarchy of struggles?'

84 El-Mahdi, 'Labour protests in Egypt,' p. 389.

85 Omnia El Shakry, 'Egypt's three revolutions: the force of history behind this popular uprising,' in *The Dawn of the Arab Uprising: End of an Old Order?*, ed. Bassam Haddad, Rosie Bsheer and Ziad Abu-Rish (New York:

Pluto Press, 2012), pp. 97–103; Walter Armbrust, 'The revolution against neoliberalism,' in *The Dawn of the Arab Uprising: End of an Old Order?*, ed. Bassam Haddad, Rosie Bsheer and Ziad Abu-Rish (New York: Pluto Press, 2012), pp. 113–23; and El-Mahdi, 'Against marginalization.' A notable, if not unproblematic, exception to this tendency is Bogaert. See Bogaert, 'Contextualizing the Arab revolts'; and Koenraad Bogaert, 'Global dimensions of the Arab Spring and the potential for anti-hegemonic politics,' *Jadaliyya*, 21 December 2011, www.jadaliyya.com/pages/index/3638/global-dimensions-of-the-arab-spring-and-the-poten, accessed 28 November 2015.

86 David Harvey, *A Brief History of Neoliberalism* (Oxford: Oxford University Press, 2005), p. 19.

87 Panitch and Gindin, 'Capitalist crises and the crisis this time,' p. 13.

88 Ibid., p. 874.

89 Marx, *Capital Volume I*, p. 875.

90 Angela Joya, 'The Egyptian revolution: crisis of neoliberalism and the potential for democratic politics,' *Review of African Political Economy*, 38(129): 367–86; Nadia Farah, 'The political economy of Egypt's revolution,' in *Egypt's Tahrir Revolution*, ed. Dan Tschirgi, Walid Kazziha and Sean F. McMahon (Boulder, CO: Lynne Rienner Publishers, 2013), pp. 47–65; Armbrust, 'The revolution against neoliberalism.'

91 Samir Amin, *The People's Spring: The Future of the Arab Revolution* (Nairobi: Pambazuka Press, 2012), p. 33.

92 David Harvey, *The New Imperialism* (Oxford: Oxford University Press, 2003).

93 Farah, *Egypt's Political Economy*; Joya, 'The Egyptian revolution'; El-Mahdi, 'Against marginalization'

94 Joya, 'The Egyptian revolution,' p. 368.

95 Ibid., p.370.

96 Ibid., p. 377.

97 Marx, *Capital*, vol. I, p. 770.

98 Cleaver, *Reading* Capital *Politically*, p. 55.

99 Gilbert Achcar, *The People Want: A Radical Exploration of the Arab Uprising* (London: Saqi Books, 2013), p. 21.

100 Ibid., p. 71.

101 Ibid., pp. 112 and 235.

102 Marx, *Capital*, vol. I, p. 175.

Chapter 2

1 Fernand Braudel, *The Mediterranean and the Mediterranean World in the Age of Philip II*, vol. II, trans. Sian Reynolds (New York: Harper and Row, 1972).

2 Gregory Gause, 'Why Middle East studies missed the Arab Spring,' *Foreign Affairs*, 90(4): 81–90.

3 Bahgat Korany, 'Egypt and beyond: the Arab Spring, the new pan-Arabism, and the challenges of transition,' in *Arab Spring in Egypt: Revolution and Beyond*, ed. Bahgat Korany and Rabab El-Mahdi (Cairo: The American University in Cairo Press, 2012), p. 271.

4 G. A. Cohen, *Karl Marx's Theory of History: A Defense* (Princeton: Princeton University Press, 1978), p. 115.

5 Ibid., p. 122.

6 Karl Marx, *Capital*, vol. II: *The Process of Circulation of Capital* (London: Penguin, 1992), p. 330.

7 Ibid., p. 135.

8 'The Suez Canal: a vital shortcut for global commerce,' World Shipping Council, www.worldshipping.org/pdf/suez-canal-presentation.pdf, accessed 21 March 2015.

9 Karl Marx, *Capital*, vol. III: *The Process of Capitalist Production as a Whole* (London: Penguin Books, 1991), p. 425.

10 'The Suez Canal: a vital shortcut for global commerce.'

11 'Saving in distance via SC,' Suez Canal Authority, www.suezcanal.gov.eg/sc.aspx?show=11, accessed 21 March 2015.

12 'Facts on Egypt: oil and gas,' International Energy Agency, www.iea.org/media/news/facts_egypt.pdf, accessed 21 March 2015.

13 Emile Zola, *Money* (London: Caxton Publishing Company, 1900), Kindle edn.

14 It was Louis Napoleon trying to get labor and capital working together in the form of large public works, after his coup, that produced the Suez Canal, and in an interesting historical parallel, in 2014 the Egyptian military similarly engaged Egyptian workers with the selling of shares to finance an expansion of the canal.

15 Bertell Ollman, *Dance of the Dialectic: Steps in Marx's Method* (Chicago: University of Illinois Press, 2003), p. 14.

16 Sara Johnstone and Jeffrey Mazo, 'Global warming and the Arab Spring,' *Survival*, 53(2): 11.

17 Ibid., p. 12.

18 Poverty Reduction and Equity Group, *Food Price Watch* (Washington, DC: World Bank Group, April 2011), pp. 1–2.

19 World Health Organization, *Urban Air Pollution in Megacities of the World* (Oxford: Blackwell Reference, 1992), p. 88. Available at: extranet.who.int/iris/restricted/handle/10665/39902.

20 Ibid., p. 89.

21 United Nations Development Programme, *Arab Human Development Report 2009: Challenges to Human Security in Arab Countries* (New York: United Nations Development Programme, 2009), p. 46.

22 'Global air pollution: what is the most polluted country and city in the world?,' *Guardian*, 26 September 2011, www.theguardian.com/environment/datablog/2011/sep/26/global-air-pollution-who#data, accessed 7 December 2015.

23 United Nations Development Programme, *Arab Human Development Report 2009*, p. 38.

24 Isabel Bottoms, *Water Pollution in Egypt: Causes and Concerns* (Cairo: Egyptian Center for Economic and Social Rights, 2014), p. 1. Available at: ecesr.org/wp-content/uploads/2015/06/ECESR-Water-Polllution-En.pdf.

25 United Nations Development Programme, *Arab Human Development Report 2009*, p. 45.

26 Bottoms, *Water Pollution in Egypt*, p. 1.

27 Ian Lee, 'Egypt hungry for "food revolution,"' CNN, 7 March 2013, www. cnn.com/2013/03/07/world/africa/egypt-food-prices/index.html, accessed 23 March 2015.

28 Jack Shenker, 'Nile Delta: "We are going underwater. The sea will conquer our lands,"' *Guardian*, 21 August 2009, www.theguardian.com/ environment/2009/aug/21/climate-change-nile-flooding-farming, accessed 23 March 2015.

29 World Bank, *Arab Republic of Egypt: Assessment of Environmental Degradation* (Washington, DC: World Bank Group, 2002). Available at: www-wds.worldbank.org/external/default/WDSContentServer/WDSP/ IB/2003/01/07/000094946_02121204015557/Rendered/PDF/multiopage. pdf.

30 Christian Parenti, *Tropic of Chaos: Climate Change and the New Geography of Violence* (New York: Nation Books, 2011), p. 5.

31 Karl Marx, *Capital*, vol. I: *The Process of Production of Capital* (London: Penguin, 1976), p. 312.

32 Ibid., p. 562.

33 Harry Cleaver, *Reading* Capital *Politically* (Austin: University of Texas Press, 1979), p. 96.

34 United Nations Development Programme, *Arab Human Development Report 2009*, p. 40.

35 Shenker, 'Nile Delta: "We are going underwater."'

36 Barnaby Phillips, 'Rising waters threaten Nile Delta,' *Al Jazeera*, 21 March 2010, www.aljazeera.com/focus/2010/03/201032017393870043.html, accessed 26 March 2015.

37 Shenker, 'Nile Delta: "We are going underwater."'

38 United Nations Development Programme, *Arab Human Development Report 2009*, p. 4.

39 Shenker, 'Nile Delta: "We are going underwater."'

40 David Harvey, *A Companion to Marx's* Capital (London: Verso, 2010), p. 203.

41 Poverty Reduction and Equity Group, *Food Price Watch* (April 2011), p. 2.

42 David Harvey, *A Brief History of Neoliberalism* (Oxford: Oxford University Press, 2005), p. 5.

43 Ibid., p. 2.

44 Susanne Soederberg, 'Cannibalistic capitalism: the paradoxes of neoliberal pension securitization,' in *The Crisis This Time: Socialist Register 2011*, ed. Leo Panitch, Greg Albo and Vivek Chibber (Pontypool: Merlin Press, 2011), pp. 224–41.

45 Wendy Brown, *Edgework: Critical Essays on Knowledge and Politics* (Princeton: Princeton University Press, 2005), p. 40.

46 Ibid., p. 40.

47 Ibid., pp. 40–3. Marx describes the sphere of circulation, the market, not the factory, as 'the exclusive realm of Freedom, Equality, Property and Bentham.' Marx, *Capital*, vol. I, p. 280.

48 Brown, *Edgework*, pp. 43–4.

49 Ibid., p. 42.

50 Harvey, *A Brief History of Neoliberalism*, p. 66.

51 Michel Dunne and Tarek Radwan, 'Egypt: why liberalism still matters,' *Journal of Democracy*, 24(1): 88.

52 Ibid., pp. 88–9.

53 Ibid., p. 89.

54 Ibid., p. 89.

55 Pew Research Center: Global Attitudes Project, *Egyptians Embrace Revolt Leaders, Religious Parties and Military, As Well*, April 2011, www.pewglobal.org/files/2011/04/Pew-Global-Attitudes-Egypt-Report-FINAL-April-25-2011.pdf, accessed 4 April 2015.

56 Subsequent parliamentary elections were also liberalized such that members of the Ikhwan, running as independents, secured a record eighty-seven seats to become the largest opposition bloc in the lower house.

57 It is instructive as to how reformist the 25 January crisis was that Nour's son was pictured on the 28 February 2011 cover of *Time* under the caption 'The generation changing the world.'

58 Dunne and Radwan, 'Egypt: why liberalism still matters,' p. 91.

59 Ibid., p. 90.

60 Ibid., p. 92, emphasis added.

61 Rabab El-Mahdi, 'Labour protests in Egypt: causes and meanings,' *Review of African Political Economy*, 38(129): 388. See also Joel Beinin, 'The rise of Egypt's workers,' *The Carnegie Papers* (Beirut: Carnegie Endowment for International Peace, 2012), p. 6.

62 El-Mahdi, 'Labour protests in Egypt,' p. 388.

63 Ibid., p. 392.

64 Karl Marx, 'The German ideology,' in *The Marx-Engels Reader*, 2nd edn, ed. Robert C. Tucker (New York: W. W. Norton & Company, 1978), p. 173.

65 David Harvey, *The New Imperialism* (Oxford: Oxford University Press, 2003), p. 145.

66 David Harvey, *The Limits to Capital* (London: Verso, 2006), p. xvi; Harvey, *A Companion to Marx's* Capital, p. 306; Rosa Luxemburg, *The Accumulation of Capital: An anti-critique*, trans. Rudolf Wichmann (New York: Monthly Review Press, 1972).

67 Harvey, *A Brief History of Neoliberalism*, p. 33.

68 Nadia Farah, *Egypt's Political Economy: Power Relations in Development* (Cairo: The American University in Cairo Press, 2009), p. 41.

69 Steven Greenhouse, 'Half of Egypt's $20.2 billion debt being forgiven by U.S. and allies,' *New York Times*, 27 May 1991, www.nytimes.com/1991/05/27/business/half-of-egypt-s-20.2-billion-debt-being-forgiven-by-us-and-allies.html?pagewanted=all&src=pm, accessed 10 December 2015.

70 Ray Bush, 'The land and the people,' in *Egypt: The Moment of Change*, ed. Rabab El-Mahdi and Philip Marfleet (London: Zed Books, 2009), p. 58.

71 Mohamed Atif Kishk, 'Mechanisms of impoverishment of the rural poor in contemporary Egypt' (Minia: Minia University, n.d.), cited in Farah, *Egypt's Political Economy*, p. 47.

72 Mohamed Abdel-Aal', 'Agrarian reform and tenancy problems in Upper Egypt' (Social Research Center, American University in Cairo, n.d.), cited in Farah, *Egypt's Political Economy*, p. 46.

73 Bush, 'The land and the people,' p. 58.

74 Helen Chapin Metz, *Egypt: A Country Study* (Washington, DC: General Printing Office, Library of Congress, 1990). Available at: countrystudies. us/egypt/84.htm.

75 Bush, 'The land and the people,' p. 56.

76 Metz, *Egypt: A Country Study*.

77 Farah, *Egypt's Political Economy*, p. 45.

78 Nadia Farah, 'The political economy of Egypt's revolution,' in *Egypt's Tahrir Revolution*, ed. Dan Tschirgi, Walid Kazziha and Sean F. McMahon (Boulder, CO: Lynne Rienner Publishers, 2013), p. 54.

79 Farah, *Egypt's Political Economy*, p. 50.

80 Harvey, *The Limits to Capital*, p. xxiii.

81 'Ecommerce in real-time: in the last 30-seconds . . .' Ever Merchant, www. evermerchant.com/, accessed 11 March 2015.

82 Eva Bellin, 'Reconsidering the robustness of authoritarianism in the Middle East: lessons from the Arab Spring,' *Comparative Politics*, 44(2): 138.

83 Robert Cox, *Production, Power and World Order: Social Forces in the Making of History* (New York: Columbia University Press, 1987), p. 21.

84 Because capital is about temporality and 'moments are the elements of profit,' time is forever being divided more finely in commodity society (Marx, *Capital*, vol. I, p. 352). A microsecond is one millionth of a second (1.0 microsecond = 1.0e-6). Computer-driven trades can now be executed in 300 microseconds. This means that more than a thousand trades can be made in the blink of an eye (Ben Moshinsky, 'Regulators outpace physicists in race to catch flash boys,' *Bloomberg Business*, 18 March 2015, www.bloomberg.com/news/articles/2015-03-18/regulators-outpace-physicists-in-race-to-catch-flash-boys, accessed 10 December 2015).

85 Cleaver, *Reading* Capital *Politically*, p. 73.

86 Harvey, *A Brief History of Neoliberalism*, pp. 157–9.

87 John C. Hull, *Options, Futures, and Other Derivatives*, 6th edn (Upper Saddle River, NJ: Pearson Prentice Hall, 2006), p. 1.

88 Ibid., p. 3.

89 Ibid., p. 4.

90 Ibid., p. 5.

91 Ibid., p. 6.

92 Ibid., p. 12.

93 Marx, *Capital*, vol. I, p. 381.

94 Ibid., p. 381.

95 Hull, *Options, Futures, and Other Derivatives*, p. 23.

96 Felicity Lawrence, 'Financial speculators responsible for rising global food prices, claims report,' *Guardian*, 13 September 2011, www.theguardian. com/global-development/2011/sep/13/financial-speculators-spiralling-food-prices, accessed 10 December 2015; Murray Worthy, *Broken*

    Markets: How financial market regulation can help prevent another global food crisis (London: World Development Movement, 2011), p. 7.

97 Stephen Leahy, 'Rampant speculation inflated food price bubble,' Inter Press News Service, 28 January 2011, 10 December 2015, www.ipsnews.net/2011/01/rampant-speculation-inflated-food-price-bubble/.

98 Baird Webel, 'Troubled Asset Relief Program (TARP): implementation and status' (Washington, DC: Congressional Research Service Report for Congress, 2013), p. 1. Available at: fas.org/sgp/crs/misc/R41427.pdf.

99 Ibid., p. 2.

100 While a zeroed interest rate can be a boon for capital it negatively affects deferred working-class wages in the form of pensions.

101 Vladimir Klyuev, Phil de Imus and Krisha Srinivasan, *Unconventional Choices for Unconventional Times: Credit and Quantitative Easing in Advanced Economies* (Washington, DC: International Monetary Fund, 2009), p. 15.

102 Justin Wolfers, 'The Fed has not stopped trying to stimulate the economy,' *New York Times*, 29 October 2014, www.nytimes.com/2014/10/30/upshot/the-fed-has-not-stopped-trying-to-stimulate-the-economy.html?rref=upshot&abt=0002&abg=1&_r=0, accessed 10 December 2015.

103 Peter Wahl, *Food Speculation: The Main Factor of the Price Bubble in 2008* (Berlin: WEED, 2009), p. 5.

104 Olivier De Schutter, *Food Commodities Speculation and Food Price Crises: Regulation to reduce the risks of price volatility* (New York: United Nations, 2010), p. 3.

105 Ibid., p. 8.

106 Ibid., p. 6.

107 Marx, *Capital*, vol. I, p. 318.

108 Leo Panitch and Sam Gindin, 'Capitalist crises and the crisis this time,' in *The Crisis This Time: Socialist Register 2011*, ed. Leo Panitch, Greg Albo and Vivek Chibber (Pontypool: Merlin Press, 2011), p. 13.

109 De Schutter, *Food Commodities Speculation and Food Price Crises*, p. 4.

110 Marx, *Capital*, vol. I, p. 255.

111 Panitch and Gindin, 'Capitalist crises and the crisis this time,' p. 9.

112 Andrew Lilico, 'How the Fed triggered the Arab Spring in two easy graphs,' *The Telegraph*, 4 May 2011, www.telegraph.co.uk/finance/economics/8492078/How-the-Fed-triggered-the-Arab-Spring-uprisings-in-two-easy-graphs.html, accessed 10 December 2015.

113 Leahy, 'Rampant speculation inflated food price bubble.'

114 'World food situation,' Food and Agricultural Organization of the United Nations, www.fao.org/worldfoodsituation/foodpricesindex/en/, accessed 10 December 2015.

115 Poverty Reduction and Equity Group, *Food Price Watch* (April 2011), p. 2.

116 Poverty Reduction and Equity Group, *Food Price Watch* (February 2011), p. 1.

117 Ibid., p. 1.

118 Ibid., p. 1.

119 Leahy, 'Rampant speculation inflated food price bubble.'

120 Carolyn Cui, 'Focus turns to Glencore's role in wheat ban,' *Wall Street Journal*, 5 August 2010, www.wsj.com/articles/SB1000142405274870465750457541175163754456, accessed 10 December 2015.

121 Logical inferences are necessitated by the fact that all of Glencore's speculation was proprietary. The limited information available was disclosed only in the process of Glencore's initial public offering.

122 Cui, 'Focus turns to Glencore's role in wheat ban.'

123 Javier Blas and Jack Farchy, 'Glencore reveals bet on grain price rise,' *Financial Times*, 24 April 2011, www.ft.com/intl/cms/s/0/aea76c56-6ea5-11e0-a13b-00144feabdco.html#axzz3txJp24in, accessed 10 December 2015.

124 Ibid.

125 Other large consumers of Russian wheat include Turkey, Syria, Iran and Libya.

126 Leahy, 'Rampant speculation inflated food price bubble.'

127 Poverty Reduction and Equity Group, *Food Price Watch* (April 2011), p. 7.

128 Geert Almekinders, Aliona Cebotari and Andreas Billmeier, *Arab Republic of Egypt: Selected Issues* (Washington, DC: International Monetary Fund, 2007), p. 42; Mary Curtis et al., *Emerging Consumer Survey 2012* (Zurich: Credit Suisse Research Institute, 2012), p. 33.

129 Nader Noureldeen, 'The risks of food subsidies,' *Al-Ahram Weekly*, 18–24 October 2012, p. 19.

130 Poverty Reduction and Equity Group, *Food Price Watch* (February 2011), p. 2.

131 Blas and Farchy, 'Glencore reveals bet on grain price rise.'

132 'Speculation in agricultural commodities: driving up the price of food worldwide and plunging millions into hunger,' Global Research: Centre for Research on Globalization, www.globalresearch.ca/speculation-in-agricultural-commodities-driving-up-the-price-of-food-worldwide-and-plunging-millions-into-hunger/26941, accessed 27 February 2015.

133 My thanks to Harry Cleaver for this historical parallel.

134 Chris Arsenault, 'Glencore: profiteering from hunger and chaos,' *Al Jazeera*, 9 May 2011, www.aljazeera.com/indepth/features/2011/05/2011572314985212o.html, accessed 28 February 2015.

135 Robert Springborg, 'The political economy of the Arab Spring,' *Mediterranean Politics*, 16(3): 428.

136 Ray Bush, 'Marginality or abjection? The political economy of poverty production in Egypt,' in *Marginality and Exclusion in Egypt*, ed. Ray Bush and Habib Ayeb (London: Zed Books, 2012), p. 58.

137 Adam Hanieh, *Lineages of Revolt: Issues of Contemporary Capitalism in the Middle East* (Chicago: Haymarket Books, 2013), pp. 2 and 173.

138 Ollman, *Dance of the Dialectic*, p. 71.

139 Joel Beinin, 'Workers' struggles under "socialism" and neoliberalism,' in *Egypt: Moment of Change*, ed. Rabab El-Mahdi and Philip Marfleet (London: Zed Books, 2009), p. 85.

140 Joel Beinin, 'Workers protest in Egypt: neo-liberalism and class struggle in 21st century,' *Social Movement Studies*, 8(4): 449.

141 Walden Bello, *The Food Wars* (London: Verso, 2009), pp. 1–2.

142 Poverty Reduction and Equity Group, *Food Price Watch* (February 2011), p. 5; United Nations Development Programme, *Arab Human Development Report 2009*, p. 125.

143 United Nations Development Programme, *Arab Human Development Report 2009*, p. 125.

144 World Health Organization, 'The National Survey on Chronic Disease and Their Risk Factors, for age group 15–65 years, Egypt, 2005–2006,' n.d., www.who.int/chp/steps/STEPS_FactSheet_Egypt.pdf, accessed 28 March 2015.

145 United Nations Development Programme, *Arab Human Development Report 2009*, p. 126.

146 World Health Organization, 'Country and regional data on diabetes,' n.d., www.who.int/diabetes/facts/world_figures/en/index2.html, accessed 28 March 2015.

147 Marx, *Capital*, vol. I, p. 381.

148 Earl (Tim) Sullivan, 'Youth power and the revolution,' in *Egypt's Tahrir Revolution*, ed. Dan Tschirgi, Walid Kazziha and Sean F. McMahon, (Boulder, CO: Lynne Rienner Publishers, 2013), p. 67–87; Dina Shehata, 'Youth movements and the 25 January revolution,' in *Arab Spring in Egypt: Revolution and Beyond*, ed. Bahgat Korany and Rabab El-Mahdi, (Cairo: The American University in Cairo Press, 2012), p. 105–24; Daniel LaGraffe, 'The youth bulge in Egypt: an intersection of demographics, security and the Arab Spring,' *Journal of Strategic Security*, 5(2): 65–80; Nadine Sika, 'Youth political engagement in Egypt: from abstention to uprising,' *British Journal of Middle Eastern Studies*, 39(2): 181–99.

149 Rabab El-Mahdi, 'Against marginalization: workers, youth and class in the 25 January revolution,' in *Marginality and Exclusion in Egypt*, ed. Ray Bush and Habib Ayeb (London: Zed Books, 2012), p. 133.

150 Gilbert Achcar, *The People Want: A Radical Exploration of the Arab Uprising* (London: Saqi Books, 2013), p. 42.

151 Marx, *Capital*, vol. I, p. 794.

152 Ibid., p. 784.

153 Cleaver, *Reading* Capital *Politically*, p. 57.

154 Karl Marx, *Grundrisse* (New York: Vintage Books, 1973), p. 128.

155 Ibid., p. 128.

156 Ibid., p. 205.

157 Ibid., p. 128.

158 In a prescient manner, Marx also says in the *Grundrisse*: '[t]he rise in the grain price is = to the fall in the price of all other commodities. The increased cost of production (represented by the price) at which the quarter of wheat is obtained is = to the decreased productivity of capital in all other forms. The surplus used to purchase grain [from abroad] must correspond to a deficit in the purchase of all other production and hence already a decline in their prices . . . the nation would find itself in a crisis not confined to grain, but extending to all other branches of production.' Ibid., p. 129.

159 Harry Cleaver, 'Food, famine and the international crisis,' la.utexas.edu/users/hcleaver/Zerowork/CleaverFoodFamine.html, accessed 31 March 2015.

160 Harry Cleaver, 'Karl Marx: economist or revolutionary,' la.utexas.edu/users/hcleaver/MarxEcoorRev.html, accessed 31 March 2015.

161 Cleaver, *Reading* Capital *Politically*, p. 95.

162 Poverty Reduction and Equity Group, *Food Price Watch* (April 2011), p. 4.

163 Cleaver, *Reading* Capital *Politically*, p. 87.

164 Marx, *Capital*, vol. I, p. 274.

165 My thanks to Harry Cleaver for this insight.

166 Cleaver, *Reading* Capital *Politically*.

167 Ibid., p. 95.

Chapter 3

1 Bertell Ollman, *Dance of the Dialectic: Steps in Marx's Method* (Chicago: University of Illinois Press, 2003), p. 86.

2 Karl Marx, *Capital*, vol. III: *The Process of Capitalist Production as a Whole* (London: Penguin Books, 1991), p. 428.

3 David Harvey, *A Companion to Marx's* Capital VOLUME TWO (London: Verso, 2013), p. 145.

4 Ibid., p. 146.

5 David Harvey, *A Brief History of Neoliberalism* (Oxford: Oxford University Press, 2007), p. 5.

6 David Harvey, *A Companion to Marx's* Capital (London: Verso, 2010), p. 42.

7 Karl Marx, *Capital*, vol. I: *The Process of Production of Capital* (London: Penguin, 1976), pp. 272–3.

8 Ibid., p. 280.

9 Ibid., p. 344.

10 E. H. Carr, *The Twenty Years' Crisis: 1919–1939* (New York: Palgrave, 2001), p. 43.

11 'Interview for *Woman's Own* ("no such thing as society"),' Margaret Thatcher Foundation, www.margaretthatcher.org/document/106689, accessed 14 April 2015.

12 Carr, *The Twenty Years' Crisis*, pp. 45–50.

13 Ibid., p. 192.

14 Samir Amin, *The Implosion of Capitalism* (London: Pluto Press, 2014), p. 139.

15 Tim Mitchell, 'No factories, no problems: the logic of neo-liberalism in Egypt,' *Review of African Political Economy*, 26(82): 455.

16 Hamid Dabashi, *The Arab Spring: The End of Postcoloniality* (London: Zed Books, 2012), p. 238.

17 Ursula Huws, 'Crisis as capitalist opportunity: the new accumulation through public service commodification,' in *Social Register 2012: The Crisis and the Left*, ed. Leo Panitch, Greg Albo and Vivek Chibber (Pontypool: Merlin Press, 2011), p. 65.

18 Walter Armbrust, 'The revolution against neoliberalism,' in *The Dawn of the Arab Uprisings: End of an Old Order?*, ed. Bassam Haddad, Rosie Bsheer and Ziad Abu-Rish (London: Pluto Press, 2012), pp. 113–23;

Hazem Kandil, 'Why did the Egyptian middle class march to Tahrir Square, *Mediterranean Politics*, 17(2): 197–215; Jack Goldstone, 'Understanding the revolutions of 2011,' *Foreign Affairs*, 90(3): 8–16.

19 Ann M. Lesch, 'Concentrated power breeds corruption, repression, and resistance,' in *Arab Spring in Egypt: Revolution and Beyond*, ed. Bahgat Korany and Rabab El-Mahdi (Cairo: The American University in Cairo Press, 2012), p. 29.

20 Abdel Rahman Shalaby, 'Presidential scion Gamal Mubarak took LE189.45 million in profits from EFG-Hermes,' *Egypt Independent*, 15 February 2011, www.egyptindependent.com/news/presidential-scion-gamal-mubarak-took-le18945-million-profits-efg-hermes, accessed 16 April 2015.

21 Lesch, 'Concentrated power breeds corruption,' p. 29.

22 Ibid., p. 30.

23 'Former trade minister and daughter sentenced to 15 years in prison,' *Mada Masr*, 20 August 2014, www.madamasr.com/news/former-trade-minister-and-daughter-sentenced-15-years-prison, accessed 16 April 2015,; Sherine El Madany, 'Court sentences ex-trade minister to 5 years,' *Daily News Egypt*, 26 June 2011, www.dailynewsegypt.com/2011/06/26/court-sentences-ex-trade-minister-to-5-years/, accessed 16 April 2015.

24 M. Cherif Bassiouni, 'Corruption cases against officials of the Mubarak regime,' Egyptian-American Rule of Law Association, 23 March 2012, www.earla.org/userfiles/file/Bassiouni%20Corruption%20Cases%20Against%20Mubarak_EARLA%20Letterhead%20(march%202012).pdf, accessed 16 April 2015.

25 Adam Hanieh, *Lineages of Revolt: Issues of Contemporary Capitalism in the Middle East* (Chicago: Haymarket Books, 2013), p. 141.

26 Ibid., p. 141.

27 Ibid., p. 141.

28 Ibid., p. 138.

29 Ibid., p. 141.

30 Ibid., pp. 138–9.

31 Ibid., p. 141.

32 Mitchell, 'No factories, no problems,' p. 458.

33 Hanieh, *Lineages of Revolt*, p. 140.

34 Ibid., p. 140.

35 Joel Beinin and Joe Stork, 'On the modernity, historical specificity, and international context of political Islam,' in *Political Islam: Essays from Middle East Report*, ed. Joel Beinin (Berkeley: University of California Press, 1997), p. 8; Joel Beinin, 'Neo-liberal structural adjustment, political demobilization and neo-authoritarianism in Egypt,' in *The Arab State and Neo-Liberal Globalization: The Restructuring of State Power in the Middle East*, ed. Laura Guazzone and Daniela Pioppi (Cairo: The American University in Cairo Press, 2009), p. 33.

36 Beinin, 'Neo-liberal structural adjustment,' p. 34.

37 Gilbert Achcar, *The People Want: A Radical Exploration of the Arab Uprising* (London: Saqi Books, 2013), p. 120.

38 Gilbert Achcar, 'Eleven theses on the resurgence of Islamic fundamentalism,'

International Viewpoint, 24 September 2006, www.internationalviewpoint. org/spip.php?article1132, accessed 19 April 2015.

39 Samir Amin, *The People's Spring: The Future of the Arab Revolution* (Nairobi: Pambazuka Press, 2012), p. 27.

40 Amira Howeidy, 'The Brotherhood's engineer,' *Al-Ahram Weekly Online*, 29 March–4 April 2012, weekly.ahram.org.eg/2012/1091/eg21.htm, accessed 1 May 2015.

41 'Interview with MB businessman Hassan Malek,' *IkhwanWeb: The Muslim Brotherhood's Official English website*, 1 December 2007, www. ikhwanweb.com/article.php?id=14751, accessed 1 May 2015.

42 Nadine Marroushi, 'Egyptian Business Development Association launching new projects,' *Egypt Independent*, 30 July 2012, www.egyptindependent. com/news/egyptian-business-development-association-launching-new-projects, accessed 1 May 2015.

43 Ammar Ali Hassan, 'The Brotherhood's abluted capitalism,' *Al-Ahram Weekly*, 25–31 October 2012, p. 18.

44 Ibid., p. 18.

45 Ibid., p. 18.

46 Marx, *Capital*, vol. III, pp. 442–4.

47 Ibid., p. 446.

48 Ibid. *Marx, Capital Volume III*, p. 444.

49 Harvey, *A Companion to Marx's* Capital VOLUME TWO, p. 150.

50 Ibid., p. 153.

51 Sameh Naguib, 'Islamism(s) old and new,' in *Egypt: The Moment of Change*, ed. Rabab El-Mahdi and Philip Marfleet (London: Zed Books, 2009), pp. 115–16.

52 Ibid., p. 114.

53 Ibid., p. 109.

54 Samir Amin, 'Political Islam in the service of imperialism,' *Monthly Review: An Independent Socialist Magazine*, 59(7): 2.

55 Wael Eskandar, 'Brothers and officers: a history of pacts,' *Jadaliyya*, 25 January 2013, www.jadaliyya.com/pages/index/9765/brothers-and-officers_a-history-of-pacts, accessed 18 February 2013.

56 Imad Harb, 'The Egyptian military in politics: disengagement or accomodation?,' *Middle East Journal*, 57(2): 272.

57 Ahmed Hashim, 'The Egyptian military, part two: from Mubarak onward,' *Middle East Policy*, 18(4): 109.

58 Achcar, *The People Want*, pp. 182–3.

59 Shana Marshall and Joshua Stacher, 'Egypt's generals and transnational capital,' *Middle East Research and Information Project*, 262 (Spring 2012), www.merip.org/mer/mer262/egypts-generals-transnational-capital, accessed 11 December 2015.

60 Robert Springborg, 'The president and the field marshal: civil–military relations in Egypt today,' *Middle East Report*, 147 (Jul./Aug. 1987), p. 10.

61 Zeinab Abul-Magd, 'The army and the economy in Egypt,' *Jadaliyya*, 23 December 2011, www.jadaliyya.com/pages/index/3732/the-army-and-the-economy-in-egypt, accessed 1 April 2015.

62 Marshall and Stacher, 'Egypt's generals and transnational capital.'

63 Clement Henry and Robert Springborg, 'A Tunisian solution for Egypt's military: why Egypt's military will not be able to govern,' *Foreign Affairs*, 21 February 2011, www.foreignaffairs.com/articles/tunisia/2011-02-21/tunisian-solution-egypt-s-military, accessed 1 April 2015.

64 Yezid Sayigh, *Above the State: The Officers' Republic in Egypt* (Washington, DC: Carnegie Endowment for International Peace, 2012), p. 9.

65 Ibid., p. 9.

66 Quintin Hoare and Geoffrey Nowell Smith, *Selections from the Prison Notebooks of Antonio Gramsci* (New York: International Publishers, 2008), p. 212.

67 Zeinab Abul-Magd, 'Understanding SCAF: the long reign of Egypt's generals,' *Cairo Review of Global Affairs*, 6 (Summer 2012), p. 155; Ahmed Morsy, 'The military crowds out civilian business in Egypt,' Carnegie Endowment for International Peace, 24 June 2014, carnegieendowment.org/2014/06/24/military-crowds-out-civilian-business-in-egypt, accessed 1 April 2015.

68 Springborg, 'The president and the field marshal,' p. 13.

69 Ibid., p. 13.

70 Marx, *Capital*, vol. I, pp. 713–18.

71 Abul-Magd, 'The army and the economy in Egypt.'

72 Marshall and Stacher, 'Egypt's generals and transnational capital.'

73 Morsy, 'The military crowds out civilian business in Egypt.'

74 Springborg, 'The president and the field marshal,' p. 7.

75 Marshall and Stacher, 'Egypt's generals and transnational capital.'

76 Zeinab Abul-Magd, 'The Egyptian republic of retired generals,' *Foreign Policy*, 8 May 2012, foreignpolicy.com/2012/05/08/the-egyptian-republic-of-retired-generals/, accessed 1 April 2015.

77 Abul-Magd, 'The army and the economy in Egypt.'

78 Sayigh, *Above the State*, p. 14. See also: Hicham Bou Nassif, 'Wedded to Mubarak: The second careers and financial rewards of Egypt's military elite, 1981–2011,' *Middle East Journal*, 67(4): 509–30.

79 Sayigh, *Above the State*, p. 14.

80 Marx, *Capital*, vol. I, p. 638.

81 Springborg, 'The president and the field marshal,' p. 14.

82 Timothy Mitchell, *Rule of Experts: Egypt: Techno-Politics, Modernity* (Berkeley: University of California Press, 2002), p. 241.

83 Springborg, 'The president and the field marshal,' p. 8.

84 Abul-Magd, 'The army and the economy in Egypt.'

85 Springborg, 'The president and the field marshal,' p. 14.

86 Morsy, 'The military crowds out civilian business in Egypt.'

87 Delwin A. Roy, 'The hidden economy in Egypt,' *Middle Eastern Studies*, 28(4): 702.

88 Ibid., p. 704.

89 Marx, *Capital*, vol. I, p. 312.

90 Abul-Magd, 'The army and the economy in Egypt.'

91 Karl Marx, *Capital*, vol. II: *The Process of Circulation of Capital* (London: Penguin, 1992), p. 229.

92 Ibid., p. 135.

93 Ibid., p. 135.

94 Mitchell, *Rule of Experts*, p. 241.

95 'National projects,' Egypt's Ministry of Defense, www.mod.gov.eg/Mod/Mod_EAA.aspx, accessed 10 May 2015.

96 Sayigh, *Above the State*, p. 16.

97 Marshall and Stacher, 'Egypt's generals and transnational capital.'

98 Ibid.

99 Nassif, 'Wedded to Mubarak,' p. 523.

100 Ibid., p. 524.

101 Sayigh, *Above the State*, p. 17.

102 'Telecom Egypt S.A.E. TEEG TE announces change to its board of directors,' *Bloomberg News*, 9 March 2011, www.bloomberg.com/apps/news?pid=newsarchive&sid=akanqTy6I1Uk, accessed 16 May 2015.

103 James Glanz and John Markoff, 'Egypt's leaders find "off" switch for internet,' *New York Times*, 15 February 2011, www.nytimes.com/2011/02/16/technology/16internet.html?_r=2&pagewanted=all, accessed 16 May 2015.

104 Marx, *Capital*, vol. II, p. 205.

105 Marx, *Capital*, vol. III, p. 425.

106 Eskandar, 'Brothers and officers: a history of pacts.'

107 Hashim, 'The Egyptian military, part two: from Mubarak onward,' p. 113.

108 Paul Amar, 'Why Mubarak is out,' in *The Dawn of the Arab Uprisings: End of an Old Order?*, ed. Bassam Haddad, Rosie Bsheer and Ziad Abu-Rish (London: Pluto Press, 2012), pp. 85–6.

109 Abul-Magd, 'The army and the economy in Egypt.'

110 Harvey, *A Companion to Marx's* Capital VOLUME TWO, p. 111.

111 Marshall and Stacher, 'Egypt's generals and transnational capital.'

112 World Bank, *Doing Business 2008: Comparing Regulations in 178 Economies* (Washington, DC: World Bank Group, 2007), p. 2.

113 Hugh Tomlinson, 'Saudis told Obama not to humiliate Mubarak,' *The Times*, 10 February 2011, www.thetimes.co.uk/tto/news/, accessed 14 May 2011.

114 Eva Bellin, 'Reconsidering the robustness of authoritarianism in the Middle East: Lessons from the Arab Spring,' *Comparative Politics*, 44(2): 131.

Chapter 4

1 Roger Owen, *State, Power and Politics in the Making of the Modern Middle East*, 3rd edn (London: Routledge Press, 2007), p. 116.

2 Joel Beinin, 'Neo-liberal structural adjustment, political demobilization and neo-authoritarianism in Egypt,' in *The Arab State and Neo-Liberal Globalization: The Restructuring of State Power in the Middle East*, ed. Laura Guazzone and Daniela Pioppi (Cairo: The American University in Cairo Press, 2009), p. 19.

3 Ibrahim G. Aoude, 'From national bourgeois development to *infitah*: Egypt 1952–1991,' *Arab Studies Quarterly*, 16(1): 13 (emphasis added).

4 Ibid., p. 14.

5 Ibid., p. 9.

6 Ibid., p. 2.

7 Moushira ElGeziri, 'Marginalization and self-marginalization: commercial education and its graduates,' in *Marginality and Exclusion in Egypt*, ed. Ray Bush and Habib Ayeb (London: Zed Books, 2012), p. 191.

8 Ibid., p. 196.

9 Zeinab Abul-Magd, 'Understanding SCAF: the long reign of Egypt's generals,' *Cairo Review of Global Affairs*, 6 (Summer 2012), p. 153.

10 Nadia Farah, 'The political economy of Egypt's revolution,' in *Egypt's Tahrir Revolution: Perspectives and Prospects*, ed. Dan Tschirgi, Walid Kazziha and Sean F. McMahon (Boulder, CO: Lynne Rienner, 2012), p. 53.

11 Ibid., p. 61.

12 Habib Ayeb, 'The marginalization of the small peasantry: Egypt and Tunisia,' in *Marginality and Exclusion in Egypt*, ed. Ray Bush and Habib Ayeb (London: Zed Books, 2012), pp. 78–9.

13 Ibid., pp. 79–80.

14 Ibid., p. 80.

15 Ibid., pp. 80–5.

16 Ulrich G. Wurzel, 'The political economy of authoritarianism in Egypt: insufficient structural reforms, limited outcomes and a lack of new actors,' in *The Arab State and Neo-Liberal Globalization: The Restructuring of State Power in the Middle East*, ed. Laura Guazzone and Daniela Pioppi (Cairo: The American University in Cairo Press, 2009), p. 103.

17 Farah, 'The political economy of Egypt's revolution,' p. 54.

18 Abul-Magd, 'Understanding SCAF: the long reign of Egypt's generals,' p. 155.

19 Philippe Droz-Vincent, 'The security sector in Egypt: management, coercion and external alliance under the dynamics of change,' in *The Arab State and Neo-Liberal Globalization: The Restructuring of State Power in the Middle East*, ed. Laura Guazzone and Daniela Pioppi (Cairo: The American University in Cairo Press, 2009), p. 244.

20 Galal Nasser, 'The army's side of the story,' *Al-Ahram Weekly*, 14–20 April 2011, weekly.ahram.org.eg/2011/1043/eg4.htm, accessed 2 May 2011.

21 Abul-Magd, 'Understanding SCAF: the long reign of Egypt's generals,' p. 155.

22 Nasser, 'The army's side of the story.'

23 Karen Aggestam, Laura Guazzone, Helena Lindholm Schultz, M. Cristina Paciello and Daniela Pioppi, 'The Arab state and neo-liberal globalization,' in *The Arab State and Neo-Liberal Globalization: The Restructuring of State Power in the Middle East*, ed. Laura Guzzone and Daniela Pioppi (Cairo: The American University in Cairo, 2009), p. 332.

24 Wurzel, 'The political economy of authoritarianism in Egypt,' pp. 100–1.

25 Frederick Engels, 'Engels to C. Schmidt, London, October 27, 1890,' in *Karl Marx and Frederick Engels: Selected Works in Two Volumes*, vol. II (London: Lawrence and Wishart, 1950), p. 450.

26 'GDP growth (annual %),' World Bank, data.worldbank.org/indicator/NY.GDP.MKTP.KD.ZG?page=1, accessed 15 October 2015.

27 Sameh Naguib, 'Islamism(s) old and new,' in *Egypt: The Moment of*

Change, ed. Rabab El-Mahdi and Philip Marfleet (London: Zed Books, 2009), p. 109.

28 Ibid., p. 115.

29 Beinin, 'Neo-liberal structural adjustment,' p. 39.

30 Wael Eskandar, 'Brothers and officers: a history of pacts,' *Jadaliyya*, 25 January 2013, www.jadaliyya.com/pages/index/9765/brothers-and-officers_a-history-of-pacts, accessed 18 February 2013.

31 Esam Al-Amin, 'Meet Egypt's future leaders,' *Counterpunch*, 9 February 2011, www.counterpunch.org/alamin02082011.html, accessed 30 April 2011.

32 Esam Al-Amin, 'When Egypt's revolution was at the crossroads,' *Counterpunch*, 9 March 2011, www.counterpunch.org/amin03092011. html, accessed 10 March 2011.

33 Ibid.

34 Quintin Hoare and Geoffrey Nowell Smith, *Selections from the Prison Notebooks of Antonio Gramsci* (New York: International Publishers, 2008), p. 212.

35 Lina El-Wardani, 'Egypt protests against anti-protest law,' *Al-Ahram Weekly*, 24 March 2011, english.ahram.org.eg/NewsContent/1/64/8484/Egypt/Politics-/Egypt-protests-against-antiprotest-law-.aspx, accessed 19 April 2011.

36 Jano Charbel, 'Labor activists organize despite legal hurdles,' *Al-Masry Al-Youm*, 15 April 2011, www.egyptindependent.com/news/labor-activists-organize-despite-legal-hurdles, accessed 16 April 2011.

37 'Summary of the Main Features of the Amended Law on Political Parties,' Egypt State Information Service, 29 March 2011, www.sis.gov.eg/en/Story.aspx?sid=54576, accessed 12 May 2011.

38 Ibid.

39 Eskandar, 'Brothers and officers: a history of pacts.'

40 Ibid.

41 Jano Charbel, 'One year on, labor revolution is stalling,' *Jadaliyya*, 24 January 2012, www.jadaliyya.com/pages/index/4139/one-year-on-labor-revolution-is-stalling, accessed 15 November 2012.

42 Jano Charbel, 'Labor law stalled as independent unions struggle for representation,' *Egypt Independent*, 26 June 2012, www.egyptindependent.com/news/labor-law-stalled-independent-unions-struggle-representation. See also Omar Halawa, 'A bill of rights for all? Economic and social provisions in draft constitution not strong enough,' *Egypt Independent*, 19 September 2012, accessed 20 September 2012, http://www.egyptindependent.com/news/bill-rights-all-economic-and-social-provisions-draft-constitution-not-strong-enough; and Jano Charbel, 'Political estrangement, legal challenges hamper labor movement,' *Egypt Independent*, 1 May 2012, accessed 1 May 2012, http://www.egyptindependent.com/news/political-estrangement-legal-challenges-hamper-labor-movement, accessed 29 June 2012.

43 'Ahead of planned strike, Egypt's army says it will not bow to threats, plots,' *Al-Arabiya News*, 11 February 2012, english.alarabiya.net/articles/2012/02/11/193874.html, accessed 16 November 2012.

44 Sarah Carr, 'Calls for civil disobedience not without criticism,' *Egypt*

Independent, 9 February 2012, www.egyptindependent.com/news/calls-civil-disobedience-not-without-criticism, accessed 11 February 2012.

45 'Call for open-ended strike divides Egypt,' *Egypt Independent*, 9 February 2012, www.egyptindependent.com/news/call-open-ended-strike-divides-egypt, accessed 10 February 2012.

46 'Criticism from "We Are All Khaled Saeed" hits at FJP paper's coverage of strike,' *Egypt Independent*, 22 July 2012, www.egyptindependent.com/news/criticism-we-are-all-khaled-saeed-hits-fjp-paper-s-coverage-strike, accessed 14 October 2012.

47 'Manpower Ministry to keep close watch on labor protests,' *Egypt Independent*, 15 August 2012, www.egyptindependent.com/news/manpower-ministry-keep-close-watch-labor-protests, accessed 15 August 2012.

48 Jano Charbel, 'No carrot, only stick: no concessions in government crackdown on strikes,' *Egypt Independent*, 19 September 2012, www.egyptindependent.com/news/no-carrot-only-stick-no-concessions-government-crackdown-strikes, accessed 20 September 2012.

49 'Statement of the Supreme Council of the Armed Forces (2),' Egypt State Information Service, 11 February 2011, www.sis.gov.eg/En/Story.aspx?sid=53693, accessed 4 May 2011.

50 'Statement of the Supreme Council of the Armed Forces (4),' Egypt State Information Service, 11 February 2011, www.sis.gov.eg/En/Story.aspx?sid=53695, accessed 4 May 2011.

51 Mostafa Omar, 'Egypt's spreading strikes,' SocialistWorker.org, 18 February 2011, socialistworker.org/2011/02/18/egypts-spreading-strikes, accessed 4 May 2011.

52 Nada El-Kouny, 'Egypt's anti-spy TV ad continues to stir controversy,' *Al-Ahram Online*, 12 June 2012, english.ahram.org.eg/NewsContentPrint/1/0/44653/Egypt/0/Egypts-antispy-TV-ad-continues-to-stir-controversy.aspx, accessed 21 January 2013.

53 'Hamas denies reports of members entering Egypt to sow chaos,' *Egypt Independent*, 16 June 2012, www.egyptindependent.com/news/hamas-denies-reports-members-entering-egypt-sow-chaos, accessed 16 June 2012.

54 'Brotherhood: Feloul, thugs, snipers responsible for Wednesday's violence,' *Egypt Independent*, 6 December 2012, www.egyptindependent.com/news/brotherhood-feloul-thugs-snipers-responsible-wednesday-s-violence, accessed 7 December 2012 (emphasis added).

55 'Update: Shater warns of "state of sabotage" ahead of referendum,' *Egypt Independent*, 8 December 2012, www.egyptindependent.com/news/update-shater-warns-state-sabotage-ahead-referendum, accessed 9 December 2012.

56 Fady Salah, 'Leading opposition figures accused of espionage,' *Daily News Egypt*, 5 December 2012, dailynewsegypt.com/2012/12/05/leading-opposition-figures-accused-of-espionage/, accessed 14 January 2013.

57 Andrew Quinn, 'U.S. pledges $150 million to help Egypt's transition,' Reuters, 17 February 2011, www.reuters.com/article/2011/02/17/us-egypt-usa-aid-idUSTRE71G5OY20110217, accessed 12 May 2011.

58 Elizabeth Arrott, 'Clinton promises support, money to new Egyptian

government,' VOANews.com, 14 March 2011, www.voanews.com/english/news/middle-east/Clinton-Promises-Support-Money-to-New-Egyptian-Government-118038774.html, accessed 10 May 2011.

59 'Clinton's remarks with Egyptian foreign minister Nabil Al-Araby, March 2011,' Council on Foreign Relations, 15 March 2011, www.cfr.org/egypt/clintons-remarks-egyptian-foreign-minister-nabil-al-araby-march-2011/p24390, accessed 12 May 2011.

60 'Remarks by the President on the Middle East and North Africa,' The White House – President Barack Obama, 19 May 2011, www.whitehouse.gov/the-press-office/2011/05/19/remarks-president-middle-east-and-north-africa, accessed 22 May 2011.

61 Ibid.

62 Ibid.

63 Amr Aref and Hania Moheeb, 'Hisham El Bastawisi: the reformist judge,' *Egypt Today*, 33(5): 68.

64 Nadine El Sayed and Hania Moheeb, 'Khaled Ali: the labor activist,' *Egypt Today*, 33(5): 82.

65 'Amre Moussa: the negotiator,' *Egypt Today*, 33(5): 35–6.

66 Khaled Dawoud, 'A revolutionary consensus,' *Al-Ahram Weekly*, 20–26 September 2012, p. 3.

67 Nadine El Sayed and Hania Moheeb, 'Ahmed Shafik: the air marshal,' *Egypt Today*, 33(5): 49.

68 Ibid., p. 50.

69 Ibid., p. 51.

70 Zeinab Abul-Magd, 'The Brotherhood's businessmen,' *Egypt Independent*, 13 February 2012, www.egyptindependent.com/opinion/brotherhoods-businessmen, accessed 14 February 2012.

71 Ibid.

72 Ibid. See also Shadi Hamid, 'Brother President,' *Cairo Review of Global Affairs*, 6 (Summer 2012), p. 127.

73 David Kirkpatrick, 'Egyptian is counting on worries of elite,' *New York Times*, 27 May 2012, www.nytimes.com/2012/05/28/world/middleeast/ahmed-shafik-counting-on-egyptian-elites-fears.html?pagewanted=all&_r=0, accessed 16 November 2012.

74 Rana Khazbak, 'Morsy strikes a power-sharing deal to shore up the presidency,' *Egypt Independent*, 1 July 2012, www.egyptindependent.com/news/morsy-strikes-power-sharing-deal-shore-presidency, accessed 1 July 2012.

75 'Egypt seeks to amend trade agreement with US, Israel,' *Egypt Independent*, 24 September 2012, www.egyptindependent.com/news/egypt-seeks-amend-trade-agreement-us-israel, accessed 26 September 2012.

76 Patrick Werr, 'Egypt's Brotherhood looks to private sector to boost economy,' Reuters.com, 6 June 2012, www.reuters.com/article/2012/06/06/us-egypt-election-economy-idUSBRE8550RK20120606, accessed 15 January 2013.

77 Stephen Kalin, 'In sukkuk, govt sees a solution to economic crisis,' *Egypt Independent*, 12 October 2012, www.egyptindependent.com/news/sukkuk-govt-sees-solution-economic-crisis, accessed 13 October 2012.

78 'Egypt balance of payments gap widens to $11.3 bln,' Reuters, 10 September 2012, www.reuters.com/article/2012/09/10/ozabs-egypt-payments-idAFJOE88901I20120910, accessed 16 November 2012.

79 'Egypt: international reserves and foreign currency liquidity,' International Monetary Fund, www.imf.org/external/np/sta/ir/IRProcessWeb/data/egy/eng/curegy.htm, accessed 16 November 2012.

80 Maggie Hyde, 'Serious govt action needed on economy, experts say,' *Egypt Independent*, 10 October 2012, www.egyptindependent.com/news/serious-govt-action-needed-economy-experts-say, accessed 13 October 2012.

81 'Morsy rules out currency devaluation,' *Egypt Independent*, 27 August 2012, www.egyptindependent.com/news/morsy-rules-out-currency-devaluation, accessed 28 August 2012.

82 Alexandre Goudineau, 'Government pursues ways to increase tax revenue,' *Egypt Independent*, 15 October 2012, www.egyptindependent.com/news/government-pursues-ways-increase-tax-revenue-0, accessed 16 October 2012.

83 'Qandil holds meeting to lure investors to Egypt,' *Egypt Independent*, 17 September 2012, www.egyptindependent.com/news/qandil-holds-meeting-lure-investors-egypt, accessed 20 September 2012.

84 'MoU with the IMF,' *Al-Ahram Weekly*, 15–21 November 2012, p. 10.

85 'Back to basics,' *Al-Ahram Weekly*, 15–21 November 2012, p. 10. The proposed income tax structure was as follows: first bracket (LE9,000–LE20,000): 10 percent; second bracket (LE20,000–LE40,000): 15 percent; third bracket (LE40,000–LE1 million): 20 percent; fourth bracket (LE1 million–LE10 million): 22 percent; and fifth bracket (LE10 million and up): 25 percent.

86 Samer Atallah, 'The visit of "Mrs. Box",' *Al-Ahram Weekly*, 15–21 November 2012, p. 10.

87 'Central Bank to start 28-day repos in July,' Reuters.com, 15 June 2012, www.reuters.com/article/2012/06/15/ozabs-egypt-repos-idAFJOE85E03320120615, accessed 15 June 2012; Sean F. McMahon, 'Forget the court ruling and elections!: Fitch downgraded Egypt,' *Middle East Online*, 27 June 2012, www.middle-east-online.com/english/?id=53081, accessed 12 December 2015.

88 Wolfgang Streeck, 'The crises of democratic capitalism,' *New Left Review*, 71 (Sept./Oct. 2011), p. 14.

89 Sara Aggour and Doaa Farid, 'Minimum income deemed "unjust",' *Daily News Egypt*, 22 September 2012, www.dailynewsegypt.com/2013/09/22/minimum-income-deemed-unjust/, accessed 21 October 2015.

90 Maggie Hyde, 'In debate over devaluating the pound, officials avoid sparking panic,' *Egypt Independent*, 4 September 2012, www.egyptindependent.com/news/debate-over-devaluating-pound-officials-avoid-sparking-panic, accessed 6 September 2012; Patrick Werr and Yasmine Saleh, 'Egypt's leader sees currency stabilizing "within days",' Reuters.com, 31 December 2012, www.reuters.com/article/2012/12/31/us-egypt-currency-idUSBRE8BS09620121231, accessed 31 December 2012.

91 'Morsy rules out currency devaluation.'

92 Maggie Hyde, 'Up against a fiscal wall, government courts foreign

investment,' *Egypt Independent*, 11 October 2012, www.egyptindependent. com/news/against-fiscal-wall-government-courts-foreign-investment, accessed 13 October 2012.

93 International Monetary Fund, 'Costly Mideast subsidies need better targeting,' *IMF Survey Magazine: Countries and Regions*, 14 May 2012, www.imf.org/ external/pubs/ft/survey/so/2012/car051412b.htm, accessed 22 October 2015.

94 Isobel Coleman, 'Reforming Egypt's untenable subsidies,' Council on Foreign Relations, 6 April 2012, www.cfr.org/egypt/reforming-egypts-untenable-subsidies/p27885, accessed 22 October 2015.

95 Ibid.

96 Patrick Kingsley, 'Bakers become the latest victims of subsidy cuts,' *Guardian*, 19 March 2013, www.theguardian.com/world/2013/mar/19/ bakers-egyptian-subsidy-cuts, accessed 22 October 2015.

97 Coleman, 'Reforming Egypt's untenable subsidies.'

98 Nariman Youssef, 'Egypt's draft constitution translated,' *Egypt Independent*, 2 December 2012, www.egyptindependent.com/news/egypt-s-draft-constitution-translated, accessed 19 October 2015.

99 Youssef, 'Egypt's draft constitution translated.'

100 Christoffer Dahl, *Comparing Egypt's Constitutions* (New York: Carnegie Endowment, 2013), p. 20.

101 Jano Charbel, 'Egypt's Constitution seen to curtail labor rights and workers freedoms,' *Egypt Independent*, 22 January 2013, www.egyptindependent. com/news/egypt-s-constitution-seen-curtail-labor-rights-and-workers-freedoms, accessed 19 October 2015.

102 Michael C. Williams and Keith Krause, 'Preface: Toward critical security studies,' in *Critical Security Studies: Concepts and Cases*, ed. M. Williams and K. Krause (London: Routledge Press, 2007), p. x.

103 Sean F. McMahon, 'Temporality, peace initiatives and Palestinian–Israeli politics,' *Middle East Critique*, 25(1): 5–21.

104 David Harvey, *A Companion to Marx's* Capital *VOLUME TWO* (London: Verso, 2013), p. 153.

105 Dahl, *Comparing Egypt's Constitutions*, p. 5.

106 'Islamist parties seek to end Parliament's farmer and worker quota,' *Egypt Independent*, 9 March 2012, www.egyptindependent.com/news/islamist-parties-seek-end-parliaments-farmer-and-worker-quota, accessed 9 March 2012.

107 Ibid.

108 Ibid.

109 Gamal Essam El-Din, 'Up for debate,' *Al-Ahram Weekly*, 18–24 October 2012, p. 3.

110 Dahl, *Comparing Egypt's Constitutions*, p. 15.

111 Ibid., p. 15.

112 Harry Cleaver, *Reading* Capital *Politically* (Austin: University of Texas Press, 1979), p. 122.

113 Robert Cox, *Production, Power and World Order: Social Forces in the Making of History* (New York: Columbia University Press, 1987), p. 50.

114 Ibid., p. 351.

115 Lally Weymouth, 'Excerpts from Washington Post interview with Egyptian

Gen. Abdel Fatah al-Sissi,' *Washington Post*, 5 August 2013, www. washingtonpost.com/world/middle_east/washington-post-interviews-egyptian-gen-abdel-fatah-al-gen-sissi/2013/08/03/6409e0a2-fbc0-11e2-a369-d1954abcb7e3_story.html, accessed 26 October 2015.

116 In a curious instance of negation of the negation, the bourgeois scaling of contradiction commercial capital realized in 2011 to its interest produced, in 2013, political demands that undid commercial capital's political form.

117 'Egypt army chief Gen Abdul Fattah al-Sisi statement,' *BBC News*, 4 July 2015, www.bbc.com/news/world-middle-east-23175529, accessed 24 October 2015.

118 Ibid.

119 Amr Adly, 'Egypt's conservative nationalism: discourse and praxis of the new regime,' Carnegie Middle East Center, 14 October 2014, carnegie-mec.org/publications/?fa=56934, accessed 24 October 2015.

120 Weymouth, 'Excerpts from Washington Post interview with Egyptian Gen. Abdel Fatah al-Sissi.'

121 Adly, 'Egypt's conservative nationalism: discourse and praxis of the new regime.'

122 Fatima Ramadan and Amr Adly, 'Low-cost authoritarianism: the Egyptian regime and labor movement since 2013,' Carnegie Middle East Center, 17 September 2015, carnegie-mec.org/2015/09/17/low-cost-authoritarianism-egyptian-regime-and-labor-movement-since-2013/ihui, accessed 22 October 2015.

123 Michelle Dunne, 'Egypt's nationalists dominate in a politics-free zone,' Carnegie Endowment for International Peace, 15 April 2015, carnegieendowment.org/2015/04/15/egypt-s-nationalists-dominate-in-politics-free-zone, accessed 24 October 2015.

124 'Egypt chief editors pledge support for state institutions,' *Al-Ahram Online*, 26 October 2014, english.ahram.org.eg/News/114013.aspx, accessed 24 October 2015.

125 Dunne, 'Egypt's nationalists dominate in a politics-free zone.'

126 Mark Levine, 'Egypt: cracking down on labor activists?,' *Al Jazeera*, 12 September 2013, www.aljazeera.com/indepth/opinion/2013/09/2013911738155508853.html, accessed 13 September 2013.

127 Mahmoud Salem, 'Egypt's gift to the world: the multibillion dollar "New Suez Canal" project makes no economic sense, but it's powerful PR,' *Politico*, 18 August 2015, www.politico.eu/article/egypt-suez-canal-sisi-regime-cairo-government-trade/, accessed 24 October 2015.

128 Heba Habib and Erin Cunningham, 'Egypt's "gift to the world" cost $8 billion and probably wasn't necessary,' *Washington Post*, 6 August 2015, www.washingtonpost.com/news/worldviews/wp/2015/08/06/egypts-gift-to-the-world-cost-8-billion-and-probably-wasnt-necessary/, accessed 24 October 2015.

129 'Full text of Sisi's speech at the New Suez Canal Inauguration Ceremony,' *Cairo Post*, 6 August 2015, www.thecairopost.com/news/163086/news/full-text-of-sisis-speech-at-new-suez-canal-inauguration-ceremony, accessed 29 October 2015.

130 Jared Malsin, 'Egypt hails $8bn Suez canal expansion as gift to world at

lavish ceremony,' *Guardian*, 6 August 2015, www.theguardian.com/world/2015/aug/06/egypt-suez-canal-expansion, accessed 24 October 2015.

131 Ibid.

132 Weymouth, 'Excerpts from Washington Post interview with Egyptian Gen. Abdel Fatah al-Sissi.'

133 Ahmed Feteha, 'Egypt shows off $8 billion expansion the world may not need,' *Bloomberg News*, 4 August 2015, www.bloomberg.com/news/articles/2015-08-04/egypt-shows-off-8-billion-suez-canal-gift-world-may-not-need, accessed 27 October 2015.

134 Ibid.

135 Heba Saleh, 'Egypt pins hopes on Suez Canal expansion,' *Financial Times*, 5 August 2015, www.ft.com/intl/cms/s/0/2c18da3a-3aa8-11e5-bbd1-b37bc06f590c.html, accessed 27 October 2015.

136 Ibid.

137 Feteha, 'Egypt shows off $8 billion expansion the world may not need.'

138 Karl Marx, *Capital*, vol. II: *The Process of Circulation of Capital* (London: Penguin Books, 1992), p. 390.

139 Ibid., pp. 552–3.

140 Feteha, 'Egypt shows off $8 billion expansion the world may not need.'

141 Amira El-Fekki, 'Despite long hours, "New Suez Canal" workers take pride in daunting task,' *Cairo Post*, 21 September 2014, www.thecairopost.com/news/125435/inside_egypt/despite-long-hours-new-suez-canal-workers-take-pride-in-daunting-task, accessed 29 October 2015; Dalia Gebrial, 'Workers' deaths reveal ugly side of Suez Canal expansion,' *Egyptian Streets*, 10 August 2015, egyptianstreets.com/2015/08/10/worker-deaths-reveal-ugly-side-of-suez-canal-expansion//, accessed 29 October 2015.

142 'Qatar to continue supporting Egypt,' *The Peninsula*, 5 July 2013, thepeninsulaqatar.com/news/qatar/243949/qatar-to-continue-supporting-egypt, accessed 30 October 2015.

143 Karl Marx, *Capital*, vol. I: *The Process of Production of Capital* (London, Penguin, 1976), p. 208.

144 In 2014, productive capital dispossessed commercial capital of the value of the Seoudi and Zad supermarket chains. Reopened after the forcible appropriation, Seoudi, and presumably Zad, sells increased quantities of commodities grown by, and bearing the surplus-value of, productive capital.

145 Ahmed Morsy, 'The military crowds out civilian business in Egypt,' Carnegie Endowment for International Peace, 24 June 2014, carnegieendowment.org/2014/06/24/military-crowds-out-civilian-business-in-egypt/, accessed 1 April 2015.

146 Amr Adly, 'The economics of Egypt's rising authoritarian order,' Carnegie Middle East Center, June 2014, p. 10, carnegie-mec.org/2014/06/18/economics-of-egypt-s-rising-authoritarian-order, accessed 30 October 2015.

147 Allison Corkery and Heba Khalil, 'Nothing new on the Nile,' *Foreign Policy*, 12 March 2015, foreignpolicy.com/2015/03/12/nothing-new-on-the-nile/, accessed 31 October 2015.

148 Rami Galal, 'Egypt hopes to lure investors back,' *Al Monitor*, 23 February 2015, www.al-monitor.com/pulse/originals/2015/02/egypt-new-law-investment-procedures.html#; Jack Shenker, 'Sharm el-Sheikh rumbles with grand promises of the international elite,' *Guardian*, 15 March 2015, www.theguardian.com/world/2015/mar/15/egyot-sharma-el-sheikh-rumbles-grand-promises, accessed 30 October 2015.

149 Dahl, *Comparing Egypt's Constitutions*, p. 20.

150 Ibid., p. 14.

151 Ibid., p. 12.

152 '2013 draft constitution: an unofficial translation,' *Mada Masr*, 13 January 2014, www.madamasr.com/sections/politics/2013-draft-constitution, accessed 3 November 2015.

153 Dahl, *Comparing Egypt's Constitutions*, p. 20.

154 Ibid., p. 19.

155 Ibid., pp. 19–20.

156 Ibid., p. 20.

157 Ibid., pp. 4–5.

158 Patrick Kingsley, 'Egypt places civilian infrastructure under army jurisdiction,' *Guardian*, 28 October 2014, www.theguardian.com/world/2014/oct/28/egypt-civilian-infrastructure-army-jurisdiction-miltary-court, accessed 24 October 2015.

159 'Comparing Egypt's 2012 and 2013 constitutions,' *Al Jazeera*, 14 January 2014, www.aljazeera.com/news/middleeast/2014/01/comparing-egypt-2012-2013-constitutions-2014114436315147.html, accessed 18 October 2015.

160 Dahl, *Comparing Egypt's Constitutions*, p. 15.

161 Ibid., p. 15.

162 Dunne, 'Egypt's nationalists dominate in politics-free zone.'

163 Marx, *Capital*, vol. I, p. 875.

164 'Egypt: retry or free 12,000 after unfair military trials,' Human Rights Watch, 10 September 2011, www.hrw.org/news/2011/09/10/egypt-retry-or-free-12000-after-unfair-military-trials, accessed 8 October 2011.

165 Joe Stork, 'Egypt's political prisoners,' Human Rights Watch, 6 March 2015, www.hrw.org/news/2015/03/06/egypts-political-prisoners, accessed 5 November 2015.

166 Menan Khater, 'Hundreds of torture cases in April: El-Nadeem Centre,' *Daily News Egypt*, 2 May 2015, www.dailynewsegypt.com/2015/05/02/hundreds-of-torture-cases-in-april-el-nadeem-centre/, accessed 5 November 2015.

167 'Egypt: security forces used excessive lethal force,' *Human Rights Watch*, 19 August 2013, www.hrw.org/news/2013/08/19/egypt-security-forces-used-excessive-lethal-force, accessed 5 November 2015.

168 Emma Goldman, 'The psychology of political violence,' in *Anarchy and Other Essays* (New York: Mother Earth Publishing, 1910), Kindle edn.

169 'Deadly attacks hit Egypt's Sinai,' *Al Jazeera*, 1 July 2015, www.aljazeera.com/news/2015/07/deaths-attacks-checkpoints-egypt-sinai-150701074350492.html, accessed 5 November 2015.

170 Rabab El-Mahdi, 'Labour protests in Egypt: causes and meanings,' *Review of African Political Economy*, 38(129): 390.

Chapter 5

1 'Muslim Brotherhood "stole" Egypt's revolution: Kerry,' *Al-Ahram Online*, 21 November 2013, english.ahram.org.eg/NewsContent/1/64/87099/Egypt/Politics-/-Muslim-Brotherhood-stole-Egypts-revolution-Kerry.aspx, accessed 22 November 2015.

2 Robert Fisk, *Robert Fisk on Egypt: A Revolution Betrayed* (London: Independent Print Ltd, 2014); Thanassis Cambanis, 'The final betrayal of Egypt's revolution,' *Foreign Policy*, 23 January 2015, foreignpolicy.com/2015/01/23/the-final-betrayal-of-egypts-revolution/, accessed 22 November 2015.

3 Jason Hickel, 'Neoliberal Egypt: the hijacked revolution,' *Al Jazeera*, 29 March 2012, www.aljazeera.com/indepth/opinion/2012/03/201232784226830522.html, accessed 22 November 2015.

4 Patrick Kingsley, 'Egypt's spring 2014: is the counter-revolution complete?,' *Guardian*, 23 March 2014, www.theguardian.com/world/2014/mar/23/egypt-spring-2014-counter-revolution, accessed 22 November 2015.

5 Menna Samir, 'Ministry of Housing denies termination of Cairo Capital MoU,' *Daily News Egypt*, 24 June 2015, www.dailynewsegypt.com/2015/06/24/ministry-of-housing-denies-termination-of-cairo-capital-mou/, accessed 24 November 2015.

6 Two interesting points of note: first, it is a common misstatement to say no bankers went to jail because of the crisis of 2007. Gamal Mubarak *was* imprisoned. Of course, in a telling move, he was subsequently released. Second, Glencore stock was driven to its lowest ever price in late September 2015. The company that accumulated capital so spectacularly at the expense of Egyptian workers in 2011 saw much of that capital centralized by other members of the finance faction. The value stolen from the Egyptian working class is now accumulating more capital for money capital.

7 Ben Sharples and Grant Smith, 'How low can oil go? Goldman says $20 a barrel is a possibility,' *Bloomberg Business*, 11 September 2015, www.bloomberg.com/news/articles/2015-09-11/-20-oil-possible-for-goldman-as-forecasts-cut-on-growing-glut, accessed 24 November 2015.

8 'Lagarde's call to action: GCC should impose taxes,' *Al Jazeera*, 15 November 2015, www.aljazeera.com/programmes/talktojazeera/2015/11/lagarde-call-action-oil-taxes-gcc-challenges-151113094249193.html, accessed 24 November 2015.

9 Joe Stork, 'Bailing out Sadat,' *Middle East Research and Information Project Report*, 56(1977): 8–11.

10 David Harvey, 'The enigma of capital and the crisis this time,' 30 August 2010, davidharvey.org/2010/08/the-enigma-of-capital-and-the-crisis-this-time/, accessed 28 November 2015.

11 Emir Nader, 'Concern as Defense Ministry sets sights on telecoms controls,'

Daily News Egypt, 12 May 2015, www.dailynewsegypt.com/2015/05/12/concern-as-defence-ministry-sets-sights-on-telecoms-controls/, accessed 26 November 2015.

12 'Is Cairo getting two more airports?,' *Cairo Scene*, 18 May 2015, www.cairoscene.com/BusinessAndPolitics/Two-Military-Airports-To-Host-Civilian-Flights, accessed 26 November 2015.

BIBLIOGRAPHY

Abdelrahman, M. (2012) 'A hierarchy of struggles? The "economic" and the "political" in Egypt's revolution,' *Review of African Political Economy*, 39(134): 614–28.

Abul-Magd, Z. (2011) 'The army and the economy in Egypt,' *Jadaliyya*, 23 December, www.jadaliyya.com/pages/index/3732/the-army-and-the-economy-in-egypt, accessed 1 April 2015.

— (2012) 'The Egyptian republic of retired generals,' *Foreign Policy*, 8 May, foreignpolicy.com/2012/05/08/the-egyptian-republic-of-retired-generals/, accessed 1 April 2015.

— (2012) 'Understanding SCAF: the long reign of Egypt's generals,' *Cairo Review of Global Affairs*, 6: 151–60.

Achcar, G. (2006) 'Eleven theses on the resurgence of Islamic fundamentalism,' www.internationalviewpoint.org/spip.php?article1132, accessed 19 April 2015.

— (2013) *The People Want: A Radical Exploration of the Arab Uprising*, London: Saqi Books.

Adly, A. (2014) 'The economics of Egypt's rising authoritarian order,' Carnegie Middle East Center, June, carnegie-mec.org/2014/06/18/economics-of-egypt-s-rising-authoritarian-order, accessed 30 October 2015.

— (2014) 'Egypt's conservative nationalism: discourse and praxis of the new regime,' Carnegie Middle East Center, 14 October, carnegie-mec.org/publications/?fa=56934, accessed 24 October 2015.

Aggestam, K., L. Guzaaone, H. Lindholm Schulz, M. Cristina Paciello and D. Pioppi (2009) 'The Arab state and neo-liberal globalization,' in L. Guzaaone and D. Pioppi (eds), *The Arab State and Neo-Liberal Globalization: The Restructuring of State Power in the Middle East*, Cairo: American University in Cairo Press, pp. 325–50.

Al-Ahram Online (2014) 'Egypt chief editors pledge support for state institutions,' *Al-Ahram Online*, 26 October, english.ahram.org.eg/News/114013.aspx, accessed 24 October 2015.

Al-Ahram Weekly (2012) 'Back to basics,' *Al-Ahram Weekly*, 15–21 November, p. 10.

— (2012) 'MoU with the IMF,' *Al-Ahram Weekly*, 15–21 November, p. 10.

Al-Amin, E. (2011) 'Meet Egypt's future rulers,' *Counterpunch*, 9 February, counterpunch.org/alamin02082011.html, accessed 30 April 2011.

— (2011) 'When Egypt's revolution was at the crossroads,' *Counterpunch*, 9 March, counterpunch.org/amin03092011.html, accessed 10 March 2011.

Albrecht, H. (2007) 'Authoritarian opposition and the politics of challenge in Egypt,' in O. Schlumberger (ed.), *Debating Arab Authoritarianism: Dynamics and Durability in Nondemocratic Regimes*, Stanford, CA: Standford University Press, pp. 59–74.

Albrecht, H. and D. Bishara (2011) 'Back on horseback: the military and political transformation in Egypt,' *Middle East Law and Governance*, 3: 13–23.

Almekinders, G., A. Cebotari and A. Billmeier (2007) *Arab Republic of Egypt: Selected Issues*, Washington, DC: International Monetary Fund.

Amar, P. (2012) 'Why Mubarak is out,' in B. Haddad, R. Bsheer and Z. Abu-Rish (eds), *The Dawn of the Arab Uprisings: End of an Old Order?*, London: Pluto Press, pp. 83–90.

Amin, S. (2007) 'Political Islam in the service of imperialism,' *Monthly Review: An Independent Socialist Magazine*, 59(7): 1–19.

— (2012) *The People's Spring: The Future of the Arab Revolution*, Nairobi: Pambazuka Press.

— (2014) *The Implosion of Capitalism*, London: Pluto Press.

Anderson, L. (2006) 'Searching where the light shines: studying democratization in the Middle East,' *Annual Review of Political Science*, 9: 189–214.

— (2011) 'Demystifying the Arab Spring,' *Foreign Affairs*, 90(3): 2–7.

— (2012) '"Early adopters" and "neighborhood effects",' in C. Henry and Jang Ji-Hyang (eds), *The Arab Spring: Will It Lead to Democratic Transitions?*, Seoul: Asan Institute for Policy Studies, pp. 27–32.

Aoude, I. (1994) 'From national bourgeois development to *infitah*: Egypt 1952–1991,' *Arab Studies Quarterly*, 16(1): 1–23.

Aref, A. and H. Moheeb (2013) 'Hisham El Bastawisi: the reformist judge,' *Egypt Today*, 33(5): 63–8.

Armbrust, W. (2012) 'The revolution against neoliberalism,' in B. Haddad, R. Bsheer and Z. Abu-Rish (eds), *The Dawn of the Arab Uprising: End of an Old Order?*, New York: Pluto Press, pp. 113–23.

Atallah, S. (2012) 'The visit of "Mrs. Box",' *Al-Ahram Weekly*, 15–21 November, p. 10.

Ayeb, H. (2012) 'The marginalization of the small peasantry: Egypt and Tunisia,' in R. Bush and H. Ayeb (eds), *Marginalization and Exclusion in Egypt*, London: Zed Books, pp. 72–96.

Barany, Z. (2011) 'The role of the military,' *Journal of Democracy*, 22(4): 24–35.

Beinin, J. (2009) 'Neo-liberal structural adjustment, political demobilization, and neo-authoritarianism in Egypt,' in L. Guzaaone and D. Pioppi (eds), *The Arab State and Neo-Liberal Globalization: The Restructuring of State Power in the Middle East*, Cairo: American University in Cairo Press, pp. 19–46.

— (2009) 'Workers' protest in Egypt: neo-liberalism and class struggle in 21st century,' *Social Movement Studies*, 8(4): 449–54.

— (2009) 'Workers' struggles under "socialism" and neoliberalism,' in R. El-Mahdi and P. Marfleet (eds), *Egypt: The Moment of Change*, London: Zed Books, pp. 68–86.

— (2012) 'The rise of Egypt's workers,' *Carnegie Papers*, Beirut: Carnegie Endowment for International Peace.

Beinin J. and J. Stork (1997) 'On the modernity, historical specificity, and international context of political Islam,' in J. Beinin (ed.), *Political Islam: Essays from Middle East Report*, Berkeley, University of California Press, pp. 3–31.

Bellin, E. (2004) 'The robustness of authoritarianism in the Middle East: exceptionalism in comparative perspective,' *Comparative Politics*, 36(2): 139–57.

— (2012) 'Reconsidering the robustness of authoritarianism in the Middle East: lessons from the Arab Spring,' *Comparative Politics*, 44(2): 127–49.

Bello, W. (2009) *The Food Wars*, London: Verso.

Bogaert, K. (2011) 'Global dimensions of the Arab Spring and the potential for anti-hegemonic politics,' *Jadaliyya*, 21 December, www.jadaliyya.com/pages/index/3638/global-dimensions-of-the-arab-spring-and-the-poten, accessed 28 November 2015.

— (2013) 'Contextualizing the Arab revolts: the politics behind three decades of neoliberalism in the Arab world,' *Middle East Critique*, 22(3): 213–34.

Bottoms, I. (2014) *Water Pollution in Egypt: Causes and Concerns*, Cairo: Egyptian Center for Economic and Social Rights.

Braudel, F. (1972) *The Mediterranean and the Mediterranean World in the Age of Philip I*, vol. II, trans. S. Reynolds, New York: Harper and Row.

Brown, N. J. (2013) 'Egypt's failed transition,' *Journal of Democracy*, 24(4): 45–58.

Brown, W. (2005) *Edgework: Critical Essays on Knowledge and Politics*, Princeton, NJ: Princeton University Press.

Bush, R. (2009) 'The land and the people,' in R. El-Mahdi and P. Marfleet (eds), *Egypt: The Moment of Change*, London: Zed Books, pp. 51–67.

— (2012) 'Marginality or abjection? The political economy of poverty production in Egypt,' in R. Bush and H. Ayeb (eds), *Marginality and Exclusion in Egypt*, London: Zed Books, pp. 55–71.

Cambanis, T. (2015) 'The final betrayal of Egypt's revolution,' *Foreign Policy*, 23 January, foreignpolicy.com/2015/01/23/the-final-betrayal-of-egypts-revolution/, accessed 22 November 2015.

Carr, E. H. (2001) *The Twenty Years Crisis: 1919–1939*, New York: Palgrave.

Cavatorta, F. and V. Durac (2011) *Civil Society and Democratization in the Arab World: The Dynamics of Activism*, London: Routledge.

Charbel, J. (2012) 'One year on, labor revolution is stalling,' *Jadaliyya*, 24 January, www.jadaliyya.com/pages/index/4139/one-year-on-labor-revolution-is-stalling, accessed 15 November 2012.

Cleaver, H. (n.d.) 'Food, famine and the international crisis,' la.utexas.edu/users/hcleaver/Zerowork/CleaverFoodFamine.html, accessed 15 November 2012.

— (n.d.) 'Karl Marx: economist or revolutionary,' la.utexas.edu/users/hcleaver/MarxEcoorRev.html, accessed 31 March 2015.

— (1979) *Reading* Capital *Politically*, Austin: University of Texas Press.

— (2012) 'Rupturing the dialectic: the struggle against work, financial crisis and beyond,' 22/23 October, la.utexas.edu/users/hcleaver/Rupturing.html, accessed 28 November 2015.

Cohen, G. A. (1978) *Karl Marx's Theory of History: A Defense*, Princeton, NJ: Princeton University Press.

Coleman, I. (2012) 'Reforming Egypt's untenable subsidies,' Council on Foreign Relations, 6 April, www.cfr.org/egypt/reforming-egypts-untenable-subsidies/p27885, accessed 22 October 2015.

Corkery, A. and H. Khalil (2015) 'Nothing new on the Nile,' *Foreign Policy*, 12 March, foreignpolicy.com/2015/03/12/nothing-new-on-the-nile/, accessed 31 October 2015.

Cox, R. (1987) *Production, Power and World Order: Social Forces in the Making of History*, New York: Columbia University Press.

Curtis, M. et al. (2012) *Emerging Consumer Survey 2012*, Zurich: Credit Suisse Research Institute.

Dabashi, H. (2012) *The Arab Spring: The End of Postcolonialism*, London: Zed Books.

Dahi, O. S. (2016) 'The political economy of the Egyptian and Arab revolt,' *Institute of Development Bulletin*, 43(1): 47–53.

Dahl, C. (2013) *Comparing Egypt's Constitutions*, New York: Carnegie Endowment, carnegieendowment.org/files/Comparing-Egypt-s-Constitutions.pdf, accessed 19 October 2015.

Dawoud, K. (2012) 'A revolutionary consensus,' *Al-Ahram Weekly*, 20–26 September, p. 3.

De Schutter, O. (2010) *Food Commodities Speculation and Food Price Crises: Regulation to reduce the risks of price volatility*, New York: United Nations.

Droz-Vincent, P. (2009) 'The security sector in Egypt: management, coercion and external alliance under the dynamics of change,' in L. Guzaaone and D. Pioppi (eds), *The Arab State and Neo-Liberal Globalization: The Restructuring of State Power in the Middle East*, Cairo: American University in Cairo Press, pp. 219–46.

Dunayevskaya, R. (2000) *Marxism and Freedom: From 1776 until Today*, New York: Humanity Books.

— (2003) *Philosophy and Revolution: From Hegel to Sartre, and from Marx to Mao*, New York: Lexington Books.

Dunne, M. (2015) 'Egypt's nationalists dominate in a politics-free zone,' Carnegie Endowment for International Peace, 15 April, carnegieendowment.org/2015/04/15/egypt-s-nationalists-dominate-in-politics-free-zone, accessed 24 October 2015.

Dunne, M. and T. Radwan (2013) 'Egypt: why liberalism still matters,' *Journal of Democracy*, 24(1): 86–100.

Egypt Today (2013) 'Amre Moussa: the negotiator,' *Egypt Today*, 33(5): 35–9.

Egyptian Center for Economic and Social Rights (n.d.) 'Water pollution in Egypt: causes and concerns,' ecesr.org/en/wp-content/uploads/2014/01/ECESR-Water-Pollution-In-Egypt-Causes-and-Concerns.pdf, accessed 23 March 2015.

Egypt's Ministry of Defense (n.d.) 'National projects,' www.mod.gov.eg/Mod/Mod_EAA.aspx, accessed 10 May 2015.

El-Din, G. E. (2012) 'Up for debate,' *Al-Ahram Weekly*, 18–24 October, p. 3.

El-Kouny, N. (2012) 'Egypt's anti-spy TV ad continues to stir controversy,'

Al-Ahram Online, 12 June, english.ahram.org.eg/NewsContentPrint/1/0/ 44653/Egypt/0/Egypts-antispy-TV-ad-continues-to-stir-controversy.aspx, accessed 21 January 2013.

El-Mahdi, R. (2011) 'Labour protests in Egypt: causes and meanings,' *Review of African Political Economy*, 38(129): 387–402.

— (2012) 'Against marginalization: workers, youth and class in the 25 January revolution,' in R. Bush and H. Ayeb (eds), *Marginality and Exclusion in Egypt*, London: Zed Books, pp. 133–47.

El-Mahdi, R. and P. Marfleet (2009) 'Introduction,' in R. El-Mahdi and P. Marfleet (eds), *Egypt: The Moment of Change*, London: Zed Books, pp. 1–13.

El Sayed, N. and H. Moheeb (2013) 'Khaled Ali: the labor activist,' *Egypt Today*, 33(5): 78–83.

— (2013) 'Ahmed Shafik: the air marshal,' *Egypt Today*, 33(5): 45–51.

El Shakry, O. (2012) 'Egypt's three revolutions: the force of history behind this popular uprising,' in B. Haddad, R. Bsheer and Z. Abu-Rish (eds), *The Dawn of the Arab Uprising: End of an Old Order?*, New York: Pluto Press, pp. 97–103.

El-Wardani, L. (2011) 'Egypt protests against anti-protest law,' *Al-Ahram Weekly*, 24 March, english.ahram.org.eg/NewsContent/1/64/8484/Egypt/Politics-/ Egypt-protests-against-antiprotest-law-.aspx, accessed 19 April 2011.

ElGeziri, M. (2012) 'Marginalization and self-marginalization: commercial education and its graduates,' in R. Bush and H. Ayeb (eds), *Marginality and Exclusion in Egypt*, London: Zed Books, pp. 191–218.

Engels, F. (1950) 'Engels to C. Schmidt, London, October 27, 1890,' in *Karl Marx and Frederick Engels: Selected Works in Two Volumes*, vol. II, London: Lawrence and Wishart.

Eskandar, W. (2013) 'Brothers and officers: a history of pacts,' *Jadaliyya*, 25 January, www.jadaliyya.com/pages/index/9765/brothers-and-officers_a-history-of-pacts, accessed 18 February 2013.

Fahmy, N. (2012) 'Egypt in the world,' *Cairo Review of Global Affairs*, 6: 91–107.

Farah, N. (2009) *Egypt's Political Economy: Power Relations in Development*, Cairo: American University in Cairo Press.

— (2013) 'The political economy of Egypt's revolution,' in D. Tschirgi, W. Kazziha and S. F. McMahon (eds), *Egypt's Tahrir Revolution*, Boulder, CO: Lynne Rienner Publishers, pp. 47–65.

Fisk, R. (2014) *Robert Fisk on Egypt: A Revolution Betrayed*, London: Independent Print Ltd.

Food and Agricultural Organization of the United Nations (n.d.) 'World food situation,' www.fao.org/worldfoodsituation/foodpricesindex/en/, accessed 10 December 2015.

Gause, G. (2011) 'Why Middle East studies missed the Arab Spring,' *Foreign Affairs*, 90(4): 81–90.

Goldman, E. (1910) 'The psychology of political violence,' in *Anarchism and Other Essays*, New York: Mother Earth Publishing, Kindle edn.

Goldstone, J. (2011) 'Understanding the revolutions of 2011,' *Foreign Affairs*, 90(3): 8–16.

Hale, H. E. (2013) 'Regime change cascades: what we have learned from the 1848 revolutions to the 2011 Arab uprisings,' *Annual Review of Political Science*, 16: 331–53.

Hamid, S. (2012) 'Brother President,' *Cairo Review of Global Affairs*, 6: 120–29.

Hanieh, A. (2012) 'Egypt's "orderly transition"? International aid and the rush to structural adjustment,' in B. Haddad, R. Bsheer and Z. Abu-Rish (eds), *The Dawn of the Arab Uprising: End of an Old Order?*, New York: Pluto Press, pp. 124–36.

— (2013) *Lineages of Revolt: Issues of Contemporary Capitalism in the Middle East*, Chicago, IL: Haymarket Books.

Harb, I. (2003) 'The Egyptian military in politics: disengagement or accommodation?,' *Middle East Journal*, 57(2): 269–90.

Harvey, D. (2003) *The New Imperialism*, Oxford: Oxford University Press.

— (2005) *A Brief History of Neoliberalism*, Oxford: Oxford University Press.

— (2006) *The Limits to Capital*, London: Verso Books.

— (2010) 'The enigma of capital and the crisis this time,' 30 August, davidharvey. org/2010/08/the-enigma-of-capital-and-the-crisis-this-time/, accessed 28 November 2015.

— (2010) *A Companion to Marx's* Capital, London: Verso.

— (2011) *The Enigma of Capital and the Crises of Capitalism*, Oxford: Oxford University Press.

— (2013) *A Companion to Marx's* Capital VOLUME TWO, London: Verso.

— (2014) *Seventeen Contradictions and the End of Capitalism*, Oxford: Oxford University Press.

Hashim, A. (2011) 'The Egyptian military, part two: from Mubarak onward,' *Middle East Policy*, 18(4): 106–28.

Hassan, A. A. (2012) 'The Brotherhood's abluted capitalism,' *Al-Ahram Weekly*, 25–31 October.

Henry, C. (2012) 'Political economies of transition,' in C. Henry and Jang Ji-Hyang (eds), *The Arab Spring: Will It Lead to Democratic Transitions?*, Seoul: Asan Institute for Policy Studies, pp. 53–75.

Henry, C. and Jang Ji-Hyang (2012) *The Arab Spring: Will It Lead to Democratic Transitions?*, Seoul: Asan Institute for Policy Studies.

Henry, C. and R. Springborg (2011) 'A Tunisian solution for Egypt's military: why Egypt's military will not be able to govern,' *Foreign Affairs*, 21 February, www.foreignaffairs.com/articles/tunisia/2011-02-21/tunisian-solution-egypt-s-military, accessed 3 May 2015.

Heydemann, S. (2007) 'Social pacts and the persistence of authoritarianism in the Middle East,' in O. Schlumberger (ed.), *Debating Arab Authoritarianism: Dynamics and Durability in Nondemocratic Regimes*, Stanford, CA: Stanford University Press, pp. 21–38.

Heydemann, S. and R. Leenders (2011) 'Authoritarian learning and authoritarian resilience: regime responses to the "Arab Awakening",' *Globalizations*, 8(5): 647–53.

Hoare, Q. and G. Nowell Smith (2008) *Selections from the Prison Notebooks of Antonio Gramsci*, New York: International Publishers.

Howeidy, A. (2012) 'The Brotherhood's engineer,' *Al-Ahram Weekly Online*,

29 March–4 April, weekly.ahram.org.eg/2012/1091/eg21.htm, accessed 1 May 2015.

Hull, J. C. (2006) *Options, Futures, and Other Derivatives*, 6th edn, Upper Saddle River, NJ: Pearson Prentice Hall.

Human Rights Watch (2011) 'Egypt: retry or free 12,000 after unfair military trials,' Human Rights Watch, 10 September, www.hrw.org/news/2011/09/10/egypt-retry-or-free-12000-after-unfair-military-trials, accessed 8 October 2011.

Huws, U. (2011) 'Crisis as capitalist opportunity: the new accumulation through public service commodification,' in L. Panitch, G. Albo and V. Chibber (eds), *The Crisis and the Left: Socialist Register 2012*, Pontypool: Merlin Press, pp. 64–84.

International Monetary Fund (2012) 'Costly Mideast subsidies need better targeting,' *IMF Survey Magazine: Countries and Regions*, 14 May, www.imf.org/external/pubs/ft/survey/so/2012/car051412b.htm, accessed 22 October 2015.

Johnstone, S. and J. Mazo (2011) 'Global warming and the Arab Spring,' *Survival*, 53(2): 11–17.

Joya, A. (2011) 'The Egyptian revolution: crisis of neoliberalism and the potential for democratic politics,' *Review of African Political Economy*, 38(129): 367–86.

Kandil, H. (2012) 'Why did the Egyptian middle class march to Tahrir Square?,' *Mediterranean Politics*, 17(2): 197–215.

Khalidi, R. (2011) 'Reflections on the revolutions in Tunisia and Egypt,' *Foreign Policy*, 24 February, foreignpolicy.com/2011/02/24/reflections-on-the-revolutions-in-tunisia-and-egypt/, accessed 15 February 2015.

Klyuev, V., P. de Imus and K. Srinivasan (2009) *Unconventional Choices for Unconventional Times: Credit and Quantitative Easing in Advanced Economies*, Washington, DC: International Monetary Fund.

Korany, B. (2012) 'Egypt and beyond: the Arab Spring, the new pan-Arabism, and the challenges of transition,' in B. Korany and R. El-Mahdi (eds), *Arab Spring in Egypt: Revolution and Beyond*, Cairo: American University in Cairo Press, pp. 271–94.

LaGraffe, D. (2012) 'The youth bulge in Egypt: an intersection of demographics, security and the Arab Spring,' *Journal of Strategic Security*, 5(2): 65–80.

Lenin, V. (1960) *Lenin on Imperialism, the Eve of the Proletarian Social Revolution*, Peking: Foreign Language Press.

Lesch, A. M. (2012) 'Concentrated power breeds corruption, repression, and resistance,' in B. Korany and R. El-Mahdi (eds), *Arab Spring in Egypt: Revolution and Beyond*, Cairo: American University in Cairo Press, pp. 17–42.

Luciani, G. (2007) 'Linking economic and political reform in the Middle East: the role of the bourgeoisie,' in O. Schlumberger (ed.), *Debating Arab Authoritarianism: Dynamics and Durability in Nondemocratic Regimes*, Stanford, CA: Stanford University Press, pp. 161–76.

Luxemburg, R. (1972) *The Accumulation of Capital: An anti-critique*, trans. R. Wichmann, New York: Monthly Review Press.

Lynch, M. (2012) *The Arab Uprising: The Unfinished Revolutions of the New Middle East*, New York: Public Affairs.

Marshall, S. and J. Stacher (2012) 'Egypt's generals and transnational capital,' *Middle East Research and Information Project*, 262, Spring, www.merip.org/mer/mer262/egypts-generals-transnational-capital, accessed 11 December 2015.

Marx, K. (1963) *The Eighteenth Brumaire of Louis Bonaparte*, New York: International Publishers.

— (1973) *Grundrisse*, New York: Vintage.

— (1976) *Capital*, vol. I: *The Process of Production of Capital*, London: Penguin.

— (1977) *A Contribution to the Critique of Political Economy*, Moscow: Progress Publishers.

— (1978) 'The German ideology,' in R. C. Tucker (ed.), *The Marx–Engels Reader*, 2nd edn, London: W. W. Norton and Co., pp. 146–200.

— (1978) 'Wage labour and capital,' in R. C. Tucker (ed.), *The Marx–Engels Reader*, 2nd edn, New York: W. W. Norton & Co., pp. 203–17.

— (1991) *Capital*, vol. III: *The Process of Capitalist Production as a Whole*, London: Penguin.

— (1992) *Capital*, vol. II: *The Process of Circulation of Capital*, London: Penguin.

Marx, K. and F. Engels (1967) *The Communist Manifesto*, London: Penguin.

McMahon, S. F. (2016) 'Temporality, peace initiatives and Palestinian–Israeli Politics,' *Middle East Critique*, 25(1): 5–21.

Metz, H. C. (1990) *Egypt: A Country Study*, Washington, DC: General Printing Office, Library of Congress.

Miller, L. E., J. Martini, F. S. Larrabee, A. Rabasa, S. Pezard, J. E. Taylor and T. Mengisu (2012) *Democratization in the Arab World: Prospects and Lessons from around the World*, Santa Monica, CA: RAND Corporation.

Mitchell, T. (1999) 'No factories, no problems: the logic of neo-liberalism in Egypt,' *Review of African Political Economy*, 26(82): 455–68.

— (2002) *Rule of Experts: Egypt, Techno-Politics, Modernity*, Berkeley: University of California Press.

Morsy, A. (2014) 'The military crowds out civilian business in Egypt,' Carnegie Endowment for International Peace, 24 June, carnegieendowment.org/2014/06/24/military-crowds-out-civilian-business-in-egypt, accessed 1 April 2015.

Naguib, S. (2009) 'Islamism(s) old and new,' in R. El-Mahdi and P. Marfleet (eds), *Egypt: Moment of Change*, London: Zed Books, pp. 103–19.

Nasser, G. (2011) 'The army's side of the story,' *Al-Ahram Weekly*, 14–20 April, weekly.ahram.org.eg/2011/1043/eg4.htm, accessed 2 May 2011.

Nassif, H. B. (2013) 'Wedded to Mubarak: the second careers and financial rewards of Egypt's military elite, 1981–2011,' *Middle East Journal*, 67(4): 509–30.

Ollman, B. (2003) *Dance of the Dialectic: Steps in Marx's Method*, Chicago, IL: University of Illinois Press.

Owen, R. (2007) *State, Power and Politics in the Making of the Modern Middle East*, 3rd edn, London: Routledge Press.

Panitch, L. and S. Gindin (2011) 'Capitalist crises and the crisis this time,' in L. Panitch, G. Albo and V. Chibber (eds), *The Crisis This Time: Socialist Register 2011*, Pontypool: Merlin Press, pp. 1–20.

Parenti, C. (2011) *Tropic of Chaos: Climate Change and the New Geography of Violence*, New York: Nation Books.

Pew Research Center: Global Attitudes Project (2011) *Egyptians Embrace Revolt Leaders, Religious Parties and Military, As Well*, April, www.pewglobal.org/files/2011/04/Pew-Global-Attitudes-Egypt-Report-FINAL-April-25-2011.pdf, accessed 4 April 2015.

Pioppi, D. (2007) 'Privatization of social services as a regime strategy: the revival of Islamic endowments (*Awqaf*) in Egypt,' in O. Schlumberger (ed.), *Debating Arab Authoritarianism: Dynamics and Durability in Nondemocratic Regimes*, Stanford, CA: Stanford University Press, pp. 129–42.

Poverty Reduction and Equity Group (2011) *Food Price Watch*, Washington, DC: World Bank Group, February.

— (2011) *Food Price Watch*, Washington, DC: World Bank Group, April.

Ramadan, F. and A. Adly (2015) 'Low-cost authoritarianism: the Egyptian regime and labor movement since 2013,' Carnegie Middle East Center, 17 September, carnegie-mec.org/2015/09/17/low-cost-authoritarianism-egyptian-regime-and-labor-movement-since-2013/ihui, accessed 22 October 2015.

Roy, D. A. (1992) 'The hidden economy in Egypt,' *Middle Eastern Studies*, 28(4): 689–711.

Rutherford, B. (2013) 'Egypt: the origins and consequences of the January 25 uprising,' in M. L. Haas and D. W. Lesch (eds), *The Arab Spring: Change and Resistance in the Middle East*, Boulder, CO: Westview Press, pp. 35–63.

Salem, M. (2015) 'Egypt's gift to the world: the multibillion dollar 'New Suez Canal' project makes no economic sense, but it's powerful PR,' *Politico*, 18 August, www.politico.eu/article/egypt-suez-canal-sisi-regime-cairo-government-trade/, accessed 24 October 2015.

Sayigh, Y. (2012) *Above the State: The Officers' Republic in Egypt*, Washington, DC: Carnegie Endowment for International Peace.

Schlumberger, O. (2007) 'Arab authoritarianism: debating the dynamics and durability of nondemocratic regimes,' in O. Schlumberger (ed.), *Debating Arab Authoritarianism: Dynamics and Durability in Nondemocratic Regimes*, Stanford, CA: Stanford University Press, pp. 1–18.

Shaikh, A. (1978) 'An introduction to the history of crisis theories,' in *U.S. Capitalism in Crisis*, New York: Union for Radical Political Economics.

Shehata, D. (2012) 'Youth movements and the 25 January revolution,' in B. Korany and R. El-Mahdi (eds), *Arab Spring in Egypt: Revolution and Beyond*, Cairo: American University in Cairo Press, pp. 105–24.

Sika, N. (2012) 'Youth political engagement in Egypt: from abstention to uprising,' *British Journal of Middle Eastern Studies*, 39(2): 181–99.

Soederberg, S. (2011) 'Cannibalistic capitalism: the paradoxes of neoliberal pension securitization,' in L. Panitch, G. Albo and V. Chibber (eds), *The Crisis This Time: Socialist Register 2011*, Pontypool: Merlin Press, pp. 224–41.

Soliman, S. (2012) 'The political economy of Mubarak's fall,' in B. Korany and R. El-Mahdi (eds), *Arab Spring in Egypt: Revolution and Beyond*, Cairo: American University in Cairo Press, pp. 43–62.

Springborg, R. (1987) 'The president and the field marshal: civil–military relations in Egypt today,' *Middle East Report*, 147: 4–11, 14–16, 42.

— (2011) 'The political economy of the Arab Spring,' *Mediterranean Politics*, 16(3): 427–30.

Stork, J. (1977) 'Bailing out Sadat,' *Middle East Research and Information Project*, 56: 8–11.

— (2015) 'Egypt's political prisoners,' Human Rights Watch, 6 March, www. hrw.org/news/2015/03/06/egypts-political-prisoners, accessed 5 November 2015.

Streek, W. (2011) 'The crises of democratic capitalism,' *New Left Review*, 71: 5–29.

Sullivan, Earl (Tim) (2013) 'Youth power and the revolution,' in D. Tschirgi, W. Kazziha and S. F. McMahon (eds), *Egypt's Tahrir Revolution*, Boulder, CO: Lynne Rienner Publishers, pp. 67–87.

Tschirgi, D., W. Kazziha and S. F. McMahon (2013) *Egypt's Tahrir Revolution: Perspectives and Prospects*, Boulder, CO: Lynne Rienner Publishers.

United Nations Development Programme (2009) *Arab Human Development Report 2009: Challenges to Human Security in Arab Countries*, New York: United Nations Development Programme.

Valbjorn, M. (2012) 'Upgrading post-democratization studies: examining a re-politicized Arab World in a transition to somewhere,' *Middle East Critique*, 21(1): 25–35.

Wahl, P. (2009) *Food Speculation: The Main Factor of the Price Bubble in 2008*, Berlin: WEED.

Webel, B. (2013) *Troubled Asset Relief Program (TARP): Implementation and Status*, Washington, DC: Congressional Research Service Report for Congress.

Williams, M. C. and K. Krause (2007) 'Preface: Toward critical security studies,' in M. C. Williams and K. Krause (eds), *Critical Security Studies: Concepts and Cases*, London: Routledge, pp. vii–xxi.

World Bank (2002) *Arab Republic of Egypt: Assessment of Environmental Degradation*, Washington, DC: World Bank Group.

— (2007) *Doing Business 2008: Comparing Regulations in 178 Economies*, Washington, DC: World Bank Group.

World Health Organization (n.d.) 'Country and regional data on diabetes,' www.who.int/diabetes/facts/world_figures/en/index2.html, accessed 28 March 2015.

— (n.d.) 'The National Survey on Chronic Disease and Their Risk Factors, for age group 15–65 years, Egypt, 2005–2006,' www.who.int/chp/steps/STEPS_ FactSheet_Egypt.pdf, accessed 28 March 2015.

— (1992) *Urban Air Pollution in Megacities of the World*, Oxford: Blackwell Reference.

Worthy, M. (2011) *Broken Markets: How financial market regulation can help prevent another global food crisis*, London: World Development Movement.

Wurzel, U. G. (2009) 'The political economy of authoritarianism in Egypt: insufficient structural reforms, limited outcomes and a lack of new actors,' in L. Guzaaone and D. Pioppi (eds), *The Arab State and Neo-Liberal Globalization: The Restructuring of State Power in the Middle East*, Cairo: American University in Cairo Press, pp. 97–124.

Zola, E. (1900) *Money*, London: Caxton Publishing Co., Kindle edn.